No Margins

No Margins

writing canadian fiction in lesbian

edited by

Catherine Lake and Nairne Holtz

Edited by Catherine Lake and Nairne Holtz

Library and Archives Canada Cataloguing in Publication

No margins : writing Canadian fiction in lesbian / edited by Catherine Lake, Nairne Holtz.

Includes bibliographical references.
ISBN 1-897178-15-8

1. Lesbians--Fiction. 2. Lesbians' writings, Canadian (English). 3. Short stories, Canadian (English)--Women authors. 4. Canadian fiction (English)-- 21st century. I. Lake, Catherine, 1964- II. Holtz, Nairne, 1967-

PS8323.L47N6 2006   C813'.01083526643   C2006-901075-7

The publisher gratefully acknowledges the support of the Canada Council, the Ontario Arts Council and the Department of Canadian Heritage through the Book Publishing Industry Development Program.

Printed and bound in Canada

Insomniac Press, 192 Spadina Avenue, Suite 403
Toronto, Ontario, Canada, M5T 2C2
www.insomniacpress.com

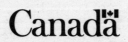

Contents

Introduction
Susan Knutson

Today, recent fiction by Canadian lesbian writers is being read in airports, living rooms, schools, and universities around the world, for it is a fact that a good many of Canada's finest and most celebrated writers are women who love other women. Do we need proof? Among the contributors to this anthology (and so, setting aside the achievements of Marie-Claire Blais and Jane Rule), we find three winners of Canada's highest award for literary achievement, the Governor General's Literary Awards: Dionne Brand (1997), Ann-Marie MacDonald (1990), and Nicole Brossard, who has won it twice (1974 and 1984). Anne Fleming was nominated in 1999. Remembering that awards can reflect dominant values and sometimes are very late in coming, it seems safe to conclude that Canadian lesbian fiction is read and respected, and that our country, which is one of four in the world to legalize the marriages of same-sex couples, is justifiably proud of its lesbian writers.

How curious, then, that this anthology, put together by Catherine Lake and Nairne Holtz, is the first of its kind—the first anthology to gather together and showcase, as such, Canadian lesbian literary fiction. [1]

The side by side placement of these texts invites analysis: what do they have in common, and what are their differences? Luanne Armstrong's "A'thyraa" differs from the others in that it is speculative fiction, along the lines of Jean Auel's *The Clan of the Cave Bear*, or Monique Wittig's *Les guérillères*. Daphne Marlatt's "Update" is unique in that it is an intertextual fiction: as she says, "part fiction and part reading" of Ethel Wilson's "Till Death Us Do Part." Writing back to the earlier Vancouver writer, Marlatt traces a ghostly lesbian line through literary history and proposes positive changes in (lesbian) women's lives. The majority of pieces in this collection, however, are representational, bearing witness to lesbian lives in all their wide variety of experience and expression. The picaresque camp of Karen X. Tulchinsky's "Ruined by Love" is a world away from Dionne Brand's passionate, decolonizing, "In Another Place, Not Here." The playful, thoughtful portraiture of Larissa Lai's "The Sewing Box" and Shani Mootoo's "The Upside-downness of the World as it Unfolds" complements the psychological drama of Lydia Kwa's "Soft Shell," and some of the issues posed by these three texts come up again in Emma Donaghue's "Here and Now," Jane Eaton Hamilton's "Wart's Ugly," and Marnie Woodrow's "Body Doubles." All of the stories are linked by an interest in sexuality, pregnancy, cultural and class histories, choices and privileges (or lack thereof), gender ambiguity, and identifications: butch, dyke, and femme.

Sexual attraction and awakening is a powerful and recurrent theme; as Nicole Brossard explains: "we need to hear about the origin, the founding moment in which we can retrace the illumination, the moment of passage when we suddenly found our self on the other side of the mirror, of the world, in a universe where surprised, stunned and relieved, we could observe *our self* drifting away from Adam's coast." Ann-Marie MacDonald's Kathleen Piper describes this moment: "I was a ghost until I tasted you, never understood the spoken word until I found your tongue. I've been a sleep-walker, sad somnambula, hands outstretched to strike the solid thing that could waken me to life at last. I have only ever stood here under this lamp, against your body, I've missed you all my life." Dionne Brand's Elizete likewise recounts her initiation into love as a coming to awareness of her own identity and destiny:

> I see Verl coming, like a shower of rain coming that could just wash me cool and that was sufficient and if God spite me for this, is so things is. I abandon everything for Verlia. I sink in Verlia and let she flesh swallow me up. I devour she. She open me up like any morning. Limp, limp and rain light, soft to the marrow. She make me wet. She tongue scorching like hot

sun. I love that shudder between her legs, love the plain wash and sea of her, the swell and bloom of her softness. And is all. And if is all I could do on the earth, is all.

This passage, which could stand beside any in world literature, also demonstrates the literary capacity of Caribbean dialectal English, and so reminds us of the multiple dimensions of meaning folded into lesbian fiction, which is never only *lesbian* fiction, but is *human* fiction, with all of the complexities that there are.

Gender identifications are explored in a number of stories: lightheartedly, as Shani Mootoo's narrator and the (sometimes) boyish Meghan face off wearing their signature blends of men's and women's scents, and grammatically, as in Ann-Marie MacDonald's nice sentence: "she is a slim young man." Marion Douglas kicks it up a notch in "Dance Hall," showing us how the "boyishness" of a girl in small town Ontario is perceived as something "weird," on a par with eating frogs, or "having a reputation": "Cora's sister, Maddy, was a girl-boy, or a boy-girl and the hero of the basketball team." The surprise ending of this story points up the enormous divide between the thoughtlessly cruel narrator and Maddy herself, who is aware that as a "boy-girl," she may not have the choice of staying in her hometown, and that the narrator's clever, urbane weariness with the milieu is a luxury she does not enjoy. Contradictions of gender and choice are taken up again in Anne Fleming's "The Pear," with its loveable but bitter bearded woman and the green-eyed girl who teases her scared, bruised heart into fantasies of love.

When it comes to choices, we do not all get the same ones, and that point is made again by Elizabeth Ruth's "tiny insurmountable hills," which explicitly juxtaposes the (non) choices of an addicted, destitute, homeless mother with those of a middle-class white lesbian couple who are trying to conceive. This story offers one of two portraits in this book of artificial or alternate insemination. Lisa, the lesbian who is trying to conceive, is hardly a picture of privilege as she suffers the anguish of a miscarriage, but she is nonetheless starkly contrasted with the out-of-doors woman who gives birth and abandons her baby on the steps of Toronto City Hall. Curiously, this story shares with others, including Lai's "The Sewing Box" and Fleming's "The Pear," a small repertoire of fertility images: plums, pears, seeds, fishes, foetuses, and homunculi. The purple plums that Lisa eats because her grandmother claimed they were good for fertility contrast with the baby born in the street, who "slid onto that dirty pink blanket on the concrete like a shiny red plum slipping from its skin."

Nicole Brossard specifies that she does not see herself as witness to her own life or to that of others: "I see myself as an explorer in language who is trying to discover new territories. I work with language hoping that it will enable me to produce and offer sequences of emotions and thoughts which, without the written word, would not exist." Appropriately, Brossard's selection from *Baroque at Dawn* closes with a little-used word that may now be used to talk about lesbian fiction: "The dark fish throw a shadow over the pinks and whites of the coral, Cybil Noland thinks before riding off again, a deep-sea wanderer aboard great incunabula." In my *Oxford English Reference Dictionary*, I read: **Incunabulum** (pl. **incunabula**): 1. a book printed at an early date, esp. before 1501. 2. (in *pl.*) the early stages of the development of a thing. [Latin *incunabula* swaddling clothes, cradle). This word, then, captures in its folds several of the meanings associated with the publishing of this first anthology of Canadian lesbian literary fiction: a book, printed at an early date in the history of Canadian lesbian fiction; and a cradle. As well, given the metaphoric framework in which Brossard places the word, we have the hotel bed upon which Cybil Noland, a global citizen in a world of signs, has made love, and upon which she now rides away towards the future prophesied in her name.

Lesbian choices, in lives and in books, have not always existed, and it still takes imagination and courage to discover and communicate them, as Dionne Brand's Elizete also notes: "I was sure of what anybody would be sure of. Spite, hunger, rain. But Verl is sure of what she make in her own mind and what she make didn't always exist. ... I like it how she leap. Run in the air without moving." Lesbian literature is new, as genres go, and has not yet attracted a great deal of scholarship, but there is more work being done all the time. L. Chris Fox, for example, at the University of Victoria, is currently writing a doctoral dissertation that argues for the existence of what she calls "nodes" in Canadian lesbian / queer women's writing: "At certain times and in certain places, an interaction with prevailing social actions and reactions seems to result in a 'queer outburst,' a concentration of publications, which may even share some rhetorical features." Fox's research focuses on a "particularly wonderful outburst of CanAsian queer women's writing in Vancouver in the 1990s," which includes several of the writers in this collection. Since publication is difficult for all writers, but especially so for non-hegemonic authors, Fox argues that it is important to explore the material conditions that encouraged this cultural bounty.

Finally, then, let us consider that the timely publication of this incunabulum—*No Margins: writing canadian fiction in lesbian*—may contribute to another "queer outburst" in our Canadian culture, and that as such, it may also help to lead us collectively towards the goals of social justice and better choices for all.

---

1. Nothing , of course, comes from nowhere, and the editors wish to acknowledge the groundbreaking work of Toronto's Lesbian Writing and Publishing Collective, which produced *Dykeversions: lesbian short fiction* (1986) and *Dykewords: an anthology of lesbian writings* (1990), both published by Women's Press; and of Lee Fleming, editor of *Tide Lines: Stories of Change by Lesbians* (1991) and *By Word of Mouth: Lesbians write the erotic* (1989), both published by Gynergy Books, in Charlottetown, PEI.

Editor Notes

The impetus for *No Margins: writing canadian fiction in lesbian* came from a conversation with a bookstore owner. I had observed that the CanLit establishment has become more inclusive in recognizing, publishing, and promoting so many authors who are lesbian. He responded that inclusivity was not the issue, but rather, Canadian fiction is currently being *defined by* our lesbian writers. We discussed the wealth of authors who are open about their sexuality and it occurred to me to create an intentional gathering of our contemporary greats into one collection. Enter Nairne Holtz with her ready research on the array of lesbian writers throughout Canada. We drew up our list and the work began.

When approaching authors, I was often asked for the "theme" of the project. I decided to re-ask them: are there recurring themes born from a lesbian identity and a Canadian geography?

We sent them a list of questions ranging from the influence of place, nationality, and sexual identity on their work to their ideas on audience, queer lit, challenging traditional narratives, and the creative process. Some authors chose to respond to all the questions, others chose one, and others made their own statement about their work and the creative process that engages them. The results of their comments are the Writer Notes that preface each work and which speak to our intersecting and layered identities.

What is critical and marvellous about this collection is that all these writers are out as lesbians. No longer content with misnomers and buried subtext, we celebrate ourselves with fervour. Visibility, particularly through the past fifteen years, has moved mountains. And as we have come out, so have our authors. Their assertive lives, their writing, themes, and content, all echo Canada's reshaping of the social and political status quo. And just as their personas and artistry have influenced our communities, so have our open lives nurtured their visibility. It is and continues to be a symbiotic relationship—reader and writer, and with much at stake societally. We are not only a readership but also a community that thrives on the words, images, and creativity of our writers. Though we share them with Canada and the world, in our hearts we feel that they belong first to us, and we to them.

Catherine Lake

Luanne Armstrong
Writer Notes

Is the geography of where you live important to your writing?
How does living in Canada inform your work?

I am a writer who identifies very strongly with a particular place and much of my writing focuses on this region, the Kootenay area in southeastern British Columbia. I am also interested in the contradictory spaces formed by my multiple identities as rural, queer, academic, social activist, mother, and grandmother. I am also a product of a politically active, pivotal period in Canadian history and I am very concerned that the issues, ideas, and visions shared by social justice movements of the last thirty years not be lost in our current social and historical turmoil.

I have been active in the lesbian community but I now feel I find multiple ways to identify and be a part of the many communities I belong to. Nor do I think there is a specific lesbian perspective in my work other than it is my work and therefore informed by all that I am. My perspective as an artist includes all facets of my identity, so although I often write about lesbian characters, I also write about men and children and animals. I would hope, therefore, to engage a wide audience of people interested in ideas, in the future, and in social issues.

I have seen a huge change in Canadian literature in the last thirty years. I think sometimes we lose sight of the fact that we have come from a place where Canadian literature was once dominated by white male writers, to a place where it now at least attempts to be broadly inclusive. However, I have often been disappointed by the conventionality of much of what is labelled queer writing. I think writing from a particular perspective is not the point. The point for me is to write from the perspective of all that I am and to include as honestly as possible the ideas and the perspectives I believe are important.

Luanne Armstrong
A'thyraa

I lay in my black tent, contented. In those days, I was mostly contented. I could hear the horses tearing at the grass outside and the soft thud of their hooves, their determined munching. I lay on my bed, warm and soft in every bone, and thought about what I might do with this new day. I might go hunting. I might work on training the new colts. I might go swimming in the afternoon. I might simply lie in my tent. I turned and nuzzled gently into the back of the woman sleeping by my side. For a moment, I couldn't actually remember who she was, but then my head cleared and I recalled the night before, the drums, dancing, laughter over the fire, catching her eye, the tendrils of heat and tenderness rising up and spinning the threads between us. And then the hours of kissing, soft crooning, moans; delight rising from my toes up to my crotch, my belly, spreading fire through my chest, up through the top of my head.

This morning, she would go back to her tent. Such was our way. Such was my way. Some women joined and partnered for weeks, months, years, even for lifetimes, though such were rare. I had never met anyone I wanted to share my tent with for long and doubted that I would. But at the gathers, I never lacked for partners. Fucking was such joy, such an endless delight and pleasure. I was quite sure the Goddess came to slide between us at times to take her share.

I had always loved to share nights of energetic lust but I also looked forward to the moments when I woke alone early in the grey dawn and slipped outside. I'd trot down to the river, slide into the cold and silky water and lie in its embrace while the sun sent slithery gold fingers down through the leaves to dance along the water ripples.

Sometimes I left the camp to ride alone among the high peaks. I wandered for days, looking into lonely valleys and over cliff edges. I tethered my pony and climbed for the sheer joy of testing myself against rocks and cliffs and handholds until I found myself in the high mountain gardens, full of tiny Goddess-arranged delights—minuscule flowers, satin streams, moss-covered gravel spills.

I lived as I pleased. I took my place among the other women when it came time for hunting, riding, herding, or trading. Most of the other women had children. When the time came, they would go to the men's camp and remain as long they chose. Most came back; some remained with the men for several seasons. But all returned home during the time when the child was to come into this place. A child was always born to a tent full of mothers and grandmothers welcoming it with singing and wonder.

I had never felt the urge for a child and so, though I played with the children and taught them riding and hunting, I left them to the tenderness of the other women. What I liked best was to wonder at the mystery I saw around me, its endless complexity. I spent hours lying on my back staring at the patterns the birds wove. I turned over on my stomach and watched the intricate insect life that went on below the carpet of grass. I decorated my tent with lichen-layered rocks, bits of wind-polished wood or dried grass. I marvelled and played, and a child, even a child beloved by many women, would take time away from this.

We didn't always stay in this place; sometimes we journeyed over the plains to other camps and occasionally to the city, which was three days slow riding or one day's fast. We went to the city for amusement and to look. We traded with them, but more for their pleasure than ours. There was little we needed that we couldn't make ourselves but the city people liked our drums, our hides, our weaving and pottery. So we traded with them. It was an excuse to visit, to drink, which we seldom did on our own, to go to the temple and listen to the goddess speaking, look at art, listen to music, and hear the gossip, which mostly struck us as funny or incomprehensible.

But sometimes it was serious. Lately, there had been news of fighting in the north. Fighting had never come to the plains in our memory and we were not sure what such a thing could mean. The people in the city seemed very concerned so we listened too.

I didn't often go to the city but when I did I got very excited by new ideas I heard in the market. Although I would have liked to have added my voice to the discussions and arguments, I remained silent. But I was a plains person and I could not speak if I didn't know that I would be heard. Our people learned to listen carefully but city people rudely interrupted each other and didn't seem to listen much at all. Sometimes I got too excited and had to ride away to calm down. I liked to think, talk, and play with words. It was a game, a bit like hunting except nothing died. But I would not have wanted to do it all the time like the city people seemed to do.

I went to the city one day with a group of women, some from my band, some not. We always dressed up for it in our bits of decoration, and rode easy on our curly-haired black ponies. We joked and gossiped about who we might meet this trip, the ways of city women, city men, and what they might be like in bed. We lied hugely about our experiences and laughed at our own lies. My own horse was one I raised as a colt. He knew my ways as I knew his. On my last trip to the city, I had traded for a red blanket for him. On this trip, I braided hawk feathers in his mane and blue beads into my own hair. I rode most of the trip sitting backwards, partly to show off and partly for ease in talking.

When we came in sight of the city, our talking and laughing quieted. Though none of us admitted it, we felt the differences in the glances that city people gave us, the differences between our plains finery and their smooth hair, immaculate clothes, and soft hands. We insisted to each other that we didn't feel any less than them, but it was clear that they thought they were more than us and they let us know. We had no way to understand or withstand such differences, since in our daily life, such behaviour was unknown to us. We were unused to the feeling of being shut in, of not being able to see the horizon, of being surrounded by people we did not know. Time in the city was time spent enduring these feelings.

When we entered the city we crowded together and I rode frontways on my horse, looking straight ahead. When we got to the market, we unloaded the pack ponies and laid out our trading things and braced ourselves for the people who would come. We had learned to give each other rest from the strain of meeting strange eyes and strange voices. So while some were trading, others were free to wander and to look.

This day, I rode through the streets to the gardens by the river. These gardens always fascinated me by their orderliness. They were like the high meadows in the mountains, but one is made by the Creator Goddess and one is made by the city people. I tied my horse and looked at the patterns of colour and order. Another woman was also there, but not looking at the flowers. She was staring at the paper in her hands. Not wishing to disturb her, I wandered from flower bed to flower bed as quietly as I could.

She looked up and smiled a greeting. Awkwardly, I nodded my head. I did not know this woman, but now that she had greeted me, courtesy and ritual said that I should also greet her. I waited. Again she looked up and smiled. This time there was a frown in the smile, that I should still be standing before her not knowing what to do next.

I waited. Since it was her place I had come into, it was her place to speak, and finally she did.

"This is a beautiful garden," she said, "and a beautiful day to enjoy it. Have you come here before?" Her voice was clear and throaty. She wore a plain white dress. Her hair was golden and braided. She had blue eyes.

"Yes," I said, "we have nothing quite like this on the plains. And it is peaceful, after the market."

"Ah," she replied, smiling kindly, "you have come to trade then."

"Yes," I agreed. After that there seemed little more to say. She went back to her papers and I went back to the flowers and then back to my pony. I didn't want her to be there and I left before I wanted to.

I went back to the market, to take my turn at trading. A crowd was beginning to gather in the square. Something was going to happen.

After a while, I saw her come from the park, mount the steps beside the square and make a speech to which everyone listened carefully, sometimes interrupting to applaud.

It was a good speech, I thought. She was warning them to prepare for fighting and to pay attention to what was going on in the world outside this small, safe city. I didn't really understand all of what she said. I wanted to ask her questions but there was a crowd of people around her. I listened and watched her from a distance and when it was over, I went back to trading.

Soon she came by the row of blankets where we were. She was still surrounded by a crowd of people chattering and laughing, some touching her to get her attention. She was talking back, lively, her arms and hands and eyes flashing. People quieted when she spoke. They listened to every word.

I bent my head over the blanket. I did not want that flashing attention turned my way. So when she stopped in front of me, I saw only her feet in sandals and then was forced to look up to meet her smile.

"This is beautiful pottery," she said. "Did you make it?"

I shook my head, for making things is not what I do. Fucking and riding horses, hunting and travelling alone in high places is what I do. But I said nothing. She picked up several bowls, frowned over them, put them back and finally chose one. She handed me some city money, which I took without looking at it.

Then she went on and the light went out of the day and I snarled at the other customers until my sisters told me to leave. I sat and thought for a while. I jumped on my horse and rode through the city in the direction I had seen her take. I had to ask directions several times but people seemed to know who I meant, and though they were startled by my question, they gave me the answer I wanted.

When I came to her house, I stopped. Her house was bigger than many of the others around it. Flowers grew everywhere. Water trickled into a pond full of white flowers floating like clouds. I rode into the yard, over stones laid flat, then stopped, unable to decide what do next. On the plains, if a door is open, one enters and if a door is closed, one does not. Her door was closed, and yet I thought that perhaps here, it meant nothing. Maybe it was a barrier I could pass through by asking.

I waited and someone came to the door to ask my business. I said I had a question to ask of the woman inside, and the young man disappeared. Soon she came to the door smiling, but I did not smile back.

She asked me to come inside and I did, leaving my horse in the yard to eat the flowers if he so chose. I took a deep breath and stepped inside. The walls closed around me. It was much bigger inside than I had supposed. The walls went up to a high ceiling and light came in from above. Rugs covered the stone floor and the walls were painted with pictures of birds and women and cattle and horses. Some of the pictures were of the plains, my plains, and I felt a flash of anger that anyone should presume to paint what they could never really know.

She took me to a place beside the fireplace and motioned for me to sit down. She left and came back with tea and something sweet on a platter.

"What is your question?" she asked when I had drunk the tea and eaten whatever was on the platter.

I looked away at the pictures on the wall, of women dancing with flowers and each other.

"How is it," I said finally, careful with my words and my tone, "that one who makes a speech about opening up walls and learning about other things outside the city, does not know the people who live on the plains outside these walls?"

She looked at me in surprise and then she laughed. Her laugh was like the river water, chuckling in the reeds.

"You're right," she said. "I don't know much about your people. But I always thought that was by your choice. We in the city think of you as wild, proud, looking down on those of us who live within walls, not wanting to talk to us. Although we live side by side and are one people, we hardly know about one another."

I laughed a little. "When have you given us a chance?" I said. "You see our rough ways and you look away, you talk to each other, or you walk on."

"Tell me then," she said, "for I would like to hear. I have always wondered and wanted to know about your people. I used to come by the market and marvel at the horses for their beauty and the easy way you ride."

"I will," I said "but you must tell me in return how to grow such flowers, why your houses are so large, how you can stand to live within walls with so many strangers, what it is you read, and what your papers say."

We talked and talked. People came in, lit the lamps, brought food, more tea and still we talked. Finally I went out to check on my horse and found him fed and brushed, enclosed and not very happy about it, in a small house attached to the big one.

I went back. It was getting late and my sisters would be wondering. They had seen the direction I took when I left so they would not wonder too much, but would wait for me to return and tell them the story.

A silence had fallen between us. I looked at the flickering candles, at her hands, lying in her lap where they had fallen among the folds of the white dress. I hesitated. It was she who moved first, taking my rough hands in her smooth ones and rubbing her thumb, over the rough places and the little hollow of the palm and between fingers. I felt my cunt loosen and shivers ran up my back. I could not look at her.

When I did, I looked at her eyes and her lips. I leaned to

kiss her. Her lips were dry and warm. I placed my hand onto the softness of her breast. I felt her move. I felt the heat grow between us and we kissed and kissed, each of us wondering when the other would speak. Finally she leaned away.

"I do have a bed," she said, "and you are welcome to share it, if you would like."

I laughed. "Yes," I said.

She led me to her room where she took off her white dress while I took off my leather and my blue beads. We lay on the bed together in the light of the lamps.

Her breasts were beautiful and the nipples rose to my tongue as she fell back on the bed in need and desire. I took my time, exploring the lift of her belly, the curved ivory of her thighs and the small spaces in the hollow of her neck. I wanted to know all of her, all the secret warm places and the taste and smells of apricots, honey, and hot summer days and the sound of her sighing when my fingers slid between her legs searching for the folded hidden warmth there. When I moved down and put my tongue where she wanted me to put it, her fingers grabbed my hair and I heard her singing. I felt it in my own body, the tension and excitement growing until her cunt convulsed. I held her there with my tongue and my fingers until, sweaty and exhausted, she pulled me up, kissed my wet face. I waited, content with whatever was to happen next. She put her hands on me, and finally in me so deep that I lost all sense of where and who I was. I only remember the Goddess singing in my blood and knew that I was lost in this woman, that between her and me there was no division. When my body cooled, I lay in her arms and wept.

At that, she was alarmed, for nothing we had done called for weeping. How could I tell her of my fear, I who feared nothing, and of my sense I had both lost and gained something indescribable? When I touched her body, it felt like my own and she said as much to me, in wonder. We were both silent, struck by the newness of something so familiar.

Finally we slept.

When I awoke in the morning, she was there and we spent the morning talking and lying flesh against flesh, until we felt the singing begin again in our blood. When I held her this time, I shivered and the bed whirled and I went deeper and deeper into myself, to where I could hear the grandmothers talking, to where the Goddess herself spread her wings like an infinite, iridescent blue butterfly. I sprawled, open and singing and moaning on the bed while she went after me and when I said, no more, she said, no, come on, more, just a little and I came and came and something in me that had been clenched and protected, let go, melted, and was gone.

After that, we got up, dressed, went out of that room and down to the kitchen for food. The woman who had brought food before was nowhere in sight but the food was there. All the time, we talked and talked, such talking as I had always longed for. Words and ideas spilled from me and her. We laughed and could hardly wait for one to say something before the other completed it. It was a glorious day, and finally, we went back to bed, exhausted.

I stayed with her for seven days. I sent a message to my sisters to go home without me. Each day was more wonderful and complete than any other, but also each day the walls closed in tighter and the sense of strangeness grew. After all, despite the time we spent in bed and spent talking, I didn't know her. Her ways were strange; her house was strange. People came and went. Food appeared and disappeared. The house had a whole life I wasn't part of. She went out, twice, to go to meetings and though she courteously asked me if I would like to come, I didn't think she wanted me to, so I didn't.

I went to bed one night, closed my eyes and thought myself back onto the plain. It was so clear that pain stuck in my heart like a fierce arrow. I awoke and didn't know where I was. In the morning I told her I was leaving. She said nothing, but closed her eyes.

"Yes," she said, and turned away. I went to the little house and got my horse, who was kicking and so fretful with loneliness for the others of his tribe that I was sorry for him. When I came back into the courtyard, she came and stood beside me. I put my arms around her and held her, and in our bodies I could feel the seal, the joining we had made, slowly ripping apart, like flesh tearing.

"I'll come back," I said. "Please know that I'll come back." I laughed a little, both with joy and sorrow, and not knowing how to live with this new feeling. "I have no choice. You are part of me and I am part of you. I am not sure how this happened or if I chose it, or even if I want it, but it is so."

She looked at me, this proud woman of the city, who made speeches, read books, and had others to do her bidding. "I will wait," she said, "I will wait here and I will have my life, but part of me will ride out onto those plains where I have never gone."

"You could come with me," I said, pleading, but she only said, "I will wait."

So I got on my black horse and came back to the plains, where everything was both the same and utterly changed. All the way home, I felt that perhaps I was a finer and better person than I had guessed, to love and be so loved, by her.

I was teased of course. And questioned. Gently. I sat at the fire that night, smiling with happiness and remembering. It was only as the days began to lengthen in number that the foolishness of what I had done began to come into me. Our elders teach us that each person is a circle connected in all directions to the world around us. I know this is so, for I have stood on the plains and seen the joining, the rays of light, go out from me to all that I loved. But now there was a torn place in me and to fill it, I would have to leave all that I love and all that makes me who I am. I waited. I slept with other women. I went riding and climbed the mountains to my favourite valley until one day, I slid onto my black horse and made the journey, riding faster than I normally would, back into the city.

At first, we were shy with each other. When I first saw her, she looked like so unfamiliar. I thought, there, now I can go back to the plains and be free. I wondered why I had ridden this long way to be with someone I hardly knew. She asked me in and had the other people bring food. When they went away, she asked me questions about my life and what I had been doing on the plains. I told her and asked her questions in turn. She took my hand, turned it over, stroked the softness there and said nothing more but only continued, stroking my hand and holding it. My heart turned over. I knew that I loved her. I saw the light begin to weave between us.

I took her hand as well. I was relearning her body, the smell of her flesh, the smooth texture along her inner arms, the soft down on her cheek, the feel of her hair, as soft and fine as a child's. Our bodies met and greeted each other with delight, toes meeting toes, hands stroking, breasts touching breasts.

We lay together on the rug by the fire for a long time, healing what had been torn. Peace came into me and wholeness. I knew that I had missed her and would always miss her until we were like this again. She found pillows and blankets and we slept there, in front of the fire like two tired children. In the night, I touched her, she touched me back and we held hands until we slept again.

After that, I divided my time between the plains and the city, but I was never easy in either place. When I asked her to come out to camp even for a few days, she always had some reason, some business in the city, which prevented her. Very quickly, I stopped asking. So the travelling, the division in my life, was mine. When I left, she wept and I carried the memory of her weeping face home with me. When I left home, my sisters wept and said I was out of balance and needed to go the healers. So I went back and forth, pulled in two directions, never able to settle in either.

I tried to live the life of the city. After a while I went with her to meet her friends, to listen to her speak. Everyone was friendly, pleased to meet me and seemed to greet our coming together with gladness. Only I saw the fear in their eyes and heard the strain in their voices when they asked me questions.

It was what they didn't say, what they didn't do, that left me out. At dinner, when all were speaking about something ordinary, the weather, or gardening and I would venture something about the plains, there would be the briefest, the tiniest of pauses, while everyone looked at me and then the talk went on as before, as if I had not spoken.

Or what they took for granted—astonishing amounts of food, servants who were well and kindly treated, but still, servants. Being among strangers and the courtesies of behaviour among strangers was new to me. The sense of being endlessly shut in, among walls and streets and more streets, made it hard to breath. The more I got used to it and accustomed to it, the more I hated it. And though I tried to tell her my feelings, it was like a fish trying to tell a bird about the water. We had no language to share for these things.

But in the evenings, as she sat on the floor, looking into the fire, I would sit and watch her. She would know I was looking. Sometimes I lay with my head in her lap, while she stroked my hair, took out my long braids and put beads in them. I knew this woman was now my heart's blood. Without her, I would be lost.

After a several trips, it settled into a routine. I would spend time with her until my longing for the plains grew too much. On the plains, I would stay until I missed her too much to bear. So I went back and forth, like some demented toy on a piece of string while the seasons wore themselves away.

We came together, each time, shy, and waiting to feel each other's presence in our bodies. We left each time, parting like souls being ripped apart. The pain would lessen and we would go back to our lives until it was time to do it over.

Finally, she came to visit, once. She said she felt left out of my life on the plains. She said each time I left her I disappeared into the midst of my sisters and lovers and friends and people.

"Come and see," I had said. "They will make you welcome." And then I wondered if I'd lied. What would my sisters do? They felt I spent too much time away already.

She came but she did not come alone, nor was I alone and in the end, it was more like a diplomatic mission than a visit. A useful mission perhaps, but not what I had imagined. The whole time she was with us, she was charming and asked questions designed to get my sisters to open up and talk. They thought she was wonderful. Only I, who knew her well, saw the mask and the fear and it made me sad and furious. At night, I lay awake beside her in the tent while she slept. When she left, I went alone to the river and wept. I didn't know what I was weeping for. I ached for the touch of her hands and yet I delayed visiting her in the city. After all, if I did not come, what difference would it make to her, with her busy life, her busy friends, her house, her garden, and the people around who served and loved her. I didn't go. I waited while summer passed into autumn and my sisters asked no questions. Still I waited.

Then one morning, I awoke from a dream of her weeping in fear, and I left before the camp was even awake, riding through the dawn-wet grass. She did not weep when I came into her house, only later, lying beside the fire. She turned away from my hands.

"I'm afraid," she wept. "I'm afraid." I was bitter because I thought she was afraid of me. I went out into the night, away from her. I was saddling my horse to leave when she came to me. We held each other for a long time. After all, there was nothing to be done. Our lives were the way we had made them. I came back into her house, with the candles lit and shining, her bed warm and inviting. I knew that as long as she wanted me there and as long as I could, I would come to her.

It was morning and we were lying in bed when we heard the rumbling. The earth shook, the wall across from her bed suddenly cracked and we could hear screaming from the city.

It was the mountain to the north, the mountain I had so often climbed and loved to play on. A long, expanding finger of smoke extended from its peak towards us and the sky darkened even as we watched. A hot wind slapped our faces. A fine, white, burning ash started falling on the city.

"My sisters!" I said. They were much closer to the mountain than we were. I ran out, ran to the stable for my horse. He was frantic with fear and the ash sparks burning his shining hide. I rode like an insane person to the gates of the city. People were fleeing everywhere; there was panic and screaming. Even as I watched, people were getting trampled. There was nothing I could do. It would take me a day to reach my sisters and if they were alive, they would be coming here, towards the city, towards the boats, towards the sea. The boats, the harbour, I thought, there might be a chance to leave that way. I stood in frantic indecision, knowing my place, my duty, my training, turned me towards my sisters.

But my love for her turned me, turned me back. The sky was darker now, almost black, except in the direction of the mountain, where it glowed orange and scarlet. I rode like a fury back towards her, back towards my love in her white dress. She was standing on the wall of her house, straining to see me, to reach out her arms towards me and even as I rode, I heard the noise, the groaning, the earth shrieking in the pain of birth and grieving and death. Fire came from the mountain covering the land.

We were lucky, my love and I. I reached her in time, gasping from burnt lungs in the hot, ash-choked air. She slid up behind me, and we rode with death behind us, rode for the harbour and the boats rocking there.

The harbour was pandemonium but I was of the plains, fierce and swift, born to run and climb. I stopped for one moment to give my horse, the friend of my youth, my willing partner for so many years, a gift of mercy. I cut his throat and left him there dying. I fought my way through the masses of crazed people with her at my back. By some miracle, we got onto a boat that was just pulling away. It was covered with people. Some were even in the water, clinging to the sides and these we helped to pull aboard.

The boat raised a sail and we flew away, over the black water, away from the burning city and I held her hand, my love's hand and felt the land, my mother, and my sisters die.

And then we were alone.

Luanne Armstrong

Luanne Armstrong is an award-winning writer and scholar. She teaches Creative Writing at Langara College in Vancouver and other places. She has published novels, poetry, and children's books. Her most recent children's book *Jeanie and the Gentle Giants* was nominated for the Sheila Egoff BC Book Prize; the Canadian Library Association Book of the Year; the Ontario Library Association Silver Birch Award; and for the Red Cedar Award in British Columbia. *Jeanie and the Gentle Giants* was also named by McNally Robinson Booksellers in Winnipeg as one of their top ten all-time best children's books. Her most recent novel, *The Bone House*, was shortlisted for the Canadian Sunburst Award for Science Fiction and the Relit Prize for Fiction.

Dionne Brand
Writer Notes

I've always wanted to write about the emergent city. And I've always wanted to write about interactions among people in that city, how it works, what happens. I think the city is a source of incredible energy. I'm not saying that it's always positive energy but I love that and I want to describe it. And I think that it has a kind of movement of its own, and just to observe it is interesting.

You're in the moments of choosing many things and time is full and long, even as you want to do everything. And that's who I see in the city and that's who I wanted to write about.

Everything changes my writing. You live. I move as the world moves as I move in it. I try to keep change as a thing I must do—so you don't step into comfortableness about your work or the world.

—from an interview with Jennifer O'Connor published in *Xtra!* May 12, 2005

Dionne Brand

excerpted from *In Another Place, Not Here*

Grace. Is grace, yes. And I take it, quiet, quiet, like thiefing sugar. From the word she speak to me and the sweat running down she in that sun, one afternoon as I look up saying to myself, how many more days these poor feet of mine can take this field, these blades of cane like razor, this sun like coal pot. Long as you have to eat, girl. I look up. That woman like a drink of cool water. The four o'clock light thinning she dress, she back good and strong, the sweat raining off in that moment when I look and she snap she head around, that wide mouth blowing a wave of tiredness away, pulling in one big breath of air, them big white teeth, she, falling to the work again, she, falling into the four o'clock sunlight. I see she. Hot, cool and wet. I sink the machete in my foot, careless, blood blooming in the stalks of cane, a sweet ripe smell wash me faint. With pain. Wash the field, spinning green mile after green mile around she. See she sweat, sweet like sugar.

I never wanted nothing big from the world. Who is me to want anything big or small. Who is me to think I is something. I born to clean Isaiah' house and work cane since I was a child and say what you want Isaiah feed me and all I have to do is lay down under him in the night and work the cane in the day. It have plenty woman waiting their whole blessed life for that and what make me turn woman and leave it I don't know, but it come. Bad spirit they say, bad spirit or blessed, it come, what make me notice Verlia' face spraying sweat in the four o'clock heat.

Because you see I know I was going to lose something, because Verl was surer than anything I see before, surer than the day I get born, because nothing ever happen to me until Verl come along and when Verl come along I see my chance out of what ordinary, out of the plenty day when all it have for a woman to do is lie down and let a man beat against she body, and work cane and chop up she foot and make children and choke on the dryness in she chest and have only one road in and the same road out and know that she tied to the ground and can never lift up. And it wasn't nothing Verl do or say or even what Verl was or what Verl wanted because even now I can't swear but is just that I see Verl coming, like a shower of rain coming that could just wash me cool and that was sufficient and if God spite me for this, is so things is.

I abandon everything for Verlia. I sink in Verlia and let she flesh swallow me up. I devour she. She open me up like any morning. Limp, limp and rain light, soft to the marrow. She make me wet. She tongue scorching like hot sun. I love that shudder between her legs, love the plain wash and sea of her, the swell and bloom of her softness. And is all. And if is all I could do on the earth, is all.

She would say, "Open your eyes, I want to see what you're feeling." I don't know what she see in my eyes but she stare into me until I break. Her look say, "Elizete, you is bigger than me by millennia and you can hold me between your legs like rock hold water. You are wearing me away like years and I wonder if you can see me beyond rock and beyond water as something human that need to eat and can die, even as you dive into me today like a fish and want nothing or so you say." Something say to me, Elizete, you is not big enough for nothing you done live and Verlia is your grace.

Isaiah gone mad catching me lying underneath Verlia, and even the sure killing in him couldn't sweep me away from the sweetness of her. I didn't even raise my head. I finished loving Verlia taking she face and she skin black as water in my hand so I was to remember what I lose something for. I never see him after that. They say he sit under a fishing net in Las Cuevas now and he talk to himself, they say he don't remember me but call out the name of the Venezuelan woman what first was his wife and what make him carry she fishing one night and when day break she was not there. They say he is like a jumbie, and is best for me and he to leave that way for it have too much between we, and is vindication what make him open the door. Isaiah was a hard man, a hard man down to his skin. Is best I didn't kill him as I plan, is best I didn't pour the milk of buttercups in his eyes and blind him, is best I didn't sling his neck off, is best I didn't rub his head with killing root. Is best I see this woman when I raise up in my swing, when the sweat was falling like rain from she. I say is grace the way it happen and is grace.

He and me story done right there, one time. It have nothing to say else about it.

Everything make sense from then the way flesh make sense settling into blood. I think to myself how I must be was sleeping all this time. I must be was in a trance because it was as if Verl wake me up to say, "Girl, put on your clothes. Let we go now." It have ways of trancing people and turning them against they very self and I suspect Isaiah now with his prayer book and his plait hair but I have no time with him. I suspect the woman I grow with and she hands that can't stop growing things. I suspect the cane. I suspect Moriah. I suspect my life. I suspect the moon. Everything. What don't meet you don't pass you.

Verl was sure. Sure of everything. And sure like that was not something in my life. I was sure that I would wake up each day, I was sure that I had to work cane, I was sure that the man they give me to was Isaiah Ferdinand. I was sure that he would illtreat me. I was sure that each night I would dream of miles of cane waving. Things like this. I was sure iguana would be thirsty enough to cross the road if the dry season was too long, I was sure birds would fly across the house in the morning. I was sure of what anybody would be sure of. Spite, hunger, rain. But Verl is sure of what she make in her own mind and what she make didn't always exist.

I like it how she leap. Run in the air without moving. I watch she make she way around we as if she was from here, all the time moving faster than the last thing she say. It come so I know where she standing in the field without looking for she. Because she moving, moving, moving all the time without moving. If I didn't like it she would frighten me.

There is a heat that looks like glass waving if you make your eyes look far. Everybody didn't like that moving but everybody eyes was on she the first time she come. She was walking in that heat and we was all in the shed eating. Some was laying down for the while and she reach and start busy busy giving out papers. She look like the transport drop she by the junction and she walk in. People get up and start going but the old ones listen to she. I know why they listen. Is not often that some young one with soft hands and skin smelling of the kind of sweat they make in the town come talking to them. They touch up she clothes and she hands and she face and say, "Who child is you?" They play with she and kiss she up. And it give them a softness like how they might have been if they live in town and if they had money and if their life was different. They give she water and they give she fry fish. They tell she don't drink fast. They love it when she just eat as if she don't scorn them but they laugh when she say what she want. They laugh long. And then they hush.

Nobody here can remember when they wasn't here. I come here with Isaiah. He show me the room and he show me the washtub and he show me the fire and he show me the road. He tell me never let him catch me at the junction. I didn't believe him but I find out soon when I catch the end of his whip. That was long time now. No need to remember. I don't even remember when I stop trying to run away, stop trying to make that junction. It was long. He would always be at that junction when I get there. I tried for a long time. I think to myself one day he is going to miss, one day. One day when he think I train, he is going to miss. But I stop. He get his way. When I see that it was his play, I resign. He stop watching me but then I could not remember why I was trying to get there. Didn't have no place to go anyway when I think of it. Trying to get to the junction

so much I forget where I was going. I know every track leading to it but when I get there and see Isaiah, it come like he was
the end of it. I used to have some place in mind I know but...
One time, I plotting my way through the mangle, one of these
old ones I never expect ask me "Where you running running
so all the time?" The spite of the thing hit me and it take me
by surprise, and I suppose I didn't have nowhere in mind
except not here. Cold water just run in my feet then. You trust
old people to know better. Why they wouldn't want good for
me? If you can't see a way for yourself, see it for somebody else
nah? So all of that is how I wear away.

Not a bone in she like that. Verlia. Hatred and anger, but
not spite. Spite is loving to see people suffer. She say to me
that you could get used to suffering. She say is what curve we
back to the cane. Is all we know. Hatred you could out and out
deal with, and anger, but not spite. It was her speed though,
the way she could make the junction still standing in front of
you, the way she could move fast in she head. People say this
is not people to trust, people who know what you saying
before you say it, people hurrying you up to move, them kinda
people busy busy going someplace soon but I was ready for
Verlia. She get send for me.

She was burning. You could see she burning bright. Before
you know it they making sweet bread for she, before you
know it washtub full of ice cream done plan. Before you know
it she invite for Sunday. I suppose not only me see rescue
when she reach.

I used to wonder who she went home to; watch she walk
to the junction in the evening half dead and wonder if her
quickness fall away on the transport, wondered if she was the
same in town, what she kitchen smell like, and if she plant
okra and what she think. Soon I was only wondering about
she. I watch she disappear up the junction and I wait for she
to break it in the mornings. Is nothing that draw me to she
but that and the way she want nothing from me and the way
she brand new and come from another life.

After the woman I lived with die on me I was given to Isaiah. She passed on when I was not yet a young lady. It seem to me that one day I wake up under Isaiah. Isaiah ride me every night. I was a horse for his jumbie. His face was like the dead over me on the floor when he cry out for the woman who leave him as he ride me to hell. Each night I hear him say these words as if I should pity him. "When I meet that Venezuelan woman it was the last day of my life. She sail me like a ship. That woman could tell stories. It was through one of her tales that I arrived at this sandpit with my back breaking and my eyes burning with this sweat, with her fine clothes and fine ideas; I laid every brick on that stone house where she take man in front of me. My hair turn red and I never scream in this place yet." With that he ride me again. These times I wander, I turn my head to the wall and travel in the dust tunnels of wood lice. I cover my self in their fine, fine sand, I slide through the tunnel and I see all where I have to go, and I try to reach where they live and I try to be like them because try as I did when I was little I never see one of them yet only the rifts on the walls. Is so they work in secret and in their own company. Is so I travel the walls of this room catching hell and Isaiah' advantage till morning. I dream every day to break a shovel over his head which he plait in braids for he read in the Bible that he should not cut his hair. Every evening when they was in season he would climb the land above the quarry to pick cashew fruit and nuts. I would stand at the bottom looking at him hoping that the bitter juice from the fruit burn him to death for I know that it is poison. I carried a mountain inside of me. The thought of him and his hardness cut at the red stone in me from sun-up to sundown. I went in the evenings after work to the sand quarry while he sleep. The salmon dank sides rise up around me and I was silent there. It was a place where I had peace, or I wouldn't call it peace but calm, and I shovelled, the sweat drizzling from my body as I think and think of escaping him. I did not sympathize with him, no matter what he said that red woman do to him. What she make him eat, how she tie his mind. It could not compensate for what he do to me. There in the damp, it make me calm, calm, calm and hollow inside me. If I dig enough it cool me and take my mind off the junction. I feel my body full up and burst. All my skin split. Until I was so tired I could not run. I dream of running though, to Aruba or Maracaibo. I hear about these place. Yes, Maracaibo. I love the sound of it yet I have never seen it. I dream of taking his neck with a cutlass and running to Maracaibo, yes. I imagine it as a place with thick and dense vine and alive like veins under my feet. I dream the vine, green and plump, blood running through it and me too running running, spilling blood. Vine like rope under my feet, vine strapping my legs and opening when I walk. Is like nowhere else. I destroying anything in my way. I want it to be peaceful there. The air behind me close thick as mist whenever I move and Maracaibo open rough and green and dense again. I dream I spit milk each time my mouth open. My stomach will swell and vines will burst out. I dream it is a place where a woman can live after she done take the neck of a man. Fearless. I dream my eyes, black and steady in my black face and never close. I will wear a black skirt, shapely like a wing and down to my toes. I will fly to Maracaibo in it and you will see nothing of me but my black eyes in my black face and my black skirt swirling over thick living vine. I dream of flying in my skirt to Maracaibo. I want to go to Maracaibo if it is the last thing I do. This black skirt will melt like soot if it get touched. And my face too. One day I will do it, for Isaiah don't know my mind in this. He too busy in his own mind now. He make his heart too hard to know anyone else. One day I will done calculate him.

The time in between as I say I don't remember but it must have been there because by the time I recognize myself I was a big woman and the devil was riding me. How I reach here is one skill I learn hard. The skill of forgetfulness. So I shovel in this pit from morning till night, cut cane when it in season and lie under this man at night until one day I see this woman talking, talking like she know what she is saying and everybody around listening. I walk past because I have no time for no woman talking. It don't mean nothing. It don't matter what woman say in the world, take it from me. This woman with her mouth flying...cheups. I hear something about co-operative. Black people could ever co-operate? This little girl too fast again. Her mouth too fast, she tongue flying ahead of she-self. Face plain as day, mouth like a ripe mango and teeth, teeth like a horse. I en't talk to she then. They tell me she is for the revo, that she is for taking all the land and giving it to people who work it all their life. Revolution, my ass. Let foolish old people believe she. Is only them have time to sit down and get wrap up in her mouth and think Oliviere and them will let go any land. Is only one thing will fix Oliviere and them and is the devil because them is the devil' son self. I pass by her going my way and didn't that woman skin she big teeth for me and look at me so clear is as if she see all my mind clear through to Maracaibo. Her look say, "I know you. I know you plan to sling off a man' neck and go to Maracaibo." I brazen she look and I pass she straight. Smelling vetiver and salt, fresh ironed clothes I pass she. Nobody from no town coming to look me in my face so. Nobody coming here to tell me what I done know. Anything she do could help me? Who she think she is come preaching here? Revolution, my backside. Then, she say "Sister." And I could not tell if it was a breeze passing in that heat-still day or if I hear the word. "Sister." I know I hear it, murmuring just enough to seem as if it was said but not something that only have sense in saying. I know I hear it silver, silver clinking like bracelets when a woman lift her arm to comb hair. Silvery, silvery the wind take it. It hum low and touch everything on the road. Things in me. I feel it cuff my back. I have to take air. A spirit in the road. It make a silence. It feel like rum going through my throat, warm and violent so the breath of her mouth brush my ear. Sweet sweet, my tongue sweet to answer she and it surprise me how I want to touch she teeth and hold she mouth on that word. I keep walking. I don't answer. But I regret every minute until I see she next.

The next time she come playing she trying to swing cutlass with she mouth moving as fast as you please about strike. Strike and demand a share in the estate. Well, look at bold face. We navel string bury here, she say, and we mother and we father and everybody before them. Oliviere use it up like manure for the cane, and what we get, one barrack room and credit in he store until we owe he more than he owe we, and is thief he thief this place in the first place. The people listen to she and smile because they know she make sense but she don't know what a hard people these Oliviere is. Is not just people navel string bury here is their shame and their body. They churn that up in the soil here too. It have people they just shoot and leave for corbeau to eat them. What left make the cane fat and juicy. She come from town and God knows where light, light and easy so. She not ready yet. One for she, she work hard. She body en't make for this, well who body make for it, but she do it.

She break my swing. It was the quiet. When I get used to she talking as I bend into the cane, when I done add she up for the swing so I wouldn't miss doing how much I need to do to make the quota, when I make she voice count in the stroke, I don't hear she no more. I swing up. What she doing now, like she tired talk at last. Good Lord! I say to myself, God wasn't joking when he make you girl. She was in front of me, staring my way, sweating as if she come out of a river. She was brilliant. I could see she head running ahead of we, she eyes done cut all the cane, she is not here, she dreaming of things we don't dream. I wanted to touch the shine of her, to dry off she whole body and say "Don't work it so hard," show she how to swing, how to tie up she waist so that she back would last, shield she legs so that the sheaf wouldn't cut. That is the first time I feel like licking she neck. She looked like the young in me, the not beaten down and bruised, the not pounded between my legs, the not lost my mother, the not raped, the not blooded, the not tired. She looked like me fresh, fresh, searching for good luck tea, leave my house broom, come by here weed. It ease me. It sweet sweet. A woman can be a bridge, limber and living, breathless, because she don't know where the bridge might lead, she don't need no assurance except that it would lead out with certainty, no assurance except the arch and disappearance. At the end it might be the uptake of air, the chasm of what she don't know, the sweep and soar of sheself unhandled, making sheself a way to cross over. A woman can be a bridge from these bodies whipping cane. A way to cross over. I see in she face how she believe. She glance quick as if unimportant things was in she way, like Oliviere, like fright. She eyes move as if she was busy going somewhere, busy seeing something and all this cane all this whipping and lashing was a hindrance. Then like a purposeful accident she eyes rest on me, and she face open, them big teeth push out to laugh for me, sweat flying, she fall again to the cutlass.

Dionne Brand

Dionne Brand is a poet, novelist, and essayist living in Toronto. Her latest novel, *What We All Long For*, was published in 2005 to great acclaim in Canada. Her fiction includes the novel *In Another Place, Not Here*—a 1998 *New York Times* notable book—and *Sans Souci and Other Stories*. Her second title, *At the Full and Change of the Moon* is a novel spanning six generations, two wars, and the violence of the late twentieth century. *The Village Voice* included her in its 1999 Writers on the Verge Literary supplement. *At the Full and Change of the Moon* was a *Los Angeles Times* Notable Book of the Year, 1999.

Dionne Brand's eight volumes of poetry include *Land to Light On*, which won the Governor General's Award for Poetry and the Trillium Award for Literature in 1997. Brand's most recent volume is called *thirsty*. In 2003 it was nominated for the Trillium Prize for Literature and the Griffin Poetry Prize. It won the Pat Lowther Award for Poetry.

Her works of non-fiction include *Bread Out of Stone*, a book of essays for which Adrienne Rich called her "a cultural critic of uncompromising courage, an artist in language and ideas, an intellectual conscience for her country." Brand's 2002 book, *A Map to the Door of No Return*, is a meditation on blackness in the diaspora.

Nicole Brossard
Writer Notes
A State of Mind in the Garden

C'est la moindre des choses que de ne pas avoir à faire tous les jours la preuve qu'on existe. C'est la moindre des choses quoique je connaisse des millions de femmes qui chaque jour doivent en faire la preuve. Certaines crient, d'autres grimacent, d'autres se tordent de rire, d'autres se frottent les mains comme pour en faire jaillir le feu, d'autres pensent qu'une existence remplie de mots c'est comme un trou noir dans le cosmos; d'autres disent qu'exister c'est parler dans la matière ou encore qu'exister c'est tracer un chemin avec sa bouche et son souffle dans l'infini recommencé de la matière.

I.

Cultures come and go. A great number of languages and species have died, others are disappearing at an incredible speed. War goes on non-stop around the world. A new civilization has started to change our notion of time, of space; is shaping differently our use of memory, of knowledge; is modifying the way humans, animals, and vegetation reproduce; is altering our certitudes about nature and the future. Yet most of the women living on this earth are enduring a non-human condition because they do not qualify as hu*man*. Life goes on, you travel, you make love, your mother dies, old friends pass away. One day you are asked to write about the self, yourself, your lesbianself and what writing can do for you. Suddenly you realize that more than anything else you are into life as others are into business.

2.

The world is changing. From memory to plain information, from depth to surface, from the reign of symbols to the reign of signs. The world is changing. Water is becoming rare and rarer. Yet I am sitting in the garden writing an article, still tracing letters with ink and pen, enjoying *le chant des cigales*, wondering if I will write about love, sex, memory, or real life. But I know that I can only write about one thing: how strongly I feel *l'immensité* in my chest and how this feeling is related to the virtuality of language. A virtuality which I cannot help associating with the idea of *making sense*. Making sense of life, of *l'immensité* in us, encountering the electrifying pleasure that sex, love, art, and nature offer us as well as making sense of death, no matter whatever its course in our life.

3.

Playing with words, enjoying them, craving them, or searching desperately for the appropriate ones to translate "*un*believable" experiences are situations in which I have found myself throughout my writing life. As I have often said, I do not see myself as a witness of my life or that of others. I see myself as an explorer in language who is trying to discover new territories. I work with language hoping that it will enable me to produce and offer sequences of emotions and thoughts which, without the written word, would not exist.

4.

I do not write to *indulge myself*, to attenuate pain, anger, or a sense of injustice. Of course, anything that is painful in my life will affect my writing. Even though it might orient my thoughts toward new themes, pain will not produce in me a desire to give in to anecdotes. Mostly it will affect the energy I am usually relying on or using in my exploration of meaning. Pain and pleasure are known to affect our breath when encountered in a vital way in life and they certainly transform the rhythm of my texts. Anything vividly experienced by the body shapes our writing and the meaning we give to life.

5.

Being a poet, a novelist, and an essayist allows me to acknowledge and process differently emotions and events traversing my life. Here, I think of the cycle: *Lovhers* (poetry), *Picture Theory* (novel), and *The Aerial Letter* (essays). Processing the raw material of desire and of sexual attraction into metaphors and the language of symbols is what poetry often does. In that sense it is very different from revisiting emotions still alive in the inner landscape of the self, hoping (as we do in prose) that they will engender a narrative voice rich with what imagination and reality are able to produce when they have altered each other to converge into fiction. Processing emotions and facts into ideas or theory also calls for another posture. Expanding the meaning of your story into the realm of social values and ideology requires that you understand where and why your story does not fit into the system and standard values. By doing so, you are forced to reevaluate the dominant forces that prevent your story from existing loudly and clearly in the public forum.

6.

Of course, it is not that simple: and in my case, genres are blurred because strong emotions in me always bring up the need to understand their source, their patterns, and their mechanics. Understanding is, therefore, a keyword in my work and this is how, for example, in the seventies and earlier eighties, while I was writing on utopia and ecstatic lesbian relationships, I was at the same time trying to figure out the tricky patriarchal logic which has been and is still so damaging to women, hoping that, once understood, it could free women at least from guilt and the double-bind.

7.

In the book *She Would Be the First Sentence of My Next Novel* (Mercury Press, 1998), I talk about my resistance to anecdote, diary, autobiography, while acknowledging the role those forms of writing have played in women's lives, be they writers or readers. I say that my *reserve* when it comes to writing down my life constitutes my *reserve* of images, of hope, and of energy. I also say that my resistance to writing down my lived experience is a way to *reserve* myself for the essential, the intuited matter that would take the form of what I would later call *theoretical fiction*.

8.

I am fascinated by the fact that no matter what our politics and our solidarities are, or our obvious belongings (gender, race, culture), one's real identity and motivations are activated by a much more complex and profound scenario than those we use for political purposes.

9.

One is first lesbian because of the pleasure shaping the intelligence and the recognition that the other woman, *she* makes sense. Lesbian desire must remain free, open, and nomadic, for it is by exploring that desire that our power to interact in the symbolic field takes effect.

10.

In the middle of our ideological discussions, *isn't each of us eager to ask* two questions of the other lesbian: when and how was it the first time? As if we need to hear about the origin, the founding moment in which we can retrace the illumination, the moment of passage when we suddenly found ourself on the other side of the mirror, of the world, in a universe where surprised, stunned, and relieved, we could observe *our self* drifting away from Adam's coast. Questions starting with where and how are questions that resemble those often asked of writers. When did you start writing? Why do you write? What is autobiographical in your books? As if being a lesbian is associated with something as mysterious, desirable, and creative as writing is.

11.

On the *Lesbian*, women and dykes can project what they don't know yet about themselves as well as what they already know. The *Lesbian* is a proposition and her proposition is sexual. Because that proposition is sexual, it astonishes and questions the good sense and the usual rationale. Her proposition questions sexual grammar, blurs the points of reference in sexual fantasies, and invites *au voyage*. It is because the lesbian's proposition is sexual that *she* has a symbolic effect that it is illuminating.

12.

There will always be a risk that a text written by a lesbian might not be a lesbian text. While the lesbian text is linguistically constructed around a sexual proposition, opening the space for other propositions to exist, the text written by a lesbian mostly relies on what she projects of her self. Her text becomes a lesbian text only if it alters the reader's sense of imagination.

> "Demain ne me demandez pas ce que fut, ce que sera ma vie. Demain, il y a mon effroyable prétention à la lucidité."

—previously printed in the *Journal of Lesbian Studies*, Volume 4, Number 4 2000.

Nicole Brossard
excerpt from *Baroque at Dawn*

First the dawn. Then the woman came.

In Room 43 at the Hotel Rafale, in the heart of a North American city armed to the teeth, in the heart of a civilization of gangs, artists, dreams, and computers, in darkness so complete it swallowed all countries, Cybil Noland lay between the legs of a woman she had met just a few hours before. For a time which seemed a coon's age and very nocturnal, the woman had repeated, "Devastate me, eat me up." Cybil Noland had plied her tongue with redoubled ardour and finally heard, "Day, vastate me, heat me up." The woman's thighs trembled slightly and then her body orbited the planet as if the pleasure in her had transformed to a stupendous aerial life reflex.

Cybil Noland had felt the sea enter her thoughts like a rhyme, a kind of sonnet which briefly brought her close to Louise Labé, then drew away to pound elsewhere, wave sounds in present tense. The sea had penetrated her while whispering livable phrases in her ear, drawn-out laments, a lifelong habit with its thousand double exposures of light. Later, thoughts of the sea cast her against a boundless wall of questions.

§

In the room, the air conditioner is making an infernal noise. Dawn has given signs of life. Cybil can now make out the furniture shapes and see, reflected in the mirror on the half-open bathroom door, a chair on which are draped a blue T-shirt, a pair of jeans, and a black leather jacket. On the rug, a pair of sandals one beside the other.

The woman puts a hand on Cybil Noland's hair, the other touching a shoulder. The stranger at rest is terribly alive, anonymous with her thousand identities in repose. Cybil

Noland turns so as to rest her cheek comfortably in the curve of the other's crotch. Neither thinks to move, much less to talk. Each is from somewhere else, each is elsewhere in her life of elsewhere, as if living some life from the past.

§

Cybil Noland had travelled a lot, to cities with light-filled curves shimmering with headlights and neon signs. She loved suspense, the kind of risk that might now take as simple a guise as strolling about among the buildings of big cities. She had always declined to stay in the mountains or the country or beside a lake, even for a few days. Her past life had unfolded at a city pace, in the presence of many accents, traffic sounds and speed, all of which sharpen the senses. Over the years she had come to love sunsets reddened by carbon dioxide. It had been so long since she had seen the stars that the names of the constellations had long ago vanished into her memory's recesses. Cybil Noland lived at information's pace. Information was her firmament, her inner sea, her Everest, her cosmos. She loved the electric sensation she felt at the speed of passing images. Each image was easy. It was easy for her to forget what it was that had excited her a moment before. Sometimes she thought she ought to resist this frenetic consumption of words, catastrophes, speed, rumours, fears, and screens, but too late, her intoxication seemed irreversible. Between fifteen and thirty years of age she had studied history, literature, and the curious laws that govern life's instinct for continuation. Thus she had learned to navigate among beliefs and dreams dispersed over generations and centuries. But today all that seemed far away, ill-suited to the speed with which reality was spinning out her anxiety with its sequences of happiness and violence, its fiction grafted like a science to the heart of instinct. As a child she had learned several languages, enabling her today to consume twice the information, commentary, tragedy, minor mishaps and prognostications.

Thus she had unwittingly acquired a taste for glib words and fleeting images. All she had learned in her youth finally came to seem merely muddleheaded, anachronistic, and obsolete.

On this July night that was drawing to a close in a small hotel in a city armed to the teeth, Cybil Noland had felt the sea rise up and swallow her. Something had spilled over, creating a vivid horizontal effect, but simultaneously a barrier of questions. The sky, the stars, and the sea had synthesized an entire civilization of cities in her when the woman came.

There between the stranger's legs, questions arose, insistent, intrusive questions, snooping questions, basic questions seeking alternately to confirm and deny the world and its raison d'être. Borne on this current of questions, Cybil Noland vowed to renounce glib pronouncements without, however, willingly foregoing the dangerous euphoria elicited by the fast, frenzied images of her century.

§

The light was now diffused throughout the room, a yellow morning light which, in movies of yesteryear, gave the dialogue a hopeful turn, for the simple reason that mornings in those days were slow with the natural slowness that suited the movements made by heroines when, upon awakening, they gracefully stretched their arms, raising arches of carnal triumph in the air.

The woman has moved her legs to change position, perhaps to leave the bed. Cybil Noland has raised her head then her body in such fashion as to hoist herself up to the level of the woman's face. The mattress is uncomfortable, with hollows and soft spots one's elbows and knees sink into.

Since meeting, the two have barely exchanged three sentences. The woman is a musician and young. *"But I'm not sixteen,"* she said with a smile in the elevator. Cybil Noland thereupon nicknamed her "La Sixtine." On arrival in the room, they undressed and the woman ordered, "Eat me."

Now that Cybil Noland has the woman's living face at eye level, her belly swells again rich with desire like a tempestuous wind. *Kiss me, kiss m'again.*[1] With fire and festivity in her eyes, the woman looks Cybil over, caresses her, then thrusts her tongue between her lips. It might have been just a kiss, but what a way she has of breathing, of pearling each lip, tracing *abc* inside Cybil's mouth with the tiniest movements, impossible to separate the letters *abc*, to stop, demon delirium *abc* a constellation of flavours in her mouth. Then the wind surges, sweeping eyelashes, drying the perspiration about the neck, smoothing silken cheeks, closing eyelids, imprinting the outlines of faces deep in the pillow. The five sibyls of the Sixtine Chapel orbit the planet and the questions return. Cybil Noland opens her eyes. There are still traces of mascara on the woman's eyelashes. She too unseals her eyes. The look they give is laughing, languid, offering an intimacy glimpsable only in the strictest anonymity. Like a love-crazed thing all of a sudden, Cybil is aburn for this anonymous woman who had caught her eye in the bar of the Hotel Rafale. Something is exciting her, something about the anonymity of this woman encountered in the middle of a huge city, something that says, I don't know your name but I recognize the smooth curvaceous shape your body takes when navigating to the open sea. Soon I shall know where your tears, your savage words and anxious gestures hide, the things that will lead me to divine everything about you at one fell swoop. Thus does imagination take us beyond the visible, propelling us toward new faces that will set the wind asurge despite the barrier formed by vertical cities, despite the speed of life that drains our thoughts and leaves them indolent. The priceless eyes of desire are right to succumb to seduction so that one's familiar, everyday body may find joy in the thousands of anonymous others encountered along the way, bodies pursuing their destinies in cities saturated with feelings and emotions.

§

The stranger gives off a scent of complex life which coils about Cybil Noland. City smells clinging to her hair like a social ego; fragrant, singularizing sandalwood, a trace of navel salt, the milky taste of her breasts. Everywhere an infiltration of life, aromatic, while the child in one does the rounds of all the smells, anonymously like a grown-up in a hurry to get thinking.

The air conditioner has stopped. There's silence. A surprising silence like the heady smell of lilac when the month of May reaches us at the exits of great, sense-deadening cages of glass and concrete. The silence draws out, palpable and appealing like La Sixtine's body. The alarm-clock dial on the bedside table is blinking. A power failure. Which means unbearable heat in exchange for a silence rare and more precious than gold and caviar. The silence is now diffused throughout the room. Surprising, devastating. An unreal silence that's terribly alive, as if imposing a kind of fiction by turning the eyes of the heart toward an unfathomable inner life.

The women lie side by side, legs entwined and each with an arm under the other's neck like sleepy reflex arcs. Suddenly Cybil Noland can stand no more of this new silence that has come and imposed itself on top of the first, which had been a silence tacitly agreed between them like a stylized modesty, an elegant discretion, a kind of meditative state capable of shutting out the sounds of civilization and creating a fictional time favourable to the appearance of each one's essential face.

§

Cybil Noland had brought the woman up to her room thinking of what she called each woman's essential face in her own destiny. Each time she had sex with a woman, this was what put heart into her desire. She was ready for anything, any kind of caress, any and all sexual scenarios, aware that you can never foresee exactly when, or for how long, an orgasm will recompose the lines of the mouth and chin, make the eyelids droop, dilate the pupils or keep the eyes shining. Most often the face would describe its own aura of ecstasy, beginning with the light filtering through the enigmatic slit between the eyelids when they hover half-closed halfway between life and pleasure. Then would come the split second that changed the iris into the shape of a crescent moon, before the white of the eye, whiter than the soul, proliferated multiples of the word imagery deep in her thoughts. This was how a woman who moments earlier had been a total stranger became a loved one capable of changing the course of time for the better.

All, thought Cybil Noland, so that the essential face that shows what women are really capable of may be seen, vulnerable and radiant, infinitely human, desperately disturbing. But for this to happen, the whole sea would have to flood into her mouth, and the wind flatten her hair to her skull, and fire ignite from fire, and she would have to consider everything very carefully at the speed of life and wait for the woman to possess her own silence, out of breath and beyond words in the midst of her present. In the well of her pleasure the woman would have to find her own space, a place of choice.

So when the air conditioner stopped, Cybil Noland felt she had been robbed of the rare and singular silence that had brought her so close to La Sixtine. As if she had suddenly realized that while the words *heat me vast*[2] were ringing with their thousand possibilities and her delicate tongue was separating the lips of La Sixtine's sex, civilization had nevertheless continued its headlong course.

Now the new silence is crowding the silence that accompanies one's most private thoughts. While groping for a comparison to explain this new silence, suddenly Cybil Noland can stand no more of it and wants to speak, will speak, but the woman comes close and reclines on top of her and with her warm belly and hair tickling Cybil's nose, and breasts brushing over Cybil's mouth, seems determined to turn Cybil's body into an object of pure erotic pleasure.

You'd say she was going. To say. Yes, she murmurs inarticulate sounds in Cybil's ear, rhythms, senseless words, catches her breath, plays on it momentarily, "That good?" she breathes. "That better?" Then over Cybil's body strews images and succulent words that burst in the mouth like berries. Now her sounds caress like violins. The names of constellations come suddenly to Cybil's mind: Draco the Dragon, Coma Berenices, Cassiopaeia, and Lyra for the Northern Hemisphere; Sculptor, Tucana, Apus the Bird of Paradise, Ara the Altar for the Southern. Then the whole sea spreads through her and La Sixtine relaxes her hold.

§

You'd say she was going to tell a story. Something with the word joyous in the sentence to go with her nakedness there in the middle of the room. Once she's in the shower the water runs hard. She sings. When she lifts her tongue the sounds crowd up from under, full of vim. Joyously her voice spews out, zigzags from one word to another, cheerily penetrating Cybil Noland's consciousness as she lies half asleep in the spacious bed.

"I'll tell you a story," La Sixtine said, opening the window before getting in the shower. The window opens onto a fire escape. The curtain moves gently. Cybil Noland watches the movements of the fish, seaweed, and coral in the curtain's design. Life is a backdrop against which thoughts and memories overlap. Life moves ever so slightly, goes through static stages, skews off, brings its humanism to the midst of armed cities like a provocation, a paradox that makes you smile. In spite of yourself. The dark fish throw a shadow over the pinks and whites of the coral, Cybil Noland thinks before riding off again, a deep-sea wanderer aboard great incunabula.

1 Louise Labé: *Baise-moi, baise m'encore.*
2 Nicole Brossard: *m'ange moi vaste.*

Nicole Brossard

Born in Montreal. Poet, novelist, and essayist, twice Governor General's Award recipient for her poetry, Nicole Brossard has published more than thirty books since 1965. Many among those books have been translated into English: *Mauve Desert, The Aerial Letter, Picture Theory, Lovhers, Baroque at Dawn, The Blue Books, Installations, Museum of Bone and Water* and *She Would Be the First Sentence of My Next Novel*. She has co-founded and co-directed the literary magazine *La Barre du Jour* (1965-1975), has co-directed the film *Some American Feminists* (1976), and co-edited the acclaimed *Anthologie de la poésie des femmes au Québec*, first published in 1991, then in 2003.

She has won le Grand Prix de Poésie du Festival International de Trois-Rivières in 1989 and in 1999. In 1991, she was awarded le Prix Athanase-David (the highest literary recognition in Québec). She won the W.O. Mitchell 2003 Prize, and she is a member of l'Académie des Lettres du Québec.

Nicole Brossard's work has been widely translated into English and Spanish and is also available in German, Italian, Japanese, Slovenian, Romanian, Catalan, and other languages. Guernica Editions published a book of essays on her work (edited by Louise Forsyth). Her most recent books published in English are *Intimate Journal* and *Yesterday, at the Hotel Clarendon*.

Nicole Brossard writes and lives in Montreal.

Emma Donoghue
Writer Notes

"Write what you know," the cliché has it, but over the course of six books of fiction I have wrung just as much delight from writing what I don't know—or rather, what I know not from personal experience but from research and imagination. And of course the worlds of the familiar and the invented often overlap. My novel *Hood*, for instance, is closely based on my memories of convent school in Ireland in the 1980s, but is all about bereavement, something I haven't yet had to suffer. Conversely, my novel *Slammerkin* is about a prostitute cum maidservant in eighteenth-century England, but the character of the employer she murders is inspired by my mother.

I am a lesbian writer, a woman writer, an Irish writer, a Canadian writer (living here since 1998), and all these identities inform my work—without setting rules for it. I have written some stories with no lesbians in them, or no women, or no mention of Ireland or Canada, and these trips away from my daily reality have given me a peculiar pleasure. But my first two novels were set in contemporary Dublin and most of my work has been about women's lives over the last four centuries. And all my books have included lesbian themes except *Slammerkin* which turned out to be my bestseller—a sign, I fear, that the mainstream fiction audience is still nervous of lesbian content.

Time Zone Tango, the novel from which "Here and Now" is taken, is extremely autobiographical in that it is about an Irishwoman falling for a Canadian woman and moving to Canada. It deals with culture clash, long-distance relationships, emigration, and other topics that have mattered to me over the last ten years. It is my first attempt to write about the social world, landscape, and startling climate of southwestern Ontario. But I am not an Indo-Irish flight attendant and my lover is not a small-town archivist with an inconvenient husband. So a novel like this one offers a writer yet another strange pleasure, that of using other actors to restage her own dramas.

Emma Donoghue
Here and Now

Walking through a strange airport always made Síle feel like she was in the opening scene of *Jackie Brown*, which was one of her all-time favourites. (There weren't many films that starred gorgeous, clever, dark-skinned flight attendants who'd never see thirty-five again.) She walked smartly, relishing the chance to stretch, aware of the movement of her hips in her purple knee-length skirt. Her red leather carry-on glided along behind her. She'd put her long sheets of hair up in a French twist and applied a lipstick called Bruised Fruit. Outside the walls of glass, she could see nothing but spiralling whiteness. Síle had spent half her life in airports, but today, Toronto Pearson—for all its dull bilingual signs and grey carpets—seemed a fairyland.

At Immigration she handed over her well-worn Irish passport. "I'm a flight attendant, but I'm not on duty," she explained.

"Visiting friends, family?"

"Mm," she said, slightly breathless. On New Year's Eve I met a girl called Jude Turner at thirty thousand feet over the Atlantic, and I haven't been the same since, she thought.

"Which?"

"A friend. She's an archivist. She lives in Ireland, Ontario," Síle added weakly. Was it true? Did two months of letters, emails, phone calls amount to *friendship*? If you'd only met once, was it ludicrous to use the word *love*? But her passport was scanned and stamped (one more mark on its tattered pages) and she was waved on.

The door slid open and she sailed through, thinking, don't stop me, if there's another minute of delay I'm going to burst...

There, behind the barrier, a narrow head on top of a huge down jacket. Síle paused, blinking. Jude didn't shout a greeting; she just raised her fingers and walked towards the gap in the barrier. She'd had a haircut; very short, very soft. Síle went stiff. She'd planned to kiss Jude boldly, with lips and tongue in the middle of the airport throng, but now the moment was come she felt barely capable of shaking hands.

Jude hugged her. Síle was engulfed in Jude's down jacket. It was like being embraced by a duvet. But on her back she could feel the hard grip of Jude's hands, and a second's hot breath on her neck. They were blocking the stream of passengers emerging from the baggage hall. "Hey," said Síle, stepping sideways. "Hey you."

"Hey."

"Oh dear, I've got lipstick on your jaw."

"Have you?" said Jude, grinning, not wiping it off, and Síle remembered what it was all about, why she'd come all this way.

Her heart drummed. "Here you are. I can't believe it. Two feet away!"

"Less," said Jude, stepping closer.

"So." Síle cleared her throat. "I thought you said spring would have come by April?"

Jude's face got serious all at once. "Where's your coat? And boots?"

"Oh, I'll be fine, this is warmer than it looks," said Síle, zipping up her long raincoat.

Jude cast a doubtful glance at Síle's high heels. "It's pretty nasty out there. We could always stay the night at the Holiday Inn," she added after a second.

Síle's mouth pursed. Spending their first night together at the Holiday Inn... "How long is the drive to Little Ireland?" She imagined how nice the village would look under a sheet of white snow.

"Usually an hour and a half—but the roads are getting worse, and they haven't been salted yet."

Síle had no idea what that meant. She took Jude's slim, warm wrist and murmured, "I'd trust your driving."

"You don't know anything about my driving," Jude pointed out.

"I can guess," said Síle, smiling back at her.

Jude picked up Síle's case, and stumbled.

"Mind, it's heavy."

"You can say that again."

"It's got wheels, look." Síle followed her through the crowd, trying to remember where she'd stowed her little kidskin gloves. Jude was still carrying the suitcase instead of wheeling it; lord, Síle thought with a mixture of dread and excitement, I didn't know she was *that* butch.

As she stepped through the sliding doors, a blast of icy wind nearly knocked her off her heels. She staggered, and felt snow like a cloud of needles against her face, in her ears, in her eyes. Where had Jude got to? This was ludicrous. Síle couldn't be expected to walk through this. The evening air was like broken glass; she couldn't breathe it. Her hands were hurting. The moaning wind flattened her lined raincoat against her; she might just have well have been naked. Turn it off! she thought. Make it stop!

A tug on her shoulder. Jude, small-faced inside a huge fur-edged hood. "Where were you?"

"Where were *you*?" replied Síle childishly.

"Don't you have a hat?"

Síle set her back to the wind and bawled, "Listen, let's go back inside the terminal till this dies down."

Jude shook her head. "It won't." And turned away, no discussion.

So Síle had to follow, picking her way across the road to the car park through several inches of snow.

Jude's car turned out to be an Oldsmobile, nibbled by rust along all its edges. The heating made a desperate whirr. "Sorry about this," Jude muttered, "but at least it's a stick-shift, so I can usually find my way out of trouble."

As they pulled slowly out of Toronto Airport, Síle sat cupping her sore ears in her hands. Her ankles were wet with melting snow. "I'm just not bred for this cold," she remarked with a self-mocking shudder.

Jude didn't answer. She was hunched over the wheel, peering past the headlights at the spot-lit direction signs. *ALL ROADS LEAD TO BRAMPTON.*

The girl was more taciturn than Síle remembered from the one morning they'd spent together at Heathrow Airport. Was this what Jude was really like in the flesh, then, or was it only a mood brought on by the howling blizzard? But then, what were any of us except a random sequence of moods?

"This climate is rather a thrill," said Síle, as merrily as she could manage. "I might have died back there outside the terminal, mightn't I, if I'd turned the wrong way in the snow and tripped over something, or just stood there waiting for you for too long? Whereas in my Ireland— Big Ireland!—you could lie in a ditch for a fortnight and end up with nothing worse than a runny nose."

She was working for a laugh, but Jude's eyes were on the dim tail lights of the jeep in front. There was no other sign that they were on a road, Síle realized. They must have turned off the motorway a while back. The signs were all matted with snow, illegible.

"Actually, this isn't really cold," Jude murmured. "When it's *really* cold, snow can't fall."

Síle absorbed that cheering information. Already she'd counted four cars off the road, one of them upside down. She craned to see whether all the passengers had got out safely, but all she glimpsed was snow and blackness. The narrow file of cars crept forward. Síle suddenly wondered whether there was a road under them at all, or whether the lead car might have veered off across some desolate field, with the rest of them following like slow lemmings.

Jude turned on the radio, searching for a weather report and for the next half hour she switched between crackling stations offering soul, opera, a panel discussion on gang culture, and Christian rock. Síle hadn't seen her have a cigarette yet.

Maybe she never smoked while she was driving, or not in difficult conditions like this. "How are your legs?" Jude asked suddenly.

"Numb to the knee, actually."

She fiddled with the heating controls. "That better?"

"Not really."

Jude turned and pulled a blanket off the back seat.

Síle tried to feel grateful for that bit of gallantry, as she wrapped the scratchy damp thing around her legs. At one point she gave her gizmo a surreptitious squeeze to light up the little screen. Eight thirty-nine somewhere in the snowbound, godless wilderness that Southwestern Ontario seemed to be. *Distance from Home City 3285 Miles.* Nearly two in the morning back in Dublin, where she could have been tucked up in her copper-pipe bed on her Egyptian cotton sheets. She wondered why she hadn't gone somewhere else for the weekend, somewhere like Tahiti.

Síle chewed her lip in frustration. Her Bruised Fruit lipstick had worn off. She hadn't noticed the jeep ahead turn off the road, but it was nowhere to be seen. The draughty Oldsmobile was alone now. There was nothing ahead of them but the menacing whiteness under their headlights and the speckle of falling snow.

"Not long now."

And that was it for small-talk for another quarter of an hour. Why, Síle asked herself, did I ever start corresponding with this immature, small-town Canadian who has nothing to say for herself and nothing to say to me?

They drew to a halt just beyond a bare crossroads, under a lone streetlight. "What is it?" asked Síle. "Don't say we're out of petrol?"

"What? No, we're home," said Jude, stepping out into the night.

She slammed the door behind her, and Síle was suddenly alone, the skin of her throat, wrists, and knees contracting in the icy air. Home? Ireland, Ontario, wasn't even a village, as far as she could tell; it wasn't anything. They'd taken the best part of three hours to reach the arse end of nowhere.

Jude opened the door again to say "Sorry, I can't pull into the driveway till it's shovelled."

When Síle stepped out, the snow came up to her knees. It was astonishing wet and cold through her ten-denier tights. She staggered and lurched after Jude's dark bulk. Snowflakes spiked on her eyelashes. At one point she almost lost one of her shoes in a pile of snow, but she reminded herself grimly, Gucci, 369 Euro, and clenched it on.

Jude was waiting for her outside a New-England style wooden house, hands tucked under her arms. "Soon be warm," she said encouragingly. Síle's teeth were clamped shut.

In the upstairs bathroom, shuddering as she rubbed some life back into her bare legs with a stiff towel, she reviewed her contingency plans. First thing tomorrow morning—if she lived through the night—she would find someone who owned a proper car in this wretched little homestead, and pay them to drive her back to Toronto Airport.

Slow steps on the stairs. Jude stood in the doorway of the bathroom. "You hate me," she said, with no preamble.

"That's right," said Síle, feeling ever so slightly better. She kept on chafing her legs, aware of Jude's eyes on them.

"What you need is a hot bath."

"Oh, I always take showers," said Síle, "they're so much faster."

There it was, Jude's crooked little smile, the one Síle had been trying to call up in her memory, all these months. "What's the rush?" Jude ran the bath till it was very deep—checking the temperature every so often, while Síle sat there on the toilet seat and watched her, suddenly aware of being drop-dead tired. Finally Jude opened a box and threw what looked like a handful of dust into the water.

"What's that?" asked Síle.

"Oatmeal," said Jude briefly, and turned off the taps.

Oatmeal? I've gone back in time. I've joined the fucking

Amish, thought Síle dizzily.

Alone in the bathroom, she immersed herself in the silky, clouded water and sank down and down till it covered her stomach, her nipples, her chin. The heat made her limbs throb. She felt as if she were drowning.

When she emerged in her towel, she looked around. Lots of wood. Warm air puffed through old wrought iron grilles at floor level. The door to a bedroom was wide open and her bag was standing there, incongruously executive-style beside the rocking chair on the rag-rug. She'd brought her silk night-shirt with her, of course, but folded on the bed were a pair of blue striped cotton pyjamas that made her think of Christopher Robin and Winnie the Pooh. So she put them on and crawled under the huge lumpy duvet.

She wondered where Jude was. Off having a fag at last, maybe.

Síle's eyelids were beginning to droop by the time Jude appeared in the doorway with a vast steaming mug. "Camomile tea."

"Sorry," said Síle guiltily, "but I can't stand the stuff."

Jude looked as if she might go away again, but instead she set the mug down on the table and sat on the very edge of the bed. "How're you doing?"

"Better," said Síle.

Jude took a sip of the camomile.

The silence was getting a little awkward, so Síle said "I brought you a little something from Dublin Airport," pointing to the Duty Free bag on the table.

Jude pulled out the box of 400 Camels.

"It's meant as an apology for telling you off at Heathrow," Síle explained. "I've always refused to buy cigarettes for my friends, but this time I decided to make the grand gesture."

Jude let out a creaky little laugh.

"What?" asked Síle. "Did I get the brand wrong?"

Jude leaned over and kissed her with precise and strong lips.

Síle stared up at her, startled. "You don't taste like a smoker," she said eventually.

"Exactly."

"You didn't!" said Síle.

"I did. I gave them up at midnight yesterday, and I've been brushing my teeth a lot since then, for something to do."

"For me?" asked Síle, marvelling. "You gave up smoking for me?"

Jude shrugged. "You were just... the occasion."

Síle smiled as sleek as a cat. "That's why you've been such a glump this evening. You're in withdrawal!"

"A glump?"

"You know exactly what I mean. Riding along in stony silence like some prison escort..."

"I was concentrating on the road. It was tough driving." Jude's voice was stern but her face was twisted with laughter. "And as for you, turning up in a blizzard in stilettos and a slinky raincoat—"

"Whose are the pyjamas?" asked Síle, changing the subject.

"Mine," said Jude, looking at her with those peculiar hazel eyes that were almost yellow, like a cat's.

"They're very soft. Are you coming in?" asked Síle at last, patting the duvet.

Jude stood up jerkily. "I dunno, I can sleep next door if—"

"Bollocks," said Síle reaching out and tucking a finger over the edge of Jude's jean pocket. "I've only got two nights and I didn't come all this way for *next door*."

Jude snapped the light off before undressing. "Puritan blood, you know," she murmured.

Síle was too tired to protest. She listened to the soft little sounds of clothes coming off, being piled on a chair. Then the bed creaked as Jude climbed in. Síle wriggled backwards till her back reached Jude's hot chest. The girl was completely naked; not such a Puritan as all that, then. It was odd, Síle thought; they'd only hugged once in their lives before, at

Toronto airport—they didn't know each other's curves and angles—and yet here they were, slotted together like this was the only way to be, like this was the only possible place to lie on a wintry April night.

Must take off these pyjamas, she thought sleepily. First times are crucial. Mustn't be wearing pyjamas. Must ravish her in some memorable way. "Lordy," she murmured at last, "cold really makes you appreciate a human body."

"There's a bit in the Bible about that," mentioned Jude.

"Isn't there always?" she groaned.

Jude quoted it in her ear: *"If two lie together, then they have heat, but how can one be warm alone?"*

Síle lay very still, planning a witty response to that.

But the next thing she knew, it was morning, and gaudy yellow sun was setting their bed on fire.

Sun in their eyes, in the crooks of their knees and elbows. It was easy, laughably so. Jude shouldn't have worried. Pretty soon she even forgot she was dying for a cigarette. She and Síle knew what to do as if the information had been waiting in their genes. Everything fit. There was startled breathing and laughter and even some roaring into pillows. It was a lucky dip, a ten-course banquet, a fruit machine where—*ching, ching!*— the coins kept spilling from the slot.

Síle's breasts lay like basking seals on Jude's hot ribs. Jude's knee cut between Síle's thighs like a river carving out its bed. Their fingers slotted together. They got so tangled up in Síle's hip-length dark hair, she had to shake it back over the headboard.

Jude played with the delicate gold chain around Síle's waist.

"Feels strange," Síle said; "nobody's touched it in a long time. It was my mother's, it's called an Aranjanam."

Jude repeated the syllables, Síle correcting her till she'd got it right. "Didn't Kathleen touch it?" she asked. There were always ghosts around a bed, you might as well invite them in, start trying to make peace with them.

Síle looked her in the eye. "Not in a few years."

Excellent! But Jude only said that in her head, and she managed to keep her face straight. She thought of saying something like *That's terrible,* but it would be tacky to triumph over her fallen foe. "Do you ever take it off?"

Síle shook her head. "Though if I carry on my love affair with Belgian pralines I may have to have it lengthened! The times I've been to Kerala, my relations tell me I look like my Amma reincarnated," she went on more seriously, "but I still feel like such an outsider. If she'd lived to raise me and Orla I suppose we'd be cultural hybrids, but as it is we're just brown Irish. I've never even slept with anyone who wasn't white as paper. Have you?"

"Well, Rizla's half Mohawk—"

"Of course. I forget to count guys," said Síle with a self-mocking grin.

Things got sweaty and noisy again, and Jude forgot how much she'd been wanting a cigarette.

Much later, Jude felt sudden wet on the side of her neck, and thought for a moment she'd burst a blood vessel. But then Síle's face lifted, and it was blotted with tears. "What is it?" said Jude, appalled. "What's wrong?"

Síle sobbed. "Nothing. Nothing at all is wrong." She licked her own salt water off Jude's collar-bone.

"Just so long as I know."

"Did you never have anyone weep all over you in bed before?"

Jude shook her head.

"You realize this is doomed?" said Síle in an indecently hopeful voice.

"What, you mean the living five thousand kilometres apart?"

"Oh dear, that sounds even worse than three thousand miles."

"I thought Ireland was metric."

"Well, in theory, but we still talk in miles and pints," Síle explained. "But yes, the distance, and also the little matter of fourteen years..."

"*That* needn't matter," said Jude. "People are always telling me I've got an old head on young shoulders."

Síle grinned. "It's two generations, musically and demographically: I'm a tail-end Boomer and you're Gen Y."

"I'd like to say in my defence that I can play 'Scarborough Fair.' Couldn't we just pretend I was born in the Sixties?"

"Play it on what?"

"Guitar. What could be more Sixties than that?"

Síle let out an exasperated breath. "How could you not have mentioned that you play the guitar?"

"I'm not that good."

"You're good enough to play 'Scarborough Fair,' which makes it a big fat lie of omission." She reached for Jude's fingertips and rubbed them. "Calluses, of course, I should have guessed," she said under her breath.

"Sorry, did they—"

"I like them," Síle told her. "So what else don't I know about you?"

"A quarter-century's worth, at least," said Jude, grinning.

Later, when Síle was in the shower, Jude stretched out and let her head dangle off the mattress. She was woozy; she was high as a kite. She had a little headache, from withdrawal, she supposed, but nothing she couldn't handle. Gwen had suggested Nicorette patches, but Jude preferred to do this cold turkey. She rolled onto her stomach and looked under the bed. There were dust balls, and a pencil, and a pair of delicate high-heeled suede shoes with salt marks on them. Jude pulled on her towelling robe and went downstairs for the desalting fluid.

She'd dabbed the worst of the marks off with desalting fluid by the time Síle emerged in a tiny towel.

They stared at each other. "Are you fondling my Gucci's?"

"Just getting the salt off before it stains."

For a moment, Síle looked as if she might burst into tears again. "That's so... so nice of you." The towel began to fall. "Whoops."

"For future reference, the bath towels are in the cupboard below the basin," Jude observed, kissing her ribs one at a time.

While Síle was dressing—wool trousers and a silk knit jumper, which still looked pretty thin to Jude for this weather—Jude peered into the Aladdin's cave of the suitcase. She saw a toiletries bag in red quilted satin, a jewellery box, a Feminique Sonic Razor, a clip-on reading light, a lint shaver, a set of voltage adaptors, earplugs, a fur-lined, gel-filled eye mask, a silk Sleep Sack, an inflatable travel pillow, a pair of what claimed to be Anti-Noise Earphones... "You come prepared," said Jude, picking up object after object. "Especially considering you're only here till tomorrow afternoon."

"Don't think about my going home yet," commanded Síle. "Anyway, this is just my standard travel bag; it's simpler to keep it packed."

"On the rare occasions I go anywhere," said Jude, "pretty much all I need is my toothbrush."

"This saves you all the work," said Síle, plucking an Electric Tooth Wand out of the jumble.

"The *work*?"

"Every 30 seconds it beeps to remind you to move on to the next quadrant of your mouth." Síle was very deadpan.

Jude couldn't stop grinning. "What're the binoculars for?" she asked, resting the compact case in her palm.

"Well, I thought maybe wildlife," said Síle doubtfully. "I didn't realize there'd be all this snow."

"Well, we'll keep an eye out for a sasquatch. And this... Watchman?" she asked, reading the name. "Seems a bit cumbersome for a watch."

"It's a TV," said Síle eagerly, putting down her hairbrush for a minute to show her Homer Simpson lumbering across the screen. "It's got a 2.2 passive matrix LCD."

"There you go, speaking Martian again. What's this?"

"A massage thimble, my sister Orla gave it to me in my Christmas stocking. The little bumps on it stimulate your acupressure points."

"Seems a bit low-tech," murmured Jude, pressing it into her wrist and wondering if it would help with cigarette cravings. "You sure do like things."

"Which translates as, materialistic and shallow?"

"No," said Jude, "I just mean you get a kick out of gadgets. Things that stand between you and the real world."

Síle's tapered eyebrows soared as she wrestled her hair into a plait. "The real world?"

Jude struggled for words. "Nature, I guess."

"But it's all real, darlin'. The birds and the bees, and the earplugs and lint shavers too." Her smile was very wry and thirty-eight.

"I still can't believe *this* is real."

"I can," said Síle, her hands decisive on Jude's hips, pulling her close. "You're no figment. I've never met anyone so here and now."

The kiss lasted long enough that Jude thought she might fall down.

That evening, Jude felt ridiculously nervous as they crunched up Main Street hand in hand, towards the solitary streetlight at the crossroads.

There were about a dozen drinkers in the Dive.

"How are my mother's snow boots?"

"Well, they do the trick," said Síle grudgingly, "but next time I'm buying more elegant ones. It must be possible to keep warm without quite so much padding."

Next time, thought Jude with a flash of bliss.

Rizla was there at the bar, sucking on his ginger ale, like most other evenings; it was warmer than his trailer, after all. It occurred to Jude for the first time that he looked like someone who'd done time. His bushy eyebrows shot up to his hairline, and he boomed "Jeez, the honeymooners managed to get out of bed!"

Jude said in his ear, "Remember I promised you could meet her if you promised not to be a jerk?"

Already Rizla had enclosed Síle's hand in his own beefy one. He helped her off with her coat, and insisted she take his stool. "Go right ahead, my fat ass's had enough sitting around."

Síle crossed her legs sexily, despite the borrowed snow boots, and smiled up at him. In her bright skirt and beaded Rajasthani jacket, she stood out against the comfortable casuals the locals were wearing, quite apart from being the only South Asian face in the village.

"Dave," said Rizla, "may I present Síle O'Shaughnessy from Dublin, Ireland?"

The bartender wore a wary smile. "Whatever you say, Riz. Now, what can I get you all? Sleeman's, Upper Canada..."

"Actually, Dave," said Síle, her accent strengthening as she leaned over the bar, "I'm not too fond of the old beer, to be honest. What I'd love is a chocolate martini, if it wouldn't be too much trouble."

Dave blinked at her. Rizla stroked his moustache smugly. "A chocolate martini?"

"Made with crème de cacao, you know?"

"I'll have a look in the back," Dave said abstractedly.

In his absence, Jude told Síle that she might have to settle for an ale. "You're not in Big Ireland now."

Síle widened her eyes. "Place your trust in the global economy."

And indeed, ten minutes later, Dave came in brandishing a dusty bottle of crème de cacao. Rizla and Síle applauded. Jude stared at it, and thought, *This woman is a magic wand.*

Dave rested on his elbows and examined the visitor more closely. "That sure is a nice accent you've got. I thought Rizla here must be pulling my leg, because you don't look Irish."

Jude stiffened, but Síle beamed back at him. "And the

funny thing is, Dave, I've been told I don't look like a lesbian either."

He took a second to register that. "Well, pleasure to meet you," he said, swabbing randomly at the counter with his cloth before heading into the back.

Rizla pounded the bar in silent mirth. "Two-nil to the Fighting Irish! You shut that dickhead up."

"Poor Dave," Síle murmured repentantly, "and after he made me a perfect chocolate martini..."

Jude felt all the strings in her body loosen.

"Yeah, this whole area was Mohawk hunting grounds," Rizla was telling Síle when Jude tuned in again, 'till we sold it to the Crown in the early eighteenth century."

"You mean early 1800s," Jude reminded him.

He ignored that. "I'm not actually Status, though," he went on.

"Sorry, you've lost me," said Síle.

"My mom married a Dutchman, that's how come my surname's Vandeloo, so she wasn't a Status Indian anymore, she had to go off-reservation; that was the law back then. She raised nine of us in a farmhouse, up north a ways. Big breeders," he commented, "like the Irish, I guess!"

"There's only two of us in my family, me and my sister," remarked Síle.

Rizla's eyebrows went up. "What happened? Your parents got bored of doing the old bump 'n grind? Took a vow of abstinence?"

"My mother died when I was two."

Rizla's face went stiff.

She grinned at him. "Now don't you feel like a crass bastard?"

"Not for the first time nor the last," he said, and insisted on buying the next round. "You've got great triceps for a girly gal, Síle," he said suddenly, gripping her arm.

She tensed it for him.

"You work out?"

"No, she lifts steel trays at 10,000 metres," Jude reminded him.

"Oh, that's right, you're a trolley dolly. *I'm Síle, Fly Me!*" he said in a lewd falsetto.

Jude glared at him. Did he have to be obnoxious, tonight of all nights, when she needed him to show his true colours?

"That's right," Síle said, deadpan, "the real money's in the sex. We only get a basic salary for all that waitressing and First Aid stuff, but it's fifty Euro for every hand job and a hundred for a fuck in the toilet."

Rizla blinked at her, and then released such an enormous laugh that two guys from the chicken factory looked up from their backgammon to see what was going on. "Good one," he said, licking his finger and chalking one on the air for Síle. "Speaking of washrooms, I gotta go shake the dew off the lily. Excuse me, ladies."

As soon as he was gone, Síle murmured in Jude's ear. "He's rather fab. Is he an alcoholic?"

"No," said Jude, startled, "he doesn't drink at all."

"That's what I mean," said Síle. "Everyone I know in Ireland who doesn't drink is a recovering drunk. Except for a few Jesus freaks who took the Pledge when they were eleven."

Jude shrugged uncomfortably, wondering whether anyone could overhear their gossip. "He drank when I first knew him, but he wasn't *that* much of a drinker; not like some guys I knew in school. At some point he just stopped, said he couldn't afford it anymore."

And here came Rizla, hitching up his belt as he slouched over to the bar, like some grizzly dressed up in men's clothes.

They had a game of pool. "I taught Jude here all she knows," Rizla explained.

"So how come I beat you nine times out of ten?" asked Jude, racking them up.

Síle kept messing up her shots. "Everything's the wrong size here, I'm getting vertigo," she complained, laughing. "The table's too low, the balls are too big, and spotted instead of red or yellow..."

"If you stayed a week you'd get the hang of it," Rizla told her, "in fact I could give you a crash course in being a Canuck."

"I already fell off a sled twice today."

"That's a start, but you gotta skate and skidoo, you gotta shoot things—"

"Don't listen to him," said Jude.

"—and above all, you gotta tell Newfie jokes."

"Newfie as in Newfoundland?" Síle guessed.

"Newfound*land*," he said, correcting the stress. "You hear about the Newfie was so lazy he married a pregnant woman?"

Jude grimaced.

"I know that one," Síle protested, "but it's about a Kerryman."

"Yeah," Jude put in, "and the Belgians probably say it about the Luxembourgers. Enough already!"

Rizla ignored her. "This Newfie goes to the hospital in St John's and says I want to be castrated You sure about that? says the doctor. Yeah yeah boy, says the Newfie, I'm telling you I want to be castrated. So after the op, he wakes up in a room with another patient. He says, Hey you boy, what operation you got done? The other guy says he's been circumcised. Damnit to hell, dat's de word I was looking for!"

Jude groaned, but Síle and Rizla were raucous with mirth. Soon the repartee was flying so fast, she could barely keep up. Rizla and Síle were testing each other out, she realized—not in a nasty way, just each of them trying to figure out whether the other was worthy of their place in Jude's life. She breathed in the stale air and thought, forty-seven smokeless hours down, only a lifetime to go. She wasn't a smoker anymore. She had a lover. Anything was possible.

But coming back from the washroom (where, as happened every couple of months, some stranger had given Jude's short hair a startled look as if to say, *This is the Ladies!*), she got the impression that the atmosphere had cooled. Síle covered her mouth to yawn, and checked the time display on her gizmo.

"Will we head home?" Jude asked.

"Fine," said Síle.

"Another quick one?" said Rizla.

"I don't think so," said Síle, before Jude could.

On the street outside, Rizla gave them both crushing hugs and strolled off in the direction of his trailer.

The night was clear and starry. "You have a good time?" asked Jude, a little uneasy.

No answer. Síle was looking down at her borrowed boots as they squeaked on the flattened snow. "Rizla was saying you must be really mad about me, to give up smoking."

"Mm," said Jude. Where was this going?

"He said, and I quote, *She's a closet romantic, is my wife*."

Bastard, thought Jude. Had he been planning this masterstroke all evening? All that broke the silence was the creak of their footsteps. "Rizla can be such a wise guy," she began weakly.

"So it's just his little nickname for you? *Wife?*"

"Well," said Jude, her chest tight, "I mean it's technically true—"

"Technically?" Síle pulled up short and almost slipped on the ice.

Jude put a hand out to steady her. "I left him nearly seven years ago."

"You're telling me you two were married?"

"Only for a year, really," said Jude, her voice shaking absurdly.

"Why the fuck," articulated Síle, "didn't I hear about this before?"

Jude shrugged. "There's a lot of details you and I haven't got around to swapping yet."

"Details?" roared Síle.

"Getting married at eighteen was an embarrassing mistake. I hadn't even reached legal drinking age. I prefer to forget it."

"Still, you could have told me. My jaw fell into my lap,

back there, I felt like a complete feckin' eejit."

"I'm sorry."

Síle started walking again, slapping her gloves together to warm her hands, and Jude thought maybe the conversation was over, which was fine by her.

"Sure I know loads of Irish dykes who used to be married," said Síle, her tone softening into exasperation. "So you got divorced, what, when you were nineteen?"

"Well, that's when I moved out." Jude made herself add, "We haven't actually got around to finalising the paperwork yet, because Rizla's always broke, and I wasn't going to pay for it all myself."

Síle's turned, her tawny eyes hawk-like in the streetlight. Cheapskate, Jude thought; I should have borrowed from the bank. I should have got around to it. "You didn't ask much about him," she said, going on the defensive, "you don't seem to count guys."

A tense pause. "Well, it's true that's my blind spot."

Moving warily, Jude tucked her arm into Síle's and headed down Main Street.

After a minute, Síle said "OK, sorry to harp on, but just to clarify—you're still legally married, but you haven't been involved in over six years."

Jude tried to swallow. *Involved*, what did that mean? One cigarette, that's all she needed. "Right, we haven't been a couple."

But of course Síle heard the equivocation, and her eyes turned on Jude like a searchlight. "The last time you slept with him," she said, spelling it out as if to a child, "it was more than six years ago?"

Messy, messy. "Well, no," said Jude, letting out a long plume of steam.

Síle had dropped her arm. "When was it?"

"Beginning of March."

"Which March?"

"This one just gone."

"Last month?" Síle stood and stared up at the cavernous

sky, breathing in and out like a horse. "Then what the fuck am I doing here?"

She was one of those women who looked superb when angry, Jude thought; her hair stood out like a crackling halo. Jude was waiting for the right words to turn up in her mouth, but—

"What exactly was the point of this mad trip to the frozen arsehole of the world?" asked Síle, breaking away to the other side of the street. "You let me believe you were single."

"Because I am. Was, till now, I mean," she corrected herself miserably. "You don't understand."

"Understand what? The erotic appeal of a not-quite-ex-husband with oil under his nails? Who *are* you?"

Jude caught her by the sleeve. "Shut up for a second."

"Oh, now you want to do the talking," Síle almost screamed. "Go ahead, delight me with some more little *details*. Next you'll be telling me there's a kid! I can't believe I left Kathleen for you."

Now that was low. "It was your decision."

"Decision?" Síle repeated, sardonic. "It was a leap in the fucking dark!"

Jude took a breath. "Why are you doing this, Síle?"

"What? What am I doing?"

"Making some big old volcano out of a molehill," said Jude. "There's no kid. There's no sinister conspiracy. So I wound up in bed with my ex once in a while, haven't you ever done that?"

"I've never been that desperate," said Síle.

"We weren't desperate," insisted Jude. "It only happened a couple of times a year. It was about... company. Comfort." She had a hunch all these words were getting her nowhere. Her newfound happiness was teetering like an icicle in a thaw. She took a step nearer to Síle. "So the last time it happened to happen was at the beginning of March, and I told Riz that was it, over and done with, because it felt wrong, because all I could think about was you."

Síle's blew into her gloved hands. "You still don't get it, do you?" she asked, gravelly. "This isn't about sex. I don't care who you slept with last month, though from this weekend on I care very much. What I can't stand is being fooled."

"I—"

"Talk about a lie of omission! You should have told me what I was walking into and you know it. I'm a stranger in this peculiar little world of yours, remember." A ragged breath. "I've gutted my whole life like a fish because you said you loved me."

"I do," Jude groaned.

"I don't just want to fuck you, I want to know you."

"I was always going to tell you the whole story of me and Riz," Jude said weakly. "There's things that are hard to explain in writing or over the phone. Sometimes it's better to wait for the right moment."

"What, like this one?" asked Síle, waving at the deserted street, the black speckled sky.

Jude almost laughed. "C'mon home before we freeze," she said.

There was a moment's pause, when it could have gone either way, and then Síle went with her.

Emma Donoghue

Born in Dublin in 1969, Emma Donoghue is a novelist, playwright, and historian who lives in London, Ontario, with her lover and son. Her books include the historical fiction *Life Mask, Slammerkin*, and *The Woman Who Gave Birth to Rabbits*; contemporary novels *Stirfry* and *Hood*; and the fairy tale collection *Kissing the Witch*. She has won the Ferro-Grumley Award for Lesbian Fiction, the American Library Association's Gay and Lesbian Literary Award, and is a five-times finalist in the Lambda Awards. For further information go to www.emmadonoghue.com.

Marion Douglas
Writer Notes

My contribution is taken from a novel, *Dance Hall Road*, which I have recently finished. It is set in small town southern Ontario, which is already on the literary map. I suppose someday I might like to write about southern Alberta, where I live, because it is so bare-bones beautiful. Step out of your car anywhere north or south of Medicine Hat and you might see only one line, the horizon. This can practically cause a person to go into a type of swoon, but I guess it takes a long time and numerous swoons before a landscape enters the bloodstream because I'm not yet totally compelled to write about Alberta.

When you're from southern Ontario it's hard to escape, even living 3000 kilometres away. Geographically, it's almost an island, surrounded as it is by five miniature oceans that create systems of oppressive weather; humidity in the summer and impassable snow drifts in the winter. Culturally, there is this legacy of unbridled Protestantism; the pronoun *I* is strongly discouraged. The first time I visited a Hutterite colony in Alberta, I felt right at home and I realized: this place feels like southern Ontario. Lots of explicit rules but even more of the implicit type, and all emotions suppressed right down to the level of the water table. It's a bit like a club or a sect that you keep thinking you really should leave.

Marion Douglas
Dance Hall

Just take the bike and go. A flat and lifeless Wednesday after-noon, sky the colour of white weather that isn't about to change, and her—redundant! Fired from the dentist's office by her very own old man. So why not go out of town on the bike? She had her license, could take the little Vega whenever she wanted, but cars were no good for stealth. You still had to ask, or at least make an announcement, explain yourself. And even with the windows down, 100 kilometres an hour, departure roaring past your ears, that car was contaminated. Owned by one Flaxian after another, passed down from Limb to Limb to Drury; the thing was full of Flax. Caked, Rose had told Adrian more than once: the car was caked with the town of Flax. Emerge from the blue interior and behold the crumbs as they fall from your lap. Could be in Mesmer with Adrian, could be in Kitchener-Waterloo with Anastasia—didn't matter. Flax was stuffed between your ears like old cake.

Away she went. Even at this age, seventeen, and on a fat-tired girl's bike, taking off without telling Dad was as good as truancy. Not that Rose was often, or even ever, truant and if she were to be, excuses would most certainly be made, her his-tory clattering like a printing press behind her back, publish-ing counterfeit notes of permission. If you looked, you could almost see the grey ink of explanation on everyone's fingers. Yes, Rose Drury, such a lovely girl despite everything, her mother and all, so long ago now, nine years, but no doubt she remembers, and a girl needs a mother, such a help to her father and that brother.

Downhill was the only realistic direction, entering humid-ity like the locker room at school, insects wanting up your nose more than the smell of sweaty girls changing. Rose had never taken this or any gravel road out of town, her best friend Anastasia living on the Mesmer Highway, the Number 4.

Though this was hardly gravel, all of the loose stones having been nudged to the edges by country tires, leaving a surface as smooth as the sweat band in Adrian's cap. Rose sped up, faster than the bugs and the time of day. Nobody else in sight, the quiet of summer heat in her ears, always suggestive—something or other might happen—and growing toward her from both ditches, dusty grasses. They reminded Rose of old people, thousands of them, stooped, greying, maybe looking for some company. Why don't you stop, girly, they seemed to be muttering. Why don't you stop?

No reason.

Here now the road became flatter with curves, grass giving way to coniferous trees and swamp. Rose kept an eye out for the mud-loving forms of life, hopping things that took off on water and popped like grapes if driven over. She didn't want to spoil her record. For more than two months now, since Skokie'd gone to sleep, she hadn't killed a single creature, not an insect or, she hoped, a blade of grass. Mosquitoes, she shooed away. Houseflies were encouraged to use the door. Yeah, well what about single-celled organisms, Anastasia had asked, finding her friend's new vigilance a little far-fetched; what about, for example, a tiny bit of mould you might wipe up and swoosh down the drain? It's anaerobic you know, can't survive without oxygen.

"I can't control everything."

"That's right," said Anastasia.

Anastasia liked to undermine the good intentions of others. No big deal; Rose was used to it. She pedalled faster, then braked, coming to a complete stop beneath the overhanging trees. Look at this: bulrushes. She walked her bike closer to the ditch. Might there be a baby Moses abandoned in the reeds? She wasn't kidding. One secret she never told Anastasia: Rose was often on the lookout for abandoned babies. Stranger things were known to happen. But not today. No crying that she could hear, still no traffic, nothing. Even the frogs shushed as she approached and so she stood perfectly still, wanting to experiment, waiting for them to think she was gone or an unusual species of tree.

Ha! They fell for it, one or two choirmasters clearing their throats and the others joining, freakishly in unison as if someone were conducting.

"Ahem," said Rose and they stopped again, all at once, apparently under the influence of one collective frog worry. Maybe they couldn't see her, but the inhabitants of these ditches were listening with their tiny flap-ears. She'd seen them in biology, during the dissections she'd never do again. The school allowed for conscientious objection, and Rose was prepared for the scoffing of Anastasia, could even predict her response. *You know, nature's not all sweetness and light. Remember that plant somebody brought into biology class last year? That pitcher plant? Doesn't that prove to you that nature isn't as nice as you might think? Nature is made up of carnivorous little throats with spiny slanting hairs that drag flies or spiders to their doom. Slowly and with malice aforethought, Rose Drury.*

Rose would admit that this road was a little like the mouth of the pitcher plant. She couldn't seem to turn around, there was no going back, and the smell was amphibian, like breath held under water for long periods of time. And here she was with nothing but a bike, no money, not even any identification, nothing but too much Anastasia on the brain. Rose looked over her shoulder. If a farmer were to drive by, would he shoot her? Such malfeasance occurred in the country, there being such a chronic lack of witnesses. Why, any outsider might be shot for target practice, left to fall into the ditch, spouting a tie-dyed bloodstain into the lonely murk. Eye-to-dying-eye with bullfrogs as big as dinner plates. A banquet for mosquitoes although you had to wonder: did they like dead people? Perhaps the freshly dead. Ask your brother; Adrian would probably know. I'm pretty sure they would not like blood blended with swamp water. That they would not go for. My guess is you would lie there forever, Rose, decomposing until you were just a few bones, unrecognizable even as a skeleton. More like pick-up sticks. What are you doing, going out there on your bike anyway?

Rose pushed off and rode further to a break in the trees, past a field of yellow grain and a green road sign. East Flax. Oh yes. Rose's knowledge of East Flax was a View-Master set of images and sensations, a dentist's daughter's three-dimensional impressions of poor teeth and disregard for higher education. But that wasn't all there was to East Flax. Don't forget the lake. Rose had been to Minnow Lake twice—for the eighth grade picnic and once on an outing with her mom, long ago, before she was even in school. By then her mother would have had the cancer but not known, or known and not told anyone, so that the day's events stood back and watched the way they did when you were keeping a secret.

They were supposed to have a good time, just the two of them, Adrian stayed home with Dad, but some man talked her mother into water-skiing, tried to convince her to go over the jump, wouldn't take no for an answer, he said. Don't be crazy, her mother had said, laughing. It was all in fun but seemed a little dangerous. Dragged by a boat over a piece of wood in the middle of a lake? She remembered how the ski jump angled out of the water like her one loose tooth and she made a deal: pull out the tooth and the ski jump will sink. But she couldn't; the rags of skin anchoring it to her gum were tough as old meat. And her mom didn't go anyway. Just as well, Rose said. Even now, eleven years later, her relief was incongruous. She supposed fun and sinister tended to overlap where adults were involved, at least from the point of view of kids.

Maybe she'd go and take a look at the ski jump: it was still there, and Adrian made frequent reference to both it and Randy Farrell. More than he liked to admit, Adrian was in East Flax, part of his secret life, along with Cheryl Decker. If only there were underground tunnels, he was always saying, instead of roads. Get up, have breakfast and disappear into a maze of passageways. No one knows where you are, no one knows where you're going.

"Why," Rose asked., "Why do you care if they know?"

"I'd just rather they didn't."

"Well, I'd just rather they did."

"Know what *I'm* doing or what *you're* doing?"

"Never mind."

Rose cycled past the dance hall road. Still no traffic. Where were all the people? Even on the sleepiest Sunday in Flax you would hear lawn mowers, screen doors or one of the Limb kids practicing the piano. Apparently, on a business day in the outskirts of East Flax, people were told to keep it down. Dogs were muzzled. Shhh. As if Minnow Lake were some big sleeping baby that might be wakened.

Now Rose could see the lake and smell it. Not a bad smell, but also not the good smell of Lake Huron with its vast capacity for washing and dissolving and rubbing things smooth. Minnow Lake was so shallow and warm, it smelled more like something cooking, the water table rising up and offering a mud casserole. And some people said not all residents of East Flax had septic systems, so who knew where their toilets flushed to. Rose did remember at the eighth grade picnic, the feel of the lake bottom curled up between your toes like wet diapers or worse. *Nobody* had wanted to come to Minnow Lake, but there were already three schools booked at Blue Lake, so that was that. Since they'd built the pavilion and boat ramp and restaurant at Blue Lake, everybody went there. And you could see why. Rose let her bike clatter into the tall weeds at the edge of the gravelly beach. Beach? Hardly. The owner of Blue Lake resort had hauled in loads of sand and strung buoys in the water to define the swimming area. If you went past them and drowned, it would be your own fault.

East Flax had definitely seen better times and so had Minnow Lake. One slanted dock and an old rowboat under three inches of water. And there stood the ski jump floating on its unsinkable oil drums, a hollow-brained tribute to the laws of physics. And up there, the dance hall, clearly visible on its so-called escarpment, watching the lake from its row of windows. Rose knew there was a store, the Farrells' rickety enterprise, but would it be open? Most places closed on Wednesday afternoon, but this was East Flax, birthplace of unlikelihood, home of the beautiful and intelligent Cora Farrell. No one for a minute thought she would be chosen school queen. Anastasia said, simply by entering the competition Cora had taken the Farrell chromosomes as far as they had ever been selected to go, that Cora was born to be a runner-up. But she beat Lillian Gee and Connie Laine.

The entire Farrell clan was weird, what with Randy and his habits, his need to have the inside of his locker just so, and that time he asked Adrian not to go in the shop wing door because he hadn't gone out the shop wing door. Their father, Frog Farrell, had swallowed a frog and their mother, Angel, had a reputation. And Cora's sister, Maddy, was a girl-boy, or a boy-girl and the hero of the basketball team, so had done some chromosome-hauling herself.

But most improbable of all was the Farrells' store. Who on earth would shop there? It would seem the road was closed to cars. Maybe in these parts people walked, in which case, would they ever arrive or would they fall asleep en route? Fall asleep in a dusty ditch, sprout little roots from the soles of their feet and, upon awakening, find they had grown leaves. No need for the Farrells' store now, honey, we've got photo-synthesis. Cancel our account.

Rose was thirsty and a drink would be nice. She didn't have a cent but maybe she could finagle one with her Flaxified charms. Worth a try. Rose rode back along the weed-rimmed lake access, turned right past a mailbox in a milk can, a long laneway ending at a metal clad house by the lake, a garage of sorts with its single Out of Order pump. More weeds, foxtail and milkweed and goldenrod crowding up to everything, green and wavy bodies intent on pushing past and under and into the relics of the human. Finally! A car, driver waving in slow motion, driving in slow motion, lifting a spectacular cloud of dust, a spawn of billows. Rose licked the grit off her teeth. No wonder frogs jumped to the nearest bog. Skin-breathers could be asphyxiated with each passing vehicle.

There was the store, plate glass windows dark as night beneath the overhanging balcony. Looked like someplace out of *Gunsmoke*, Miss Kitty's sister's place perhaps. Empty, no doubt, closed for the afternoon. Everybody out hunting varmints or settling feuds. But to Rose's surprise the Drink Pepsi door opened into an unlit habitat, the nocturnals' exhibit at the zoo. Her eyes adjusted to the gloom. Where she anticipated wombats and opossums, were three old men in chairs, hillbillies she presumed, and at the till, the beautiful Cora Farrell.

"Hi, Cora," Rose said, six night vision eyes of the old men fixing on her, Geiger counters divining her history, DNA, purpose in this store and on this earth.

Cora was not bothered by the unexpected; Rose Drury shopping at her parents' store probably made as much sense as she herself working there.

"If you're looking for Maddy," Cora said, "she's up at the dance hall."

Of course. She should be looking for Maddy. Maddy was her contemporary, also heading into grade twelve whereas Cora was finished, a graduate and a queen. Rose wouldn't be here to inquire about her plans. And she couldn't very well claim to be visiting for sociological reasons, or would they be anthropological? *Yes, I'm conducting some research for the University of Mesmer, and I've been wanting to interview Maddy Farrell for quite some time now. It's about that ridiculous orange hat she wears in the winter. She's so tall and well, what both I and Anastasia Van Epp would like to know, as well as the public in general, I'm sure: Does she think she's a character in a Dr. Seuss book? Does she think she's living on Mulberry Street?*

"Well, in fact, I was just out for a bicycle ride, finding myself unemployed because my father, the dentist, George Drury—maybe you know him, maybe you wish you didn't know him—anyway, he decided he doesn't really need me working in his office and so I thought, why not go to East Flax? Maddy might be around." Rose saw her voice landing on the shelves of dry goods and from there, watching the action wonderingly. "I'd buy a drink but I didn't bring any money. Not a single dime."

"Dentist's daughter should have a dime," said one of the men from his old and mud-coloured armchair. Alfred Beel, Rose now saw, an occasional patient. The other two, opposite him, sat on wooden chairs, mute and slouchy, soft-spined in appearance, creatures who had just yesterday made the switch from water to land and weren't quite sure what to make of the move.

"Yes, she should. That is true enough."

"Well, have a drink," Cora offered. "My treat. What do you want? Orange? Root beer? Cream Soda?"

Was this place even wired for electricity? No lights. But behind Alfred, the glass-fronted cooler emitted fluorescence. Designed for cuts of meat, most likely salvaged from an old butcher shop, here in East Flax it contained single bottles of pop arranged in rows and off to one side, packages of wieners and Velveeta cheese stacked in, Rose had to admit, rather decorative pyramids. That would be the renowned work of Randy Farrell.

"So what'll it be?" Cora was behind the cooler, sliding the door open.

"Cream soda."

"Good choice." And Cora, moving her arm like a mechanical device to the head of the cream soda row, withdrew the lead bottle, edged the others forward a spot, and said "Here. You likely know Randy likes to organize. If we don't keep the pop in rows and the other stuff in stacks, he gets a little fidgety or something. Anyway, the opener's on the counter. See that string? If we don't tie it down, it grows legs." She was busy finding a replacement cream soda from a carton behind the cooler. Apparently, the bottles on display were required to line up and take turns.

Having engineered the free drink, Rose was ready to spend some time with Maddy. Could be educational and she didn't want these four mouths speaking unkindly of her when she left, in particular the two mushy-looking men on the wooden chairs, didn't want them hissing and bubbling judgments through their gills.

"I guess I'll go find Maddy now."

"Sure. You know where the dance hall is?"

"Yes. Oh yes. Everybody knows where the dance hall is," and she left, the door slamming shut behind her, its rusty spring unsoftened by years of sunlight and use.

Hard to believe that out here, even in East Flax, arrangements had been made. Rose had not thought the vast trellises of Flax, able to support the monstervine of familiarity would have made their way to the inhospitable climate of East Flax, but they had. Apparently, uncluttered movement through uncluttered time was not possible. Now she would *have* to see Maddy Farrell because later today Cora would ask, "Did that Drury girl come to see you at the dance hall? She dropped by the store looking for you." Maddy shrugging, saying no. But weeks later at school, still wondering, watching Rose from her position below the trellis, not far from where the stalk met the mud, yet never daring to ask: Why were you in East Flax? Did you come to laugh at my orange hat?

Tall, weird Maddy would have to be seen.

Dance Hall Road. Here it was already, complete with the steepest hill for miles and such a case of washboard bumps, Rose had to push the bike. You'd think the place would be quiet but yahoos were forever driving out here to spin their tires to the top of the hill, stretch their white arms out the windows, and hurl empties over the roof and at the trees as hard as possible. A type of sport, Rose had heard, called bottle darts. And in the winter cars made a habit of sliding into the snowy ditch, trees looking a little ashamed in the headlights, possibly embarrassed for the drivers. Nothing happening today, though, unless you were to count the panting of Rose and the wind in the trees.

At the crest of the hill Rose stopped, to breathe and reconsider. Funny that the dance hall still felt like the dance hall, even in broad daylight. She guessed the place had memories, as did this very parking lot, home to seventy years, at least, of dance anticipation. Even Rose was experienced enough to know it wasn't so much the event or even the hall as the stepping out of the car or roadster or buggy and into the plans, the thinking: maybe I'll see someone, or better, maybe I'll be seen. The shadows of the leaves could in reality be what remained of the secret criss-crossings of a thousand hearts. You never knew. Rose gave a little shudder. Seven or eight weeks until the September dance, always the best of the year.

All right. She had come this far, too late to turn back now. What was the protocol? Did one knock at a dance hall? Better do. To walk in might give Maddy a scare. But how would she hear above all that thumping? To open the door and call Maddy would be a ridiculous intimacy, like opening the door to Dr. Graham Rochon's mental health office and calling, Graham? Graham? Are you in? I have some new confessions for you.

She knocked again. Knock, knock, knock. And again, louder. KNOCK, KNOCK, KNOCK. An ominous silence and then the door swung open.

"You have a guest," said Rose.

At a rumoured height of six feet, one-and-a-half inches, Maddy Farrell was taller than most boys at Flax Composite High. Everything about her was long and narrow, including her face, which she lengthened and narrowed by tying back her frizzy, paper-bag coloured hair with a paper-bag coloured elastic. She looked puzzled right now, but that was normal. Even at predictable events such as the lunch bell or assemblies, Maddy conveyed puzzlement, as if each event she saw had somehow been snipped from its short little history and its inconsequential little future and was free-floating, without context.

"Do you know who I am?" asked Rose, inflecting towards neutral, veering into arrogant.

"Yeah," a little defensive. "You're Rose Drury, the dentist's daughter and Adrian's sister. My brother knows Adrian."

"Yes, they're friends. Or at least they seem to spend time on the ski jump. Anywho, I was riding my bike and wound up in East Flax and went to the store and your sister said you were up here, so I thought I'd come and see you."

"Oh." The puzzled look, appropriate in this case since there was no context. "Well, come in. It's not exactly my house as you can see, it's not really set up for hospitality, it's a dance hall. But it's not really set up for basketball either and yet, here I am shooting baskets. Quelle surprise," she said, her voice flat and unsurprised. "We could play some one on one if you want."

"No thanks. I'm no good at basketball. Half-good at volleyball except last time I played, my wrist turned purple," said Rose, extending a tanned and healthy wrist for emphasis, showing off, well, why shouldn't she?

"Oh."

Now what? "Can I look around the dance hall?"

"Sure." And Maddy lead Rose through the place like a realtor would a prospective buyer. "Here's the kitchen. And the cupboards. As you can see, dishes for five thousand. Ever seen that many identical cups and saucers?"

"Nope."

"It's almost like art, maybe, or something really symmetrical or in a giant pattern. Or it could be Randy's been out here putting things in place. I don't really know what I'm talking about."

Art? Anastasia would have something to say about this.

"So the Women's Institute holds meetings here, and sometimes they all come together in a passel, my dad says. A passel of women. It's kind of funny," Maddy said, watching Rose's smiling, unlaughing face, "or maybe not. I mean, like a herd of cows or a pride of lions. It's actually my dad's sense of humour, not mine. And these are the eight mysterious roasting pans. Only two ovens, that's the mystery. Want to see the men's washroom? It's really the best part."

"Definitely."

They walked to the wrong side of the darkened basement, pushed open the scraping men's door, and there were three urinals backed against the wall, respectful, ghostly. "Welcome to the stand-up world of men," Maddy said.

"My friend Anastasia would love this tour."

"Oh. Her." Two conflicting opinions of Anastasia Van Epp clattering against one another in the pause. "Do you want to see the stage? There's a microphone."

Rose would be honest. This was not the sort of girl she had expected. Where were the misconjugations, possibly gap-toothed for emphasis? The basketball prodigy with no knowledge of sound equipment? But seconds later, squeal, "Testing, one, two three," Maddy's voice, important as the mayor or someone who might tell a joke or two.

"Well, without further ado," Rose said, grabbing the mike, determined to extemporize more and better than Maddy Farrell. "I've brought you here today to ask you the following. Okay. How many of you, given the chance, would move away from Flax?" More squeal of feedback.

"I'm from *East* Flax," said Maddy, seated now on the edge of the stage, long legs bare and crossed.

"Oh right, right. Let me rephrase this. How many of you, given the chance, would move away from Flax *proper* tomorrow?" And Rose returned the microphone to its cradle, jumped to the dance floor, faced Maddy, raised her hand—"I would"—then leapt, not as nimbly as she had hoped, back onto the stage.

"Now. How many of you," taking a deep breath, "given the same opportunity, would move away from *East* Flax?"

Craning herself around to look at Rose, Maddy answered, "Realistically? I'd probably stay."

Marion Douglas

Marion Douglas was born in Walkerton, Ontario, and grew up on a farm not far from there. In 1981, she moved to Calgary and stayed. Marion Douglas started writing short stories in 1985 and published several in literary journals, then began writing novels: *The Doubtful Guests*, *Bending at the Bow*, and *Magic Eight Ball*. "Dance Hall" is an excerpt from her almost-finished fourth novel, *Dance Hall Road*.

Anne Fleming
Writer Notes

It was understood, in 1983 and '84 and '85, which is when I was coming out, that with a few notable exceptions, lesbian writing was bad. My friends and I passed books around amongst ourselves. We read them. We laughed at them ("Wait, wait, listen to this. They're having sex. 'It was like stirring soup.' Oh, yeah. Stir my soup, baby.") We bemoaned the dearth of anything better. Once you'd read Colette and Jane Rule and one Rita Mae Brown, what was left? (Lots, I know. You don't need to make a list; just grant me my snappy if not literally true sentence, okay?)

Around the same time, I began to write. I didn't set out to correct the lack of good lesbian stories but neither did I have any clear idea what I wanted to write about. The result? More bad lesbian writing.

There is an odour about the deliberately lesbian story as there is an odour about the deliberately anything story. One wrinkles one's nose. At the same time, it seems to me many straight people mistake a story by a lesbian with any lesbians in it at all with the deliberately lesbian story. ("When she's not on her little lesbian soapbox," my mother reports her friends saying, though I suspect it is what she herself thinks, "she's really quite good.")

All of this frightens me off now, when I hope I have a greater subject than the little lesbian smiles we used to give one another when recognizing a stranger's dykeness on the street (yes, the subject of one of my first (thankfully unpublished) stories, called, inventively, "Little Dyke Smiles"). Doesn't stop me writing about lesbians altogether, but it makes me self-conscious about how it will be received. I wish this were not so. I would like to write equally self-consciously or unselfconsciously about all my characters and storylines. If there is an upside, it is that I am forced to be as honest as I can possibly be.

I doubt it's all due to the legacy of bad lesbian writing that lesbians are now writing non-lesbian stories as often as not. Nor is it the greater chance of finding book-world respectability and literary regard. It's that the world is so big and has so many people in it and some of them are queer and some of them are not and there is an 'isness' about certain characters: they come to you whole. They are what they are and you cannot make them something they are not. A sort of character-creation essentialism, maybe. I don't know.

What I do know is that twenty-some years after my coming out, fiction can be lesbian fiction and can also be stunningly, heartbreakingly good. There's a freedom that wasn't there before. Then, "serious" writers tended not to write lesbian books, and lesbian books tended to be written by amateurs.

This is why Jane Rule means so much to me. She was out and she was good. *Is* out, *is* good, yes, but the past tense is important here. *Desert of the Heart* was published in 1964, the year I was born. I didn't know about its existence until I was nineteen and my first lover stole *Lesbian Images* from the public library and we tracked down and devoured every book in it. Good lesbian writing *was* out there. The whole time. Saying *do it, do it. It can be done.*

Anne Fleming
The Pear

One way to begin is to describe the pear, grapefruit-shaped and golden, rough to the touch, hefty in the palm, its weight surprising for its size, promising succulence. Liquid is heavy. I am mostly liquid, too, and also heavy. There are one hundred and fifty-six pounds of me in this world. Is that not a strange thought? Not that we weigh a certain amount, but that we contain mass, a more or less fixed supply of matter, and this mass, particularly arranged as it is, is us. Nothing beyond that mass is us; everything beyond it is not-us; and yet, that's not the way it feels. It feels as if... well, there is no good way to describe it, but it feels as if my consciousness is as large as all I can see and hear and taste and smell—not that I need to go through all of the senses, although, duh, there's only one more, so okay: touch. But if my consciousness is as large as all that, and contained within myself, a mere one hundred and fifty-six pounds on the planet's surface, well, there's clearly a disjunction there, isn't there? Everything in one person's purview; a body maybe a tenth of a cubic metre in volume and one hundred and fifty-six pounds in mass. It doesn't fit.

I will eat the pear she gave me. Its mass will join my mass. I will encompass it, though I will not become it; it will be gone, and I will persist. I will try to live the life the pear would have wanted for itself.

No. Wait. Scratch that.

What life would a pear want? To ripen and fall to earth, to be nibbled by ants, pecked by crows, phaged by phages, to rot nicely in the soil around its life-encasing pips, osmosing its best organic wishes to its small, nutty hopes for propagation?

Hey.

Maybe I *will* try to live the life the pear would have wanted for itself.

I will eat the pear. With each bite, I will tell you how it

was, our meeting, our time together, our parting. That's how to tell stories like ours, isn't it? Though that order is not necessary, I suppose.

All right. Bite one: my teeth slide bluntly over the flat curve of finely pebbled skin, denting and bruising it to a darker brown before catching and slicing through to the pearly flesh. After stopping suddenly in mid-conversation on Keefer, she darted into a store, leaving me jawing to blank-faced shoppers rifling the produce stalls. We were talking about extreme sports and then I asked her a question about something else, but she had already taken two pears cashierward and I never got my answer.

Befuddled, abandoned on the sidewalk, I wanted to explain myself. This has always been my fault, to want to explain myself. Here I am, explaining myself to you and I have done nothing wrong.

A woman squeezed in front of me to examine the lychees, giving my badly placed self a clucking look. Sara emerged from the store. She had heard my question.

Here. Have a pear, she said.

What she meant was, Sometimes it's better to eat fruit than to talk about things we mean. I had become expert at that point at deciphering what she meant. We had known one another precisely one week.

Bite two: the pear fills its promise of succulence with a surge of juice bursting forth from the broken walls of its cells. We met on the train. She didn't know where she would stay, buoyed with confidence the world would take care of her. I was tempted to let some other soul offer to share a room, but I did think I'd like to see her face again with its quick eyes and faint freckles, its red, red lips. She liked to think she was a free spirit. I liked to think she was a free spirit. I'm not sure she was. Reader, I invited her to share my room.

Bite three: My intentions were chaste.

Can you say that? That intentions are chaste or unchaste? You are chaste or you are unchaste. Intentions be damned.

No, my intentions *were* chaste. My intentions have ever been chaste. It's the intentions of others that have kept me from a life of chastity. Oren, the hired hand. Helmut, the greenhouse supervisor. Gwendy, in that strange arrangement that worked so secretly and so long.

The night before I left home when we talked the whole night through, my sister told me she and Rona Friesen had agreed I was asexual. Until Gwendy, I thought they were right. It was a comfort to think so. Afterwards, I reverted best I could.

With Sara, I did not wish for some sort of barter arrangement, that was never my plan. I imagined she'd, in the lingo of youth, *crash* here only, that I'd give her a key and she'd come and go on her own schedule. I imagined she'd be out day and night, a bebackpacked youth meeting other bebackpacked youth. And so she did.

Bite four: time is getting out of whack here. On the same day that she gave me the pear I savour, she took sixty dollars from my pockets and caught a ferry, caught a VW van full of lean young bodies full of love, leaned her full young body into all of theirs. They spoke a vague, wistful language.

From a gulf island farm, she writes: Your rooms were too small and there were no geese. I want to live as if timelessly. I know you loved me and I'm sorry.

She *knows I loved her?*

I held the postcard as if to rip it in half, then did not.

Did I love her? There was no reason to love her. No, that's not true, I don't know why I said that. You could love her just for those freckles, just for those green eyes, just for the green apple she was eating when I got on the train at Winnipeg after visiting my sister and her new baby, my first niece, the continuation of our family that had for so long seemed threatened with extinction after the two of us. (Pear juice drips down my chin.) She said hi first, giving me a glance then going back to the window and digging her incisors into the fruit. After a cool greeting, I dug my book out of my bag, not just because

I wanted to read, though I did, but because I wanted to demonstrate I was not going to be a hassling seat-mate, nor did I want to be seated next to same.

We pulled out of Winnipeg into prairie—what else?—and she nibbled her apple down to thread and cartilage, peeling the flesh off the translucent carapace with her small teeth.

She folded the seeds up in her hand and asked what I was reading. I showed her the cover of the book. Is it any good? she asked.

Yes. I think so.

It's about cod?

Yes. Codfish.

That never made sense to me, she said. Codfish. Tunafish. We don't say robinbird, we don't say chickenbird. Why tunafish?

Bluebird? I said. Mockingbird, mynah bird, hummingbird. I knew there were more but I was running out of them, those were all I could think of. Even as I spoke, the rebuttal to my argument was obvious and I blushed with embarrassment. Except for mynah, perhaps, which I would have to look up, they were all adjective-birds, whereas tunaness was not a particular attribute of a fish. Or was it? From whence did *tuna* stem? This, too, I would have to look up. (And now I do: Latin, thunnus. Mynah is from Hindi. No meaning given. They are just names.)

If she noticed my shoddy logic she certainly didn't care. She had made her point. She had moved on. So tell me about codfish, she said. Are you from Newfoundland?

No.

Okay. Tell me about codfish.

Would it make a difference if I was?

I'm just wondering why you'd be interested in codfish.

Isn't everyone? Aren't you?

I am now, she said.

So I told her what the book had told me, about cod wars and ghost nets, nets separated from their ships that rise with their bloated, useless catch and fall, rise and fall.

Have you ever caught a codfish? she asked. I shook my head.

We should go cod-fishing when we get to the coast.

My first thought was that Pacific cod are a garbage fish, that you wouldn't want to catch one, but I didn't say that. I said, Okay.

How did she know I was going to the coast? I might have been going to Medicine Hat.

In the observation car, she befriended others, introduced me to them. She got us to play Murder, a card game in which the person who gets the queen of spades must kill the other players by winking at them. It was the unlikeliest thing, this crowd of fat American tourists and well-heeled Japanese tourists and a bright, white-haired Saskatchewan farm wife whose husband had died and who was going to visit her daughter in Vancouver, and two young white dudes from rich Ontario families going out tree planting. They kept trying to hit on my friend. To my pleasure, she quite obviously preferred the white-haired farm lady to the two boys, and quite possibly me to the white-haired farm lady.

Back in our seats trying to settle down for the night, I read more about cod and she read a novel. Then she asked me what I'd been doing in Winnipeg and I told her. She asked if I got along with my sister and I said yes, anyone would get along with my sister, she was wonderful. I asked if she had any siblings, and she said yes, three sisters and two half-brothers. Their allegiances were constantly shifting; lately they were all off on her, but that was all right because she didn't really like any of them either. She guessed she was running away.

I couldn't tell what kind of family she might come from. She might be the child of a carpenter and a nurse in a small Ottawa Valley town, of a wealthy anglo banker with a French-Canadian wife from Montréal, or a wealthy francophone banker with an anglophone wife. She might be an orphan from Nova Scotia, a dental hygienist's daughter from Fredericton, a professor's daughter from Guelph, a mill worker's daughter from Sudbury. When I asked where she was from, she said she'd lived a lot of places. Military, I thought.

As we rode the train together, I was—I realize in retrospect—careful where my arm rested, which way my head flopped as I dozed in the rocking of the train. You're too old for her, intimated the furtive, wordless homunculus lodged in the crypt of my inner mind. You're the wrong sex. I think. (The homunculus and I have ever been foggy on such matters.)

I assumed, as I am wont to do, that she couldn't possibly be interested in me. This had so often happened to be true that I had long given up its ever being otherwise. I was like Jack Lemmon in *Some Like it Hot*. I was very like Jack Lemmon in *Some Like it Hot*.

And so I took the sympathetic looks, the seeking out of my eyes, my understanding, the resting of her forearm next to mine, of her cheek on my shoulder, as carelessness.

The pear, actually, to tell the truth, is a bit mealy. I don't know how to tell a love story. There is so very little to it. Two days on a train. Five days in Vancouver. We were supposed to go fishing the next day. I had us booked. I put it on my credit card.

I've let it sit too long, the pear.

We arrived in Vancouver late Friday afternoon and took a taxi to my house. It was early summer and my horticulturally-inclined downstairs neighbours Burt and Val were out putting in new grasses in their ever-evolving garden.

They asked how the baby was, how my sister was. They pretended to take the presence of my companion in stride.

You must be Val and Burt, she said, before I could answer. Nice to meet you.

I blushed. This is Sara, I said. Sara's going to stay with me a few days.

Great, said Val, raising her eyebrows at me.

Hey, said Burt to Sara, raising his eyebrows at Val.

The baby's marvellous, I said. A wonder. Her little hands,

her little eyebrows. You could count the hairs. Verna is over the moon.

Sara clutched my arm. Your sister's name is Verna? she said. I am the biggest idiot. Why didn't you say something? Why didn't you punch me?

Burt and Val raised their eyebrows at each other. I knew what they meant. There was a falseness to this intimacy. Sara didn't know me but was acting like she did. Despite being embarrassing, this gave me pleasure.

Inside, she examined my apartment, peering at the bookshelves, the CDs, the pictures on the wall, the pictures on the fridge (exhausted-looking sister with newborn; Gwendy at the bird sanctuary, holding Bob's arm and smiling), the contents of the fridge (scant). She was finding out all about me in the way that two kinds of people do— people who are curious about everyone and want to know everything about how other people live (she *was* one of these people) and people who wouldn't normally do this but want to eat everything up about this person they've just met. She might have been one of those people, too.

On the train she'd asked what I worked at.

I am a parasitologist.

I didn't ask what you are, I asked what you work at.

There is not really any difference. I work at studying parasites.

Why do you have to have an *-ologist* to define yourself? If you lost your job, say, and no longer worked at that thing, what would the *I am* mean then? You are more than your job, the wholeness of you.

I would be an unemployed parasitologist.

She was quiet and I thought she was sulking, but after a moment she said, You just like saying the word, don't you? Parasitologist.

No.

I lifted my book to my face and read for what in conversational terms was a long time, twenty seconds maybe. Then I said, wrapping my tongue lovingly around the word, Parasitologist. Parasitologist.

It was our first big laugh together. My first big laugh in a long time. She took it up, too, *parasitologist*, and for the next few days we'd say it out loud, reverently, as if to ourselves, when the other was not expecting it.

Do you study parasites in cod? Codfish?

No. Fish, fish aren't my thing.

What is your thing?

Animal parasites, domestic animals, farm animals. These days, poultry.

Poultry? Chickens?

Turkeys. Ducks. Geese.

I want to keep a flock of geese.

Okay, I said.

And what sort of parasites do poultry have?

The usual sort. Worms. Bugs.

We were quiet. We fell asleep. When I awoke I felt her eyes on me. Her accusing eyes.

You work for the poultry industry, don't you?

I work for the university.

But who funds you?

There is some poultry money, yes.

Do you eat chicken?

I do.

You know how they are treated.

Free-range. I eat free-range chicken.

You'll take their money, but won't eat their chickens?

I shrugged. I grew up on a farm. After a pause, I went on. Actually, free-range chickens are more apt to have parasites than wire-grown chickens. It's the contact with the ground. That's one of the things I've been studying: how do you control parasites in organic flocks?

Really? Her face just beamed. And? How do you?

I think she was genuinely interested. I really do.

Why don't you live on a farm now? she asked.

I wouldn't be doing what I'm doing.

Oh, come on. You could live on a farm somewhere, couldn't you?

I'd rather not.

Why not? I'd love to live on a farm. You grow food, you eat it. What could be more beautiful than that?

Many answers ran through my head: A painting? A symphony? A good book? That is the most simplistic thing I've ever heard. You have no idea, do you?

Nothing. Nothing, I said. That's the thing. But she was not interested in subtleties.

Why don't you want to live on a farm?

And the next string ran through my head. The responsibility. The bank. The stress. Rats. The hired man. (When Dad had his stroke and had to move into the nursing home, I fired him.) The way it never stopped. Failure. I couldn't save the farm. I tried. It burns me to this day, the memory of selling it, the thought of who I sold it to.

I've never found anyone to live on a farm with, I heard myself saying.

I'll live on a farm with you, she said.

Of course, she was being glib. I knew that. She was joking. *Parasitologist.* We had only just met. But if I am to be truthful in my recollection, I must register that her words caused a sensation in my abdomen, a tightening, a shimmering, noted not so much by my conscious mind as by the part of my brain that dealt with low-level daily idiocies of feeling that as a foolish and unloved person I experienced. (Not the homunculus. A blob next to it.) Down, Rover, down, that part of the brain would have been saying if it could ever rouse itself to speech.

Okay, I said. Next stop, let's get off, buy us a farm.

I'll need a farm name, she said.

Not me, I've already got one. I laughed, but this kind of joking was like a knife. Elmers and Velmas, the town kids called us. *Oh, Jesus, would you look at the Velmas.*

Call me Verna, she said.

My eyes stung. But I laughed. I did. I laughed. Already she had me. Already I'd given up part of myself.

I want you to show me hidden Vancouver, she said that night. I didn't know hidden Vancouver. When my sister or cousins came to visit, I took them to an assortment of: the aquarium, Stanley Park, the Museum of Anthropology, the Cypress lookout, a sushi restaurant on Cambie, Granville Island, the Endowment Lands, Second Beach, Denman Street, Robson Street, Van Dusen Gardens, Gastown. In short, all the tourist places.

So she said, all right, we'll find it together. We clinked glasses and I got her sheets and blankets for the chesterfield and both of us made up the bed she would lie in.

Thanks, she said. You're a sweetheart. The universe will repay you for your kindness.

Sure.

It will. Her eyes were green and clear as a tropical lagoon.

I place all my faith in the universe, I said. Good night.

It's just the weekend, I thought. She knows I won't be working on the weekend and wants to use her tour guide while she has one.

You've got a beard, she said the next morning as I poured coffee. She reached out to stroke it where it had grown since the day before. I tilted my head away. Do you shave it every day?

I nodded.

You're a bearded lady.

Yes. Thank-you.

Sorry.

There are more of us than you'd think. Seriously. Start looking. You'd be surprised. This is true. Bearded ladies—and mustachioed ladies, let's not forget them—are everywhere. We are successful. We are down at heel. We have boyfriends, girlfriends, husbands. We are tall and short, fat and thin, Italian and Greek. Sorry, bad joke and not true either. Look at me, German by descent. Look at the other bearded women I know: Scandinavian, Punjabi, Iranian, Welsh. My bad joke endangers my point, which is that we are—as members of minority groups often say—just like everyone else.

Have you ever thought of growing it?

Ask me next if I've thought of joining the circus.

Have you?

I gave her a look.

You asked me to ask you.

Though what bearded lady hadn't? There were times I longed for the old days when I could've made a living at it instead of being a freak in no ways but one and having no talent for it.

A woman I worked with wanted me to grow it, I said. In the eighties. She had just come out—one of those come-out-screaming lesbian-feminists. She was convinced it was only a matter of time before I did too. How I would screw the patriarchy by growing a beard was beyond me. I went for electrolysis instead.

Was it?

Was it what?

Just a matter of time.

No.

Her green eyes focused on me like an owl's on its prey.

Later, on the skytrain out to Surrey (her idea—Nobody ever shows you the suburbs, why is that?) she asked, If you went for electrolysis, how come you still have—and instead of saying beard again, she reached out and stroked that stretch of jawline. A ludicrous pounding erupted in my chest.

Infection, I said with a rush of shame at not only having a beard, but not being able to get rid of it properly. I pulled my face away, though I longed to do the opposite, lean it into her long, tree-froggy hand.

In the afternoon, I showed her the UBC farm, introduced

her to Chris, my grad student, showed her our chickens.

This, she said, looking around, this is hidden Vancouver. I could live here. She wanted to stay all afternoon. She wanted to help with the chores.

Awesome, said Chris, taking her to meet the other enthusiastic scrubbed young things who ran the market garden. She said she'd make her own way home.

That's it, I thought, she's gone. Youth has won her. This struck me as beautiful, the idea of youth winning youth, the idea of me as a conduit, delivering her to them, them to her. Tears of recognition of the sublime ran down my face as I walked to my office, where I stayed until nine.

My home was dark as I approached. Yes. Gone, I thought, opening the door. Then my nostrils twitched: a baked something with garlic and cheese. I flicked on the lights.

Where've you been? Sara squinted from the chesterfield. I made eggplant parmigiana for us.

At dinner she told me she'd decided to stay and volunteer at the farm for a while. I don't have to stay here. I could move to the youth hostel if—

No, no, no—unless you'd—

No, I'd—

Cause if you—

I'd rather stay with you. She grinned in a particular way then that made me hop up and clear the table.

Every day for the next week, we rode the bus together to UBC, she spending her days at the farm, I starting off there, then going to my office and crunching data.

Late Wednesday afternoon, I went back to the farm under the pretence of straightening out data discrepancies with Chris only to discover that he and Sara had gone to Wreck Beach. Knowing he'd have to be back to coop the chickens for the night, I left a message. He called at eight. Sara was not with him. Nor was she, as on eggplant parmigiana night, at home.

At 3:45, I heard the door click. Although I relaxed, I could not fall back to sleep. Once I realized I wouldn't sleep, I wanted to read, but was afraid if I turned my light on, Sara would interpret it as a) a veiled admonition for coming home late and waking me, or b) evidence I'd been worried about her like a waiting-up parent. I lay in the dark, telling myself she was acting exactly as I had thought she would initially, and that this was as it should be.

In the morning she was up at seven as usual. What was I doing that night? she asked. Someone she'd met was doing a fire dance for the summer solstice on Granville Island. We went. The dancers were beautiful, as naked as they could get, with their skin painted. Both men and women were muscular and graceful, like panthers or snakes. Sara danced with leaping, long-skirted, dyed-haired, nose-pierced types while the drummers drummed and the rest of us bobbed in place and the fire-dancers swung fire around their heads and behind their backs and around their fronts and under their feet, and the jugglers juggled fire and ate fire and we all felt the beat of the drums and the heat of the fire and knew instinctively that this was what civilization was all about, that primitivism and civilization were the same thing, and this was it: sun, earth, humans, drums, fire.

As we were leaving, we passed a VW van with the side door open and three people playing hacky sack outside it, two girls with army shorts and spaghetti-strap T-shirts, scarves wound through their hair, and a boy in India cotton drawstring pants. They blew kisses at Sara and called out some goddess greeting or other, Kali, Inanna, I don't know.

The next morning, before she had a chance to allude to plans she might have had, I suggested breakfast at the Ovaltine.

What's the Ovaltine?

A diner. I wonder if they serve Ovaltine. My mother used

to drink Ovaltine.

Ovaltine?

Kind of a cross between hot chocolate and coffee and malted milk.

Ovaltine.

Parasitologist.

Can we get a newspaper? I love going out for breakfast with a newspaper.

I grabbed a fold of *The Vancouver Sun* and draped it over my head. Off we go, I said.

How come nobody's snapped you up?

My heart stopped. I don't know, I said. They just haven't. Ugly, is what I thought. Big teeth, big jaw, eyebrows like old toothbrushes used to clean silver. Beard.

Off we went to the Ovaltine. A drunk with a husky on a rope stopped us to ask for a light and oh yeah, how bout a loonie, how bout your life savings, what the hell, come on, how about yer ar-ar-ess-peeees, how bout you leave me in yer will and die tomorrow, har har har, coughing fit, no, no, I'm kiddin' ya, no, I'm unna die first I'll bet you that, you're all right, you two, you're all right, thanks, me and my cur we thank you, you have a nice day now.

After breakfast we walked down to Crabbe Park, another place I'd never been, though I knew it was there, don't know how. My stomach felt all loopy. We stopped by the stone for the women who'd died in the Downtown Eastside and she leaned against my shoulder, folding herself into my side. Such a beautiful place and then this, she said, hushed, clinging to me. My hands hung at the ends of my arms, my arms hung out of my shoulders. What was going on here? What was going on?

She changed topics. Doesn't it make you want to go for a swim, just seeing the water?

No.

Come on. She took my hand. Let's strip off all our clothes and go for a swim.

She was touching me. She was touching me a lot. She was holding my hand. She was taking my arm. She was taking me back to Chinatown and we were talking about extreme sports because we didn't want to talk about prostitution and drugs and poverty and cultural genocide. I thought extreme sports were evidence of a decadent culture and she thought they were the perfect expression of human nature, the urge to test ourselves, the urge to go beyond, the urge to be in our bodies, the urge to compete, the urge to folly. And I said, Sara? What's going on? It was the bravest thing I'd said in about eight years, but she didn't answer and instead bought me the pear, a Japanese pear shaped like an apple, flecked and golden-russet-coloured and now half-eaten, discarded. I spit the last bite out; close to the core it's like eating a still-wet but drying sponge.

I'll save it for later, I said about the pear, putting it in my pocket.

Come on, let's go home, she said, grabbing my hand.

Home. That was the word she used.

At the bus stop she stood in front of me, right in front, her back touched my front. She drew my arms around her waist. On the bus she leaned her elbow on my shoulder to look out the window.

You tell me. Was this a romance or wasn't it?

We got home and played Scrabble. I booked the fishing charter. In the late afternoon, I had a bath. I thought... I thought she might join me. Instead, I was leaning back with a washcloth over my eyes when she called my name and said she was going out. I became aware of a rumbling from the street, a characteristic rumbling. A Volkswagen rumbling. I waited for and heard what came next, a low zhoosh as the van door opened, zhoosh, shut. The shift from idle into gear.

That night I did wait up.

The next day I heard from Chris that the van people knew about a farm on Saltspring where you could stay as long as you liked provided you helped out.

And today I got a postcard: Dear Edna, Your rooms were too small and there were no geese. I want to live as if timelessly. I know you loved me and I'm sorry.

This is to say: Sara, don't flatter yourself. I would have loved anybody.

Anne Fleming

Anne Fleming's most recent book is *Anomaly*, a novel. Her first book, *Pool-Hopping and Other Stories*, was shortlisted for the Governor General's Award, the Ethel Wilson Fiction Prize, and the Danuta Gleed award. Anne Fleming lives in Kelowna, BC, and teaches creative writing at the University of British Columbia Okanagan.

Jane Eaton Hamilton
Writer Notes

"Wart's Ugly" came about when I was thinking about children and sexual identity, children and enforced heterosexuality. As a society, we are invested in funnelling children into gender roles that are meant to cement and last a lifetime, and the intransigent—the tomboys, in the case of some lesbians—are to some greater or lesser degree shunned. They are given the message that they don't measure up. The slights—names like Wart, teasing, ostracism—go in deep, and last a lifetime. What happens when a little girl falls in love with another little girl, and no one notices?

Jane Eaton Hamilton
Wart's Ugly

The children were not allowed to leave the property, but the property at thirteen acres was large enough for injury. Both of the older children and many of their friends had fetched up wounded over the years. Casey had broken his ankle jumping out of the hayloft onto a hill of straw, and had also had a flap of flesh from the tip of his thumb consumed by a snapping turtle. They had all of them been stung by bees, wasps, hornets. A man in a trench coat had exposed himself to Wart while she crouched on her knees nursing a flap-winged killdeer. Another man had touched Wart when, topless, she had manned a corn-on-the-cob and lemonade stand with Casey at the end of the driveway. It had been August; it was hot; even the dog had been panting and dragging (that's why they were called *dog days*, Wart's father said). Casey was bare-chested, so why couldn't *she* be? She didn't have boobies, knockers, bazooms. Her chest looked exactly the same as Casey's, only littler.

"You a girlie?"

Wart had stubbed her thongs on the grass, had looked up at him with thinned eyes. He was just a regular man. When she'd admitted, surly, that sure she was—who wanted to know?—the man reached out a thick, stubby index finger and rubbed its end over her left nipple, causing it to pucker. Wart knocked his hand away. When he got back into his Oldsmobile, she threw his nickel after him. It rolled on edge down Porcupine Hill before guttering out.

Casey's friend, who was also named Casey, had whopped Wart's brother with a maple branch and slashed open his cheek so it needed stitches. Wart had fallen off her bike so many times she didn't know what scabless knees looked like. Wart had tried to balance across the paddock fence and had taken a tumble, spraining her wrist. Wart was thrown off horses and suffered cut lips and bloody noses; sometimes at night she picked her nose, and things commenced to bleeding until she could tease out ropes like red licorice from where they had coiled somewhere inside her—veins, she figured.

Wart's best friend Wendy had cut herself on glass when Wart smashed out one of the little multiple panes on the locked tack house windows so she could slip her hand in and unlock the window latch, then swing herself over the sill and pull Wendy up behind her. (They had to buy the replacement windows for twenty-five cents apiece at the hardware store and putty them back in themselves. That was always the penalty Wart's father meted out.) Wart had taken Wendy's wrist in her hand and sucked off the blood, then chased Wendy around the tack house hooting like a vampire. Wendy said Wart should cut herself too, so Wart did, and they mashed their wrists together as blood sisters. Wart's other sister was baby Delora. Wart had stolen her baby-bottle warmer and used it to boil a pocket full of rhubarb stalks she mixed with sugar. Being able to make her own rhubarb stew and dole it out on a twisted kitchen spoon mouthful by mouthful to Wendy satisfied her. There were built-in bunks in the tack house, and Wart and Wendy curled up tight reading Archie comics. They tugged off the horsehair mattress and slats below so they could crawl under the built-in table that joined the bunks—their fort—before teasing the mattress back on top to be pitched into blackness. Wendy was scared and always had to cuddle into Wart for protection, but Wart had matches for light and pretzels to smoke, the ends of which reluctantly began to smolder with enough porosity for an imitation of draw. They were eight years old, but they imagined they were sixteen.

Casey, Wendy's brother, broke his finger in one of the stall doors. Wendy bashed her ear falling against the workbench. Casey and Wendy were big brother and little sister, but even though the boys had the same name, and Wendy and Wart had the same first initial, they were not the same family. The name thing was just *coincidental*, a word Wart's wordsmith father shared and that Wart was fond of.

The children were allowed to get injured in all manner of ways. It was expected. The children were only enjoined from dying.

Before she was pregnant with Delora, Wart's mother had been in the hospital. Wart's father had taken her there. It was a special hospital for *people like your mother*. There had been a lot of screaming and throwing of the *Globe and Mail*; Wart's parents not realizing Casey and Wart were roped around the staircase spindles, spying. A couple days later, her father led Wart's docile, bruised, stumbling mother to the Chevy by her wrist and pushed her into the back seat as if she were a suitcase. The housekeeper came to stay with Casey and Wart. Elsie had a rule that every child must have a bath before bed, and when she tucked Wart in, she opened her pajama top and spread Vicks VapoRub on her chest while she talked about Wart's mother. "Such pretty lady, but oh, cuckoo. What is cereal? Fruit Loop. She fruit loop, your mama. You know what is this?" She lifted a finger thick with Vicks to her temple and circled it.

Wart thought of the cuckoo clocks that chimed on the hour. "My mom's getting better," she said. "She's going to come home."

"Maybe I always to be look after you."

"My mom's coming home," insisted Wart and twisted away to face the wall.

As if by magic and wishes, Wart's mother did reappear, but she was not the same mother. She was pinched around her mouth as if by staples, and if it had been hard to ignite her attention before, it was worse now. Wart's mother sat at the kitchen table with her shoulders slumped, crying. Sometimes she threw coffee cups that broke against the range. Elsie snorted and packed up her bags and carried them up the road to the bus stop. Wart's mother paced and muttered and obsessively twirled a finger in her hair. The days and months passed. She got pregnant; she bore Delora, then jiggled her like a basketball she was trying to hold aloft.

Wart knew her mother just wanted them out of her hair. Her hair, she often insisted, was a robin's nest (or a bear's nest, or a rabbit's nest lined with down, depending on her mood). Where before her hair had never looked the part, after the hospital it did. She hardly ever washed it. Her twirling finger caused snags like the clumps of used straw Wart shovelled from the horse stalls. Wart's mother maintained that she had eyes in the back of her head, which allowed sight of her children's misdeeds. Wart was skeptical while in general awestruck by adults' superior deductive powers. Her grade three teacher, for instance, had accepted a note excusing Wart from gym and had pulled Wart aside. Had Wart's mother really written it? Wart had wracked her brain over how Mrs. Kilmore had seen through her duplicity, and finally realized that writing the note in pencil had given her away. Wart's mother always knew when Wart had eaten an illicit Wagon Wheel. She knew when Wart was just pretending to sleep. At night, while they watched Ed Sullivan or Carol Burnett, Wart cocooned in her baby doll pajamas, Wart finger-combed her mother's knotted dreadlocks looking for the fabled pair of extra eyes. Her mother swatted her hand away and told her to stop being a bug. She hated having kids in her hair. Wasn't Wart smart enough to grasp that? Her mother was busy with the baby.

After lunch—Wart's mother was babysitting Casey and Wendy for the day, which to Wart was having heaven fall in her lap—their mother had told them to skedaddle, but to stick close by. "Stay where I can find you," she said. "You might have to go over to your grandparents' later." She eyed them suspiciously. "Stay in the house."

Casey grabbed a can of their father's frog legs (of the order Anura, Wart's father had said, lifting one of the slimy things to his mouth, winking). Wart ran after her brother chanting, "Casey's a big old Rana catesbeiana, Casey's a big old Rana catesbeiana." Casey yelled back that Wart was the ugly one. "Wart's ugly, Wart's ugly, Wart's ugly," he screamed. "Wart has warts!" Wart felt the short bristles of her near brush cut. Sister and brother leaped into the basement past the gnawed dog's bed and the newspapers Casey claimed would spontaneously combust (like fat people, he said) to the root cellar with its spider webs and wet dampness, its mouldering shelves, its exposed light bulb, its dirt floors. The Caseys flipped the latch behind them and blocked the door so Wart and Wendy couldn't leave. They pried open the can of frog legs and tried to make the girls, who squealed, swallow some. Wart's mother yelled down to cut out the racket. The boys puffed their chests up and held their noses and let the webbed feet of the frogs slide down their esophaguses. The boys were hoping to give themselves botulism or ptomaine poisoning, which Casey, Wart's brother, insisted was what would happen if the atom bomb went off. Casey, Wendy's brother, said they would have to grab all the frog legs in the cupboard and rush down here where they would have to live until they were old. Wart stared at the shelves of dusty preserves.

"Know how you have to get under your desk at school when the drill goes?"

Wendy nodded.

"You have to stay like that for months."

"Do not," said Wart, but she wasn't positive.

"With your hands over the back of your neck," added the other Casey.

After Wart's mother had come home from the hospital,

Wart's hair had fallen out. Until then, she had been a little girl in braided pigtails fastened with tiny plastic pink bows, her fine hair pulled tight against her skull, but afterwards stray hairs began to ripple from her hands to the floor. It didn't alarm her more than the long clots of blood she pulled from her nose. She was a tomboy. Tomboys had all kinds of weird things happen.

Wart's mother got around to grooming her.

"Where do you get this snaggledy mess?" said Wart's mother, exasperated as she yanked through a comb. She looked down at it, then lifted up Wart's chin to get a better look. "Your hair is falling out."

"No, it isn't," said Wart.

Wart's mother snorted. "You haven't *noticed*?" Wart's mother stroked the child's hair with her fingers and caused a rain around Wart's face. She wearily shook her head, stood up, and paced as if she didn't realize where she was. She sighted Wart again like looking down a telescope. "Genevieve, understand this. Listen to me closely because this is important. I am the electrical current gone wonky, the spark, the sizzle in the wires behind the walls."

"What?"

"The income tax," said Wart's mother. "The sales tax. The audit. I am the 'F' in Arithmetic, the mumps and the measles, the scraped knees."

Wart had thought only kids could be those things.

"I am the fly in the Campbell's mushroom soup, the coons in the trash cans. The stillborn foal in the barn. Your father's flat rubber tire. Who did it? It's a foregone Clue game: me in the kitchen with a milk bottle."

Murder? Who did *murder*? thought Wart.

"You kids spread around Jerseyville like DDT. You're weeds, Genevieve, you and your brother."

"We're not weeds," said Wart. Her father killed weeds in the lawn with a spray can. All the grass around them shrivelled up and died.

"A man and a woman lay a frame of two-by-fours and pour forth a child." Wart's mother's hands exclaimed, fluttering around her head like fledgling swallows. She looked into the distance. Wart looked too, but all she could see was a night-black window. "Don't you get it? If the frame is weak, it breaks and the child gushes out any which way, drying with each passing day until she is set so hard only a jackhammer can pierce her."

Wart frowned. She knew about jackhammers. A bubble-head boy had crawled into a pothole on their road and been crushed by a car; men came and jackhammered the road apart. (Also, thought Wart, right around there a huge turtle had gotten squashed, and its guts had looked like spaghetti noodles.)

"Genevieve, I am the mouse that ate through the baseboard."

"You're not a mouse, Mommy," said Wart. This she knew. This she could have confidence about. She herself had nurtured a shoebox of mice babies, feeding them with an eyedropper; she knew everything about mice.

Wart's mother blinked, then looked at her daughter and seemed to actually see her, not just as a prop but as someone real, someone she knew, and she sank onto the edge of the bed and touched Wart's cheek. "I'm not? Little you know, oh spawn-of-mine. Then where's the mouse?" She snatched up Wart's hand too hard, circled her index finger on Wart's palm. "Round and round the garden, goes the teddy bear. One step—" And here her fingers hopped up Wart's arm. Wart laughed and screamed. "—Two steps. Tickle you under there. Three steps, four steps—" She tangled her fingers in Wart's hair. "How'd that mouse get in your hair?" When her mother took her hand away, they both stared at it. It was covered with a snarly clump that dangled like an oriole's nest.

Wart's mother took her to the doctor. Wart sat on the cold edge of his examining table while he shaved her bald. She had a paintbrush spatter of freckles over her nose and now exposed warts on her scalp, too—six warts that looked like periods on the ends of many missing sentences. Wart's mother sewed baby bonnets for her in robin's egg blue corduroy. They tied under her chin in bows. In school, when Wart felt her head, the bonnet was moist with leaking medicine.

The children clappered up to the attic. They passed the fat, doomed flies buzzing around the grimy windows, then rummaged through stacks of newspapers about the war and a guy named Winston Churchill their mother had a crush on, then through their father's wartime trunk. When Wart had asked her father what he'd done in the RAF, her mother had laughed.

"Did you see action?" Casey had asked.

Her father picked his banjo and looked up at him to smile. "Sure I did," he said. "I was stationed in England."

"The only action your father ever saw," interrupted their mother dryly, "was the blade of a moving potato peeler."

In the trunk were medals, which Wart pinned on Wendy's chest over the boys' objections, and thick socks with holes, and sepia photographs, and a uniform, and a sharp smell of mothballs.

Wendy unpinned the medals and threw them at her brother. The boys ran downstairs to make a balsa wood plane. Wendy said, "Uh? We could play Barbies." She opened her Barbie carrying case and showed off a brand new doll with waterfalling yellow hair that she'd gotten for her birthday. This Barbie wore a tight skirt that came down below her knees like the ones Wart's mother wore for appointments, along with a sweater set in green, and a chain of tiny pearls. All Wart's Barbie dolls had brush cuts Wart had given them, along with missing limbs, scratches, and discolourations. Wart preferred them. Most of their accessories were lost. She still had one tiny pink mule with feathers on the toe and one alligator handbag, but otherwise the accessories had all gone missing, tiny high heels and hats vacuumed up into Elsie's Hoover. Wendy crooned to her Barbie as if it were a baby with a pull cord who was going to answer. Wart felt stirrings of jealousy.

"*I* know," said Wart and dug through silver-belled boxes that contained her mother's wedding gown and the dresses her bridesmaids had worn, which were the same but in blue. She threw a dress to Wendy, which surrounded the girl like a dress-up cloud. They weren't supposed to go near the white one itself, but the bridesmaids' gowns were fair game as long as they were *exceedingly* careful. (Wart's father said the word *exceedingly*, a four-syllable word, was to be used to refer to excess.) Wendy took her top and shorts off but left on her undershirt and panties. Wart left all her clothes on. They struggled into the flounces and swishes of material and pointed at each other, giggling maniacally. The dresses were far too big; the straps hung down past their chests; the waists coddled the tops of their thighs. They slipped into old, unmatching high heels that had belonged to Wart's mother and clunked around the attic pretending to be society ladies with cigarettes in holders and glasses of champagne.

When that game wasn't fun anymore, Wendy knelt down and gathered up her Barbie, roping its hair into a ponytail between her thumb and index finger, carefully tucking it back into the carrying case with its Barbie-sized closet. There was a space for clothes, too, with miniature plastic pink hangers from which hung ball gowns easily as fancy as the ones the girls wore.

"How come *you* don't have long hair?" Wendy asked.

"'Cause I was bald."

"I know, but you're not bald anymore, so how come?"

"Beats me. My mom won't let me."

"But short hair is ugly. It's for boys."

"Let's go outside," said Wart. She could feel heat on the tips of her ears, knew she was flaming with blush. If Wendy thought she was ugly, then Wart wanted long hair.

"Your mom won't let us," said Wendy looking up.

"Will so. She always does."

"My mom and dad will be coming to get us."

"Not till after dinner, Mom said," said Wart. She couldn't bear it when Wendy had to go home; the rest of the night was like flat Ginger Ale.

"We're moving," said Wendy.

Wart thought about the word moving. One time, a kid in school had moved from one house to another house on the next street over. "No way," she finally said.

"Yes, way. We are." Wendy nodded. She was painstakingly itemizing accessories, organizing hats and purses and a mink stole the size of a Band-Aid. "That's where my parents are. They're at our new house. They took us last weekend."

"You never told."

"We weren't allowed." She glanced up at Wart. Wart could see she was nervous "'Cause it's in Toronto."

Toronto was not in their town. Once, a kid in school had gone to India for a year, but it was more like he was a Casper the Friendly Ghost who winked gone for a while, and then winked back. "That's not true."

"Is so," said Wendy. "Wednesday is my last day of school. We have to move for my dad's work. I have to go to a new school. My new teacher's name is Mrs. Morris."

Wart had memorized every inch of Wendy. Everyone said they looked like sisters, except for Wendy had long hair and darker eyes. Wart knew how Wendy turned her head. She knew how she looked laughing and crying. She knew which games she was good at—Double Dutch and Red Rover Come Over—and which she was bad at—baseball, basketball, volleyball. She knew which subjects Wendy liked and that she hated Wart's favourite thing, reading, which was why Wart always read to her instead of the reverse. They had been in the same class since kindergarten. Wendy had ridden bareback behind Wart, her sweaty body clinging as they went over jumps singing *It was an itsy, bitsy, teeny weeny, yellow polka dot bikini.* They took swimming lessons together. They took ballet lessons together. They took figure skating lessons together. They spent every free minute together in a way Wart's father called *inseparable* (five syllables). Wart couldn't talk. She wanted to throw her hands over her ears and scream in her loudest voice. She said, "Last one down is a rotten egg," and yanking the bridesmaid dress up above her knees, she sprinted for the stairs.

In Casey's room as Wart hovered, Wendy bent to smooth a decal on the boys' biplane. Wart said she'd forgotten something and ran back up to the attic. She kept an ear out for Wendy. She opened Wendy's Barbie case and snapped the head off Wendy's new doll. She stuck her hand down the chest of the dress and stuffed it in her shorts pocket.

A couple nights earlier, Wart had seen her father grab her mother's elbow and whisper harshly, "This has to stop."

"Don't touch me," said her mother.

They stood glowering at each other, buzzing like the electric fence in the field, then he said, "I saw you."

"Let me go," said her mother, twisting away, nursing her elbow.

Wart's father noticed Wart. "Genevieve, go to your room." When she didn't move, he said, "At once, young lady!" He looked back at Wart's mother. "You're not too big to take over my lap."

"I'd like to see you try it." Her mother's ribs rode in and out.

"I will try it, you bitch."

"Like you've ever been a saint," said Wart's mother. "Like you're a bloody war hero."

"At least I'm not a lunatic."

"At least I'm not *you*," said Wart's mother and spat at his feet.

They looked like they had just finished a relay race. Sweat was popping above Wart's father's upper lip; her mother looked winded.

The next day, on the back porch, Wart had found her

father's banjo shattered in pieces like a split apart bale of straw, bits scattered everywhere. His hard-shelled suitcase was upright, a thin piece of worn undershirt protruding from its side. She bumped it over, flattening banjo bits, and tried to open it, but it was locked. A bobby pin worked. Her father's clothes—his jodhpurs, his suits, his dirty socks and underwear, his riding boots and spurs, his ties—were mashed into a big muddle.

After the kids had played an exuberant game of horse, neighing and galloping from the den through the kitchen and foyer and dining room back into the den, chasing each other with Wart's father's spanking paddle (which hung by the telephone: *Show your family you really care, spank them soundly bottoms bare*), shrieking, and had begged for cookies, and milk, and bugged her for Play-Doh, Wart's mother's patience finally wore thin. It was something like toffee being pulled to its breaking point, she explained—did they *want* her to break? "Vamoose," she said, jiggling Delora. "Scram. Don't leave the property. Do *not* leave the property. Do *not* drown." The children understood that their mother really meant: *Don't get into any trouble I need to get you out of*, and, *Don't go near the valley*.

Water was considered to be the most dangerous of all the perils awaiting the children. Water could prove fatal and in fact the prior owners had lost their teenaged son in the pond when his ankle had become snared by weeds. When Wart had been nearly two and her inattentive mother had been sunbathing, she misplaced Wart. Her mother thought the child was playing by her feet, but when, sometime later, she woke up shivering, the sun was behind a cloud and the girl was nowhere to be found.

"Where's your sister?" Wart's mother took off her sunglasses and stared at her son. He was only four and shrugged. His mother took his shoulders and shook. "I said, where is your sister?"

Wart's mother panicked, frantic—frantic to find the baby, but just as frantic about what people would think. She skittered across the property searching the tack house, the window house, the chicken coop, the tool shed, the garage, the garbage lean-to. Finally, hoarse from calling, with Casey whining as she tugged him, she bolted into the house to call the firemen. They arrived ten minutes later with sirens blaring, their red trucks taking out low maple boughs as they sped up the driveway. They searched the property fruitlessly, ranging further afield with Wart's mother in tow, finally weaving at the lip of the murky pond with its reeds and grasses, its unnameable depths, scanning for a sign of ruffled diaper, Wart diving like a duck, tail in air. An older man pointed out where the previous child had gone under. Two others conferred about plans to dredge; they were sorry, they said, their eyes slipping to where Wart's mother's shirt was undone, her baby blue polka-dotted bikini top exposed, her hip canted; they were sorry for the tanned young mother in orange pedal pushers.

It was then a fireman loudspeakered down from the house—the baby had been found between the front door and the screen, had rolled into the foyer like an orange off a grocery pile, perfectly round, perfectly unblemished, perfectly fine.

Even so, Wart's father had the pond drained.

"You go with Casey," said Wart's brother. "Me and Wendy'll play."

Wart grabbed Wendy and clung tight. "Nuh-uh, she's mine. That's the rule. Boys together, girls together."

"Not for *Bum Show Club*," said Wart's brother.

"They're babies," said Wendy's brother Casey. "Dumb old babies. Let's go." The boys leaped the stream and disappeared into the aspen forest. The girls were too small to jump, but down by the mouth of the marsh there were stepping stones. The marsh was the best place for finding the strings of frog eggs in long ropes of mucus that looped like nosebleeds, each egg the size and shape of a cap gun cap on a red paper strip. It was the best place to fish tadpoles from the water; the best place to spy warty toads; the best place for sinking in gooey mud to your knees—quicksand, Wart and Wendy always pretended. Wart helped Wendy cross over, and they tracked the boys. When they found them, the boys were undressed and jumped around cupping their privates and ordering them to bugger off. Wart and Wendy retreated to the edge of the grove, where the light was dappled, and stood around uncertainly. Usually the boys orchestrated the activity, yelled over what to do. Wart was *discombobulated* (a really good six syllables; almost as good as *supercalifragilisticexpialidocious*) and sort of mad. Mad like the niggle of a knife down her *esophagus* (good for its great gutlike sound). When Wendy asked Wart what they should do, Wart replied, "Well, I dunno. Take your clothes off, I guess."

"I don't want to," said Wendy and formed an 'X' of her arms over her chest.

"Do it, though."

"No. I won't. You can't make me." Wendy's eyes thinned.

"You have to."

"No way, José."

Wart stuck out her tongue and turned her back. She supposed Wendy would stomp off, but she was curious to see. She waited, but instead Wendy touched her shoulder. "Don't be mad," Wendy whispered in a skinny voice. "Wart, come off it. I'll do it, okay? I will. I'll be good."

"You don't get to wear *anything*," Wart said between gritted teeth. She refused to turn around. "It's the *Bum Show Club*."

"But I don't want the boys to see."

"They don't care." Wart planted her arms emphatically across her chest. "They don't even know we're alive."

She heard a susurration and wheeled. Wendy had stripped down to her underwear and a second later she was naked.

Suddenly, Wart hated everything about Wendy—her shapeless, powerless girl's body, the planes of her too familiar face, the knobbly-knock knees covered with healing scars, the pale skin where her bathing suit went. She *wanted* Wendy to move away. She heard a muffled scream across the copse and stepped around a tree trunk to look. Her brother was slung over the crotch of a tree, his bottom tilted into the air, an unnerving, exposed pink. Wendy's brother was using the paddle. It gave Wart a queasy feeling. She didn't quite trust boys, their bigness, their body strength, the way Casey always dragged her across fresh cut grass until she was stained green as an inchworm, how he made her kiss his feet before she could leave the house.

The dress was a blue pool at Wendy's feet, like a pond she had just stepped into that was rising to drown her. Wendy tried to make the bifurcated 'V' at her lower torso vanish by crossing her legs in contorted ways.

"No," said Wart, "don't. Just stand."

Wendy shot a worried look to Wart. Her eyes were as dark as tarnished silver, subterranean and flashing. But she did it. She gave in. The fluid lines of her body shifted, her shoulders straightened, her nothing hips fell into line. This was a new Wendy, one Wart had never seen—calm, self-possessed, reconciled, challenging. Wart was *flummoxed* (two syllables, but a word that sounded harder) and awestruck. She leaned forward and touched the tiny pink mouse nose of Wendy's right nipple. She strummed it as her father strummed "Clementine" on his banjo.

Captivated, she watched her finger, felt the nipple stiffening beneath it, watched goosebumps break out across Wendy's body until the hairs on her arms stood up in the backlighting of the lowering sun like sparkling frosting. Wendy intook her breath. Wart strummed "Home on the Range," then stopped, looked up. Something turned over inside Wart, a desire she had been denying harbouring. She wanted to be Wendy's husband. Wart dropped her finger. Their faces were two inches apart. Wart took Wendy's chin between her index finger and thumb the hard way her mother did it to her to comb her hair and put her other arm around Wendy's waist, pulling her close. She didn't know what to do after that except kiss her, so that's what she did; she kissed Wendy's lips and was surprised at how soft they felt. Sometimes Wart kissed mirrors or glass to leave an oily, puckery imprint of her lips, but this was not cold and hard like that. This was warm and pliable. Wendy started to kiss her back, her lips parting, but then Wendy's tongue wiggled towards Wart like a snake, surprising her, and something between them shattered, a spell, and Wart let go suddenly, and Wendy stumbled backwards, her feet catching in the net of dress, and she fell backwards, her left hand finding purchase on the loam of the forest floor. Her legs flung apart and Wart saw the inside of her privates. Wendy saw her see.

Wendy scrambled up, pushed Wart, grabbed the dress and ran, sobbing. Wendy was only ten feet away at the edge of the marsh, when she looked around wildly and found a rock the size of a baseball, which she heaved overhand like a girl. She couldn't throw, she was known as a terrible thrower, but Wart knew the rock was going to hit its target anyhow. She didn't move. She felt its impact on the side of her head at the same instant that out of the corner of her eye she registered the boys coming closer and the ball of blue nude that was Wendy fleeing across the marsh, hopping from stone to stone, the dress dangling in the water, picking up mud and lily pads. At the far bank, she scrambled up on hands and knees, then turned and stared back at Wart, her chest heaving. Wart saw rather than felt blood splashing on her own dress and skin. With as much dignity as she could muster, Wendy yanked on the bridesmaid dress and stomped up the hillside through long, impeding grasses and gopher holes.

That night when Wart was in bed, the light on, reading a Nancy Drew book, her mother dropped out of nowhere onto the side of her bed and hovered there like an anxious mosquito. She said that Wendy's mother had called and that Wendy was missing her new Barbie doll's head. Had Wart seen the goddamned thing?

"No," said Wart.

"You stole it, didn't you? That would be so like you." Wart's mother picked at her eyebrows, which were already so thin from her thinning that she had to draw them in in pencily arcs. She also didn't have any eyelashes left. "Let me check that scalp." She picked at the dried blood on the side of Wart's head.

Wart twisted away. "No. I didn't take her dumb old doll head. Dolls are for sissies."

"Tell me what happened today. Those dresses are ruined."

"I told you. I fell. It was an accident."

Her mother let out a long, mad sigh. Wart wondered if she was opening the hidden eyes that could see Wart's crimes. She narrowed the set Wart could see. "Know something? It doesn't matter anyway. Who cares if you took it? The little bitch is moving. You're not going to see her again anyway. I never liked her, and I never appreciated that holier-than-thou mother of hers making me babysit. Like she never lost track of one of her goddamned kids. Like the milk in her fridge never went off."

Wart was scared. She wanted to say Wendy *couldn't* move, that someone had to stop her. She wanted to say that *she* liked Wendy plenty, that she always had, that Wendy was her best friend, her *bestest* friend and she loved her. Except that she didn't. She *hated* Wendy. "Why's Dad's stuff outside?"

Her mother snorted.

"What happened to his banjo?"

Wart's mother popped up like a jack-in-the-box. She twisted opened Wart's closet and swiped dresses and blouses and Wart's jodhpurs off hangers and flung them onto Wart's floor. She took out Wart's cardboard suitcase and snapped it open on the end of Wart's bed. The mattress barely bounced. "Genevieve, your asshole fath—"

"What?" said Wart. "What?" Her mother started scooping undershirts and underpants from her dresser, cramming them in the suitcase, sweeping the clothes on the floor into her arms and adding those. Wart felt a lump of panic forming in her chest. She was going out on the porch with her father's clothes, she just knew it. She was being vanished. She said, "I mean it. I didn't take any stupid doll head, honest. And I'm sorry we wrecked your dresses. It was an accident."

Her mother looked at her. "You're going to stay with your grandparents, Little Miss Tomboy-too-big-for-her-britches. I expect you to behave like a big girl. No *whining*. I will talk to Mrs. Kilmore and get your homework."

"I don't want to. Why do I have to?"

"Well, you *are* going," said Wart's mother, "and your brother too. And Delora. And that's the end of that." She threw in bobby socks and patent leather shoes, a kilt, Wart's saddle shoes, play clothes and snapped the suitcase closed. She brushed her hands together with finality.

Wart didn't want to cry—tomboys didn't—but she just hated her grandparents' guest room. There were framed Audubon prints of falcons with yellow eyes and sharp beaks, and the bed was higher and harder than her own, the pillow fatter. The feathers in it made her sneeze. She wanted her mother; nobody would tell her when she was coming to pick them up, or when Wart's dad was. "Don't you worry your little head about *that*," their grandmother had said, ruffling Wart's scruffy hair, careful of its bandage. "You let the grown-ups worry about *that*. You just concentrate on having fun."

"Was it because I was bad?"

"Were you bad, sugar? Well, that would be just *coincidental*, I'd guess."

Wart couldn't have fun; when she woke up in the morning, she didn't even know for a minute where she was. It was a school day, Monday, only she wasn't going to school. She wondered what Wendy was doing this exact minute. She tried to think what Toronto would be like and who Wendy's best friend would be, and whether she'd have her own room, or horses, and whether her teacher would be prettier than Mrs. Kilmore.

Wart had thought they were bound to get a licking for ruining the bridesmaids' dresses, but when she'd gotten back from the valley, her mother had been screaming on the back porch, wielding scissors, tossing cut bits of Wart's father's clothing into the yard. Wart had trailed around to let herself in the front door. At first she couldn't see Wendy, but then she found her sitting cross-legged, crying silently beside the freezer. She had her own clothes on and was holding on to her Barbie doll case for dear life.

Wart sat down beside her. They could hear Wart's mother on the porch. "Never mind my mom. She just gets like this."

Wendy said, "You're bleeding."

"It already dried up," said Wart. The blood was splashed down her dress, rusty rain on blue, freckling on a robin's egg.

"I want my folks to come *now*."

"They are." Wart's stomach growled. "Soon."

"My mom says your mom has bats in her belfry."

This was a new phrase for Wart. She turned it over. A bat had come down the chimney and she had taken it to Show and Tell. "What's a belfry?"

Wendy shrugged. "Does your head hurt?"

Wart shrugged. "Want to go up to my room and wait? I could read to you." Wart pushed the bridesmaid's dress off her shoulders and stepped out of it, gave Wendy a hand. "Getting married is dumb anyhow. I hate dresses." She picked the gown up and turned to go upstairs. The material overflowed in a bridal train. A musty smell of moth balls wafted after her.

They lay on Wart's bed while Wart oozed blood onto her pillow, Wart reading *Mary Poppins Opens the Door*. They heard the boys come in, and finally they heard a car and got up to look. Wart's mother was revving across the grass in her green and white Comet, leaving ruts on the lawn, finally shooting out the driveway. A while later, Wendy's parents arrived. Wendy's mom exclaimed over Wart's head, but Wart said not to, it was just *superficial*. (Four good syllables. Her mom had said her dad was just *superficial*. It was something that didn't mean much.) Wendy's mom cleaned it up anyhow, but Wart didn't know if there was any gauze anywhere, so Mrs. Farrell left it unbandaged. Wart stood at the back door in the hail of fallen clothing and banjo pieces as Wendy's father carried her away.

"So, bye," Wart had said waveringly.

"See ya," Wendy had said, her eyes locking with Wart's.

At her grandparents' house, Wart didn't hear anyone else up yet, even Delora. She pulled on her clothes from the day before and crept down the back stairs to the kitchen, looked through the drawers until she found a spoon, and let herself out the heavy back door with a vacuumy whoosh. There was dew on the grass and Wart's bare feet left prints. Her grandparents had a statue of a little boy holding the scales of justice. Wart stepped over a clipped box hedge and rubbed the boy's cold cement cheek and gave him a kiss on his stone lips. But he didn't feel like Wendy. Wart took the Barbie doll head from her pocket and looked at it. She fondled the yellow hair the way Wendy had, making a ponytail then releasing it to see it swing out. It felt fake. Wart ran her finger over Barbie's plastic face, too, her plastic eyes and plastic nose and plastic lips. They felt fake. Wart tried kissing her, but she didn't feel like Wendy, was cold and tiny and pointy. Wart smelled her—she smelled like *chemicals* (three syllables). She took the spoon and dug a hole into the sandy ground, using the handle as a pickaxe until it torqued. Into the hole, she dropped the Barbie head. She didn't need it. She didn't need anyone.

Jane Eaton Hamilton

Jane Eaton Hamilton is the author of six books, most recently the Ferro-Grumley nominated collection of short fiction, *Hunger*. She has won numerous awards for her poetry, nonfiction, and fiction, including first prize in the 2003 CBC Canadian Literary Awards and twice, first prize in the Prism International short fiction award. Her work has recently appeared in the anthologies *The Spirit of Writing*, *Best Lesbian Love Stories 2005*, and *The Writer's Presence*.

Lydia Kwa
Writer Notes

I have interests in idiosyncrasies of mind and habit. Language is very musical, even the way people and characters don't or can't utter words close to their deepest truths. There's the languor of silences and what's trapped or embodied in them. Queerness isn't fixed. Queerness is more than who sleeps with whom. Being a foreigner or outsider informs much of my imagination. In my writing, I like to create—or hint at—such experiences and locate them in the so-called centre, rather than at the margin, without explanation or justification. I'm more interested in not spelling everything out, challenging readers to complete the narrative with their own projections. Or perhaps, asking readers to rethink their expectations of what lesbian narrative is, for instance. Is this a stable form with clear boundaries? Not for me.

Lydia Kwa
Soft Shell

"This is the first time you've been detected, so it goes without saying..."

"Without saying?"

"I'm surprised. You can't possibly believe that you would escape our detection?"

"No... I suppose not... well, I didn't even think that far ahead."

"A problem. Can't afford to be slack, a dyke of your standing. What you've done is a serious crime. Imagine what a bad influence you could become on the young ones."

"What crime?"

"You've thought it. The unacceptable."

"But surely, we've gone beyond the dark times of the 21st century? I mean, hadn't they done all the important work so that we..."

"That was a mistake."

I turned towards Cui and shook her shoulder roughly, "Wake up, you're having a bad dream."

She blinked several times and mumbled, "It's too scary to be a figment of my imagination."

"What was it this time?" I asked, unable to conceal the irritation. How long has it been? Every night for two weeks. Ever since we arrived in Kyoto.

At Nishiki market, most shops still had their roll-up aluminum doors partway up from ground level. A memory of Cui's sleep-laden eyes, that half-drowned look, flitted through my mind. I peered through the gaps and caught sight of legs in trousers, mostly white or blue cotton, moving about briskly. It was just after dawn, cool enough to walk the narrow alley between shops without sweating.

I went to my favorite tofu shop. The woman had figured

out I wasn't Japanese on my first visit at the beginning of July, when I only managed a few stuttered words. Today she flashed me her usual toothy smile. I watched her deft, wrinkled hands as she used a wooden spatula to scoop the freshly made tofu skins from the inside of a wooden bucket, and fill a plastic container full of the steaming strands. Then she filled the container almost to the brim with soymilk from the same bucket. I licked my lips eagerly. There are some things I will never tire of.

Further down the alley, I bought some pickled octopus, a packet of large bonito flakes, and a small flask of Okinawan saké, Cui's favorite. I was about to head home when I spotted the big basin of soft-shell crabs. That would be good for dinner, I thought, and bought two medium-sized ones, bound by rattan twine and wrapped in the previous day's newspapers.

I wanted to linger at the market, but I knew that if I took too long, the thickening crowd would become oppressive. I decided to escape instead to a café to reward myself with a shot of espresso *kohi* before heading back.

At the apartment, I placed the container of tofu skins and the packet of bonito onto the counter, and then tucked the saké away into the cupboard. Left the crabs in the sink, reluctant to slaughter them just yet. I put on some jazz to help me focus. Seated in front of my laptop, I tried to concentrate on the short story I was working on, but found myself wondering about Cui instead.

The most restless and fretful I had seen her in all our years together. Was it because of her work at the studio? Or being stuck with me in this tiny apartment, away from our familiar surroundings? But we had known only too well, we desperately needed a change, needed to leave Vancouver and seek refuge in Kyoto, a place appealing for its mix of ancient and modern, its shrine and shadow worlds.

Hours later, I was jolted out of writing by the sound of keys jangling as they landed on the floor. The routine never deviated, no matter where we lived, the dropping of keys onto the floor. Yet I still startled that afternoon. I looked up to catch the frown between her eyes.

"How's the sculpture coming along?" I asked, glancing quickly at her then back to my screen. But I was only pretending to concentrate on the story, wondering instead why Cui, so far, hasn't told me a thing about her nightmares.

"I don't know. Maybe it's not a good idea, trying to build a giant spider with fibre optic cables and bubble wrap. Would Louise Bourgeois approve of how I'm quoting her work?"

"Ever thought of trying to contact her and asking?"

"Good idea," she replied in a disinterested tone.

She peered into the sink and her voice instantly perked up, "Wow, what a treat. Do you want me to kill them?"

"Don't worry about it." I waved my hand at her, saved the paragraph I was working on, and got up from the writing desk. At the stove, I placed a pot of water on high heat. Carefully placed a rack inside. I poked at one of the crabs, on the top of its shell. It flinched a little. I retrieved the kitchen scissors, snipped off the front quarter-inch of that crab behind the eyes and mouth, flipped it over to expose the pale grey gills and then cut them off at the base along one side, then the other. I found the flap at the back of the crab, lifted it with the scissor blades, and snipped it off. Did the same on the other side.

"You don't seem bothered. And you do it so well."

"Old trick," I said, and went through the same procedure swiftly with my other victim.

I threw the two back into the sink, which I filled with cold water, and cut off the twine around their claws and shells. The crabs twitched imperceptibly. Good, I thought, as Cui continued to stare wide-eyed at the crabs.

When the water came to a boil, I placed the crabs onto the rack in the pot, with scallions, cooking saké, soy sauce, and ginger. Then I grated some ginger and mixed up a sauce to spoon over the tofu. Whipped up some *zarusoba* on the side while the crabs cooked. I didn't pay much mind to Cui hovering around me, since I was rather pleasantly engrossed in the cooking.

"We have to excise that tendency from you, I'm sure you know that already."

"Why do you say that?"

"What?"

"That I know already."

"Of course you do. You know everything I'm about to say."

"You're the one who's the Thought Police, not me."

The interrogator laughed and switched off the light. In the dark, burdened by the encroaching sensation of loneliness, I felt a craving for steamed crab. Wanted to bite into the soft and yielding insides.

"Well, you can't have it, that's just the way it is," Cui muttered in her sleep.

I was surprised because she hardly spoke aloud during her dreams. I drew up to her face and felt the whispering breath of her words caress my cheek. I moved closer, so close that my lips were almost touching hers. She continued to sleep, mumbling. Another unusual occurrence, I noted, as I drifted back to sleep, relieved for the reprieve.

"We have to remove the urge from you before it's too late."

"It shouldn't be a crime."

"Thinking the wrong thing always has been a crime."

"Imagination can't be contained. Just because I'm a lover of other women doesn't preclude me from fetishizing other bodies."

"Men's bodies."

"Don't you think it's hypocritical? I've seen you pack a dildo without hesitation day and night. It's become your fashion accessory. Yet you condemn me for having lust for cocks?"

She woke me up with her hand stroking my pelvis, her breathing slow and relaxed.

"I'm hungry," she said, licking my earlobe.

She moved her face down and parted my thighs. I had the odd sensation of feeling aroused while slipping back into sleep, at first only vaguely aware of the light strokes of her tongue, then jolting awake when her mouth sucked at my clitoris. I raised myself up on my elbows, and closed my eyes, fully awake.

Hunger was contagious. I was about to close my mouth over her breast when she said, "I want you to pry me open. Imagine ripping apart the soft gills and reaching in for the roe."

Cui hadn't been so forthright with me before. I nodded in the dark, dazed. I stumbled over to the CD player and put on *Tokyo City Lights*. With the bamboo blinds thudding lightly against the windows, the sound of the sax and vibraphones cruising above the humidity, I returned to Cui. As I entered her, I closed my eyes tight, to better feel the soft shell breaking open in my palms.

The music was somewhere else, fading away into a dream. We fell asleep quickly, entwined. Just before daybreak, I was roused by sounds of moaning. At first I wasn't sure whether it was pleasure or another nightmare. I sat up and looked down at her.

She spoke up, her voice husky yet defiant. "You can't keep me here any longer. See? I'm walking away."

She looked so serene saying goodbye, I wondered why.

Lydia Kwa

Lydia Kwa was born in Singapore but has lived in Canada since 1980. She published *The Colours of Heroines*, a collection of poems, with Toronto's Women's Press in 1994. Her first novel *This Place Called Absence* (Turnstone, 2000) was nominated for the Amazon.com / Books in Canada First Novel Award and the Lambda Literary Award. Her third book, *The Walking Boy*, is published by Key Porter Books.

Larissa Lai
Writer Notes

I still believe in the importance of claiming lesbian identity for political reasons, though as I get older and my life becomes more fluid, I'm sometimes concerned about the accuracy of making such a claim. Much of this novel-in-progress, which I've been working on since the 1995 publication of *When Fox Is a Thousand*, is in fact about trying to understand the ways in which we inhabit the labels we use to describe ourselves. The terms we use in a politics of liberation are never sufficient to describe lived lives, and yet, they are necessary in order to have those lives. In this project I'm trying to draw a picture of what it was like to be in one's twenties in 1990s Vancouver, trying to make sense of community, family, race, class, gender, and sexuality. The two main characters, Lynda and Ilene, share a house and a tenuous, often volatile friendship.

Larissa Lai
The Sewing Box

The flowers on my mother's sewing box have faded to ghosts of what they were. I suppose they are roses, although all that remains are little flecks of pink, some dark, some light, and the traces of leaves, like skeletons left behind after winter has claimed the living parts. There might have been birds there too, although all you can see is the possibility of a wing here, a white throat there. Inside the box, all her things lie neatly just where she placed them before she died. There are wooden spools of thread in different colours lined up in a compartment on the side. There is a pair of scissors in black steel, with wide looping handles and short, sharp blades. There is a crochet hook, a tool for picking seams, and patterns of her own design cut in ancient yellowing newspaper or brown paper salvaged from supermarket bags. There is an embroidered satin pincushion in the shape of a star. A variety of pins and needles stick out of it, all deadly sharp though stained with age.

There are buttons in a little round tin that once held cherry candies. These buttons are the holding pegs of memory— rhinestone buttons for the splashy red flowered dress she wore for her fortieth wedding anniversary; big purple plastic buttons from the coat she made for my first day of school; smooth shiny gold buttons left from the Sunday jackets she sewed for my brothers; a few small elegant black buttons for the silver satiny dress she gave to my elder brother's wife. There is one dark button left over from the simple black dress she hurriedly assembled to wear to my father's funeral.

The only thing I remember from that day was that I had to wear a dress with elaborate shirring in front. She had gone to some trouble to learn how it was done, but the result was that the dress itched terribly. I complained about the discomfort so plaintively and persistently that she finally asked my youngest brother (who was then in his early thirties) to drive me home to change. I think, in retrospect, she was more hurt than angry and I still sometimes get brief pangs of guilt about my behaviour that day, since it turned out to be the first day of the last week of her life. There is still a small coil of the elastic she used for the shirring in her sewing box.

I was a miracle baby, born in the late evening of my mother's life. She was fifty-nine. A lot of people thought it was scandalous, revolting even, to think of a body so wrinkled and flabby parading its fertility as though it were forty years younger. Akin to an elderly lady wearing jeans and a halter top and smearing her lips a too-sexy red. But personally, I don't think there's anything wrong with it. My brother Wilson's wife Abbie thinks the "abnormal" circumstances of my birth are the source of my bad manners, but I chalk it up to the fact of having been raised by men. Not that I'm complaining mind you. I can change a tire faster than any of my friends. I can clear a plate of steak and potatoes faster than any trucker and I'm not in the least bit perturbed by cleaning out successful mousetraps, regardless of the degree of carnage.

Anyway, my mother never was the jeans and halter top type. She was cool and elegant and reserved and always kept herself to herself, which is more than I can say about Abbie.

It's true, though, that I've always been a bit of a pain in the neck. Even I can't deny it.

How my mother could have become pregnant at fifty-nine I can't imagine although I am sure there is something odd about my family's biology— something not noted in the official genealogies, even the most recent entries that record things like blood type and history of heart disease. Apparently she had already hit menopause, so my conception was just a jot short of immaculate, but I'm no Jesus Christ and that's for sure. Quite the contrary, actually, although I wouldn't say *the opposite*. I wasn't all bad you know, only mischievous. There are worse flaws in a child.

To begin with, I turned my mother's life upside down. She was planning on a quiet retirement. Her sons were more or less grown, although somewhat less in Wilson's case, but he was as grown then as he would ever get. It's true she had always wanted a girl, but I was hardly the daughter of her dreams. I broke dishes and knocked boiling pots from the stove. I stuck my fingers into electrical outlets. I pinched my brothers, stole eggs from the fridge, and broke them on the good living room carpet. I stuck gum in my hair. I ate garden snails, crunchy shell and all. I taunted dogs on chains, I dropped kittens into bathtubs, I unlocked doors at night practically inviting burglars to help themselves.

The most uncanny thing was that I could talk about it, almost from the very beginning. From the day after my birth, I spoke in full sentences. The first thing I said was "Forget her, forget her." When my brothers asked me about it later, I couldn't explain it, although a psychic once told me that the memory of my previous life had not been properly erased.

I dream more intensely than most people. I can't explain this either but I know I do. I dream of a house with a room where all the walls are red. I dream of a wall behind which I can hear the sound of water. Sometimes it is a bathroom. There is a woman sitting in a tub ladling water over her head so that her hair streams into her face. She squeezes her eyes shut and breathes out through her nose. She sighs with contentment. Sometimes that water sound is more ominous than that, as though the ocean itself were behind the red wall and threatening to spill through like blood at any moment.

My mother might once have wanted a daughter, but at fifty-nine she had little energy for a child. Besides, she had already had enough child trouble for one lifetime. My first brother, David, was born six months after my parents' wedding, and in the forties this was a scandal of great proportions. My mother was a lounge singer from America ("worse than an actress," said the tut-tutting aunties) and my father was a grease monkey from South Vancouver. He met her at the

Smiling Buddha supper club off Hastings by sending her, after a show, flowers he could ill afford.

"White chrysanthemums," she told him, "are for funerals." But she accepted his dinner invitation anyway. He took her to the BC Royal for steak and mashed potatoes and found himself in possession of both her heart and her underpants two weeks later. Six months after that, they were married. This, unfortunately, was not soon enough to stop the whispers that hissed through Chinatown. Because by that time, my brother David was already half-formed and hanging contentedly upside-down in her womb like a ripe pear waiting to drop.

The aunties were well aware that it takes more than six months to make a baby. For this, my mother paid dearly in behind-the-back whispers until the boy was almost five. The whispers kept her womb from maintaining its grip on anything that grew inside until David was seven. Then out popped Wilson, nice and respectable-like, and he remains that way to this very day.

My mother was not the type you would expect to find at the eye of so much scandal. She was cool, serene, and reserved—no short red dresses and back-seamed hose for her. By day she dressed in modest browns and greys with matching pillbox hats, by night in elegant, not-too-tight evening gowns that demurely covered her ankles and exposed only the faintest hint of cleavage. The whispering eventually died down, and all was forgotten until I came along.

When I look into her sewing box, its obsessive orderliness, I can't help thinking that there is some kind of secret she was keeping, a secret carefully disguised through rigorous self-discipline. When I say so, my brother Wilson laughs and calls me a dreamer.

I was helping David at his auto repair shop the day I got a letter saying a certain Maureen Mo Ling Wing had died and willed her house to me.

"Get Wilson to take care of it," said my brother David with a sharpness uncharacteristic of his gentle, slightly nervous nature.

"Strathcona's an up-and-coming neighbourhood," said Wilson. "I could make you a bundle." He was going through a phase as a real estate agent and, as with everything else he touched, was enjoying a success so instant and unabating that I said no to him out of pure spite. "I think I'll move in," I said, mostly to see what kind of reaction I could get.

"Please don't," said David, his voice dark with horror.

"Why not?" I said. "Who was Maureen Mo Ling Wing?"

"Nobody you want to have anything to do with," said David, "alive or dead."

I looked at Wilson to see if he might be a little more forthcoming. Wilson shrugged. "It's a good time to sell. Prices are high."

Maureen Mo Ling Wing's house was not the dusty, cluttered hovel you might imagine a spinster dying in. She had been meticulous at keeping the place in good repair and had occasionally renovated with a remarkably tasteful eye, so that the wood floors were not hidden by nasty shag carpets. The windows let in lots of light and fresh air. In the public areas, the furniture was dark and gentlemanly—a stuffed leather armchair, a smooth black couch, a deeply stained mahogany coffee table with space underneath for magazines—*Time*, *Maclean's*, *The New Yorker*, *Atlantic Monthly*, as well as home repair and automobile magazines, and oddly, the occasional *Astronomy Today*. So Auntie Mo was a stargazer! Well, why not? Atop the coffee table sat a small tray made of dark wood, deftly jointed so that not a nail was needed to hold it together. Inside lay the reddish curve of a pipe and a pouch half full of tobacco. The whole house, in fact, had an underlying tobacco smell, not the acrid stench of cigarette smoke, but the sweet buttery scent of pipe tobacco, like some bearded old professor's library.

The bedroom was similarly dark and lush—a Persian carpet flowered in reds and blues on the floor. There was a chair and a squareish vanity in dark wood. But the bed was romantic. It flowed with white linens like a bride. It was strange to think of the old woman dying here.

I opened one of the drawers of the vanity, and that was where I found her sewing box, similar in design to my mother's although without the adornment of flowers. Inside lay spools of thread, scissors, a lemon candy tin full of buttons, as though this box were the sister of my mother's and contained the same memories.

I can be superstitious, and I can be squeamish. But there was something strangely comfortable about this house, and this bedroom. I washed the white linens in the machine in the basement, put them back on the bed, and slept there that night as soundly as a baby.

"Please reconsider," said David, with whom I had, up to that point, lived all my life since my parents' deaths.

"Why?" I said. "What's the big deal?"

"It's just strange. She's not a member of our family. It's true she didn't have children of her own to will it to, but she had nieces and nephews. It will make the old ladies whisper."

"Who was she?"

"I don't know exactly. She was a friend of Mom's before Mom married. She came to my school once to see me. Dad told me and Wilson to stay away from her."

"But you don't know why?"

"No. Only that Mom and Dad would turn over in their graves if they knew about this."

If David could have one thing in the world, it would be to have the family living together happily under one roof. He hates it when we fight and he was irked with me for having been so rude to Wilson when Wilson was only trying to help. David knows that Wilson is a shallow, money-grubbing little so-and-so, but he still wants us to get along. Which is a noble cause, I suppose, but it annoyed me that he wanted me to accept Wilson's behaviour and, to add insult to injury, have that acceptance swept under the carpet.

"You could've just said 'no, thank you,'" he said, as I lay underneath Bill Chow the grocer's Subaru trying to figure out what was wrong with the driveshaft. I had been working at David's auto repair shop ever since I was fourteen. It paid better than Starbucks, although I had to admit I was getting sick of David's bossing.

Due to the circumstances of his birth, David was mostly the meek and mild type, except when it came to me. It was as though the circumstances of my birth made me the only thing in the world beneath him, and he ruled his one-child fiefdom like a petty despot.

"Why don't you do something to make us proud for once?" he said.

"Us who? You and Wilson? Since when are you and that used carpet salesmen in the same league?"

"Don't you get cheeky with me, missy," he said. "At least have some respect for your dead mother."

"How do you know she wouldn't have liked it? Maureen Wing must have willed me the place for a reason. Maybe she was it."

"No doubt she was, but you don't know what kind of reason. You wouldn't like it if you knew."

"How do you know?"

"Because," he said, beginning to get exasperated. "Because I'm older than you."

"You're just bigger," I said. "Bigger and dumber."

"Fine," he said. "Stay there. You'll see what I mean. Maybe when you grow up you'll do something we can all be proud of like going to med school."

This, I knew was a jibe at my drawing. I have always wanted to be a cartoonist or an illustrator of children's books and had been amassing a portfolio ever since junior high, but Wilson said it was impractical and David agreed. I'd been saving up for art school for years, since neither of them want to invest in that kind of future for me.

"Med school?" I said. "Give me the money and I'll go."

"You don't have the perseverance."

"Watch me."

He looked at me quizzically. "I don't understand you," he said, "but if you're serious, I'll talk to Wilson. I'm sure we can raise the money."

Wilson the Conqueror, as I called him—mostly to bug David, since Wilson couldn't care less—was amassing a small fortune selling leaky condos to Torontonians and Asian immigrants sight unseen. He sent them elegantly drawn architectural drawings with lots of shrubbery to cover up the design flaws, and outrageous price quotes. Eager to establish homes for themselves amidst mountains and water, they bought, sacrificing the present for the future. Wilson's bank account swelled.

It was on this money that I studied bio-chemistry for three years and then transferred into med school, going for a specialization in diseases of the ear, nose, and throat. Under Auntie Maureen Mo Ling Wing's old brass desk lamp, I studied cell biology and evolution, drug therapies and bedside manners, until my eyes were red and my body swelled thick and flabby from too many Ichiban noodles and Kraft Dinners. I wasn't unhappy. I have an analytical mind. The mechanics of the ear are very interesting.

What I wasn't prepared for was all the death. I met Meg on the day of my first human dissection. The body was male and grey. It reeked of formaldehyde. I could hardly bear to touch the clammy flesh. Brazen Meg offered to make the first incision. She cut deftly and neatly without showing the least sign of distaste. Afterwards, I couldn't stop thinking about her.

I felt more settled in Auntie Mo's house after Meg moved in. I dropped med school, much to David's anger and disapproval. But Meg finished. Now she runs a family practice in a nearby medical building and volunteers at a community clinic once a week. Resources are well-enough in place that it doesn't matter how sporadic my work as an illustrator for children's books is. The mystery of how this house came to me has faded to a less urgent place, all the more so after we began to discuss having a baby.

So we're here at Toby Sushi to discuss the options. Meg wants to eat teriyaki, which is her business. Personally, I think it's a sin to eat cooked food in a Japanese restaurant. Bring on the raw fish! My favourite is sea urchin with a quail's egg cracked over the top—so sweet and slippery and delicious. Still, since Meg's conventional tastes in cuisine are her worst fault, I consider myself pretty lucky. She'll be a great second mother to my child if I can only figure out a safe and palatable way to get the damn sperm. Meg and I are not quite desperate, but getting there. We've been talking about this for over a year now. I'm twenty-eight, which is nearly thirty, and this is something I really want. If I've found someone who's willing to do it with me, then I figure there's no time like the present. My health is still good. But who knows how long it will last? We'd really like a sweet little girl in our lives. Or a little boy, I guess. That would be okay too.

Meg says she knows this really nice straight guy who'd like to help. "He's not very healthy or good looking—has bad acne, wears Coke-bottle glasses, and probably couldn't touch his toes to save his life, but he's kind and gentle and caring. Only worrisome thing is that he hasn't had a girlfriend in years."

"No way!" I say. "Those are the kind of guys that turn out to be child molesters and psychopaths. Or at the very least, he'll change his mind halfway through the pregnancy about wanting to be a benevolent outsider and try to sue for custody rights or something."

"Beggars can't be choosers," says Meg, but then her teriyaki arrives and so does my sashimi plate and a little wooden board with the uni sushi artfully placed just off centre and decorated with a slice of fake greenery in bright plastic, a little heap of pink pickled ginger, and a dollop of wasabi. I stop talking and slurp the suckers back.

A mental picture of the guy Meg mentioned hovers in my head. Weird the things life hands you, I think. Though no weirder than the circumstances of my own birth. What will I say to David?

As it turns out, the pimply guy with the coke bottle glasses is Chinese-Canadian. And also, he only has two zits— discreetly positioned just to the side of his nose. His glasses aren't exactly paper thin, but I wouldn't call them *Coke-bottle*. I think he's kind of cute, in a brotherly sort of way.

"You totally exaggerated," I say to Meg. I also want to say, *Don't you know it's really uncool to say things like that about Chinese guys.* But I don't because I don't want to get into a long argument about race politics, and maybe I don't want to admit to myself that Meg is less than perfect.

"Yeah well, I thought you'd be less disappointed this way than if I said he was stunningly gorgeous."

"And you didn't say he was Chinese. That makes all the difference. Chinese guys never turn out to be violent psychopaths."

"Haven't you ever heard of Charles Ng?" says Meg.

"Charles Ng is Vietnamese," I say.

Meg gives me a strange look.

"Well, compared to how many Caucasian psychopaths there are out there," I begin, but then let the sentence trail off to nowhere. This kind of conversation can only get worse.

We had kind of been hoping to find a man who looks at least a bit like Meg, but as she says, beggars can't be choosers.

So we make plans with Garrett Yee. We spend an afternoon in the park with our dogs.

He's tall and gangly. If you forget about the glasses, he's actually not unattractive— he has a kind of pensive, aristocratic scholar sort of look, if you imagine flowing robes instead of Levi's and a blue Vancouver Aquarium sweatshirt with whales on it. Not that the aristocratic look is what I'm going for, mind you, only it's less objectionable than a lot of things. It turns out Garrett's pockets are full of dog biscuits. That's a good sign.

"So where do you work?" says Meg, sounding just like her mother.

"Shoppers Drug Mart," says Garrett. "I'm a pharmacist."

Sometimes I think it's funny how fast all your political ideals go out the window the minute you start to think of becoming a parent. I mean here I am, rejoicing that the potential father of my child is a nice, traditional, middle-class man with a professional job. If my old friend Lewis were here, he'd probably whap me over the head for being so politically regressive. Yet I'm still obsessing about the psychopath thing. I mean, what about Charles Ng? And then, on the other hand, I'm really glad this man is Chinese, although I would never say so to Meg. I know she wants so badly to make some kind of genetic contribution to this child, even if it exists only in our imaginations. I think with Garrett she'll find it a stretch. I know there's no such thing as a purebred and I know that such ideas are completely socially destructive, but it doesn't stop a secret part of me from silently rejoicing. That is, if this works out.

"Why do you want to help us?" says Meg.

"Well," says Garrett turning a really quite endearing beet red, "I'm twenty-nine years old. I haven't had a girlfriend since I was twenty. I'm just afraid the family thing is never going to happen for me, you know. I mean, it still could and that would be great, but just in case it doesn't, I'd just like to know that a little part of me will go down in posterity. If I was a painter or a writer or something, I guess that would be another way to deal with it, but I'm a pretty normal, boring sort of guy, you know what I mean?"

Having revealed a potentially very embarrassing kernel from the depth of his soul, Garrett looks up, not at Meg, but at me, with a doggy-eyed plea for approval. Something inside me cringes at his awkward vulnerability. There's a kind of sadness behind it. Half of me wants to turn away, pretend he never said a word. The other half wants to reach out and hug him.

"That sounds like good logic," says Meg amicably. For some reason, I want to punch her.

There is a moment of silence, but then our discomfort with one another melts away. We start playing Frisbee with the dogs. At one point, Meg tosses and Garrett and I both run to catch it. She's right. He is clumsy. He smacks right into me and I slip and fall. When I get home, I notice sweet grassy smelling stains in the knees of my jeans. I try to imagine a bespectacled little girl with Garrett's round face. It's not a completely horrible image.

Meg and I are at a fundraiser for a new Asian Canadian magazine, organized by Lewis. I'm dressed most smashingly in a long red velvet dress with a plunging neckline that Meg found for me at this funky second-hand clothing store. I feel electric, and not just because of the dress. I'm surprised that everyone in the room is not staring at me in utter amazement. I feel voluptuous but also completely transparent as though people can see right through the dress and right through my skin and flesh too, can see the little creature swimming inside me, swelling by the minute into something increasingly human. "Hey everyone!" I want to yell. "I'm pregnant!"

I would have been willing to sleep with Garrett, if that was what it was going to take. I didn't even really think of it as that gross, but he wasn't into it, got all awkward and funny. So that was a relief in a way, although I have to admit, I had this unnerving, gritty curiosity about it. Like a shy, needy dog inside me that was disappointed when it didn't happen. Meg said she was okay with it, but I suspect she wasn't. So it is probably for the best. The syringe was not much fun, but Meg and I just giggled the whole time and then next thing we knew it was done. I know a lot of people have to try hundreds of times before anything happens. Guess I must be a real egg factory.

Ilene, Meg's foundling, Lewis's on-again-off-again girlfriend, and now our downstairs tenant shows up at the fundraiser drunk as a skunk. She comes up to me. "How's it goin'?" she says.

How can she not see? I always thought the girl was a bit of an idiot, but now I really think so. "Fine," I say. "I'm pregnant."

"Wow. Really?" I can tell she's not really impressed but is just trying to be polite. I decide not to tell her about Garrett, or the turkey baster. Next thing I know she's launched into some tirade about a craft fair at the university, at which she sold three mugs in six days. She didn't even come close to covering the cost of the booth, not to mention her time. And if it counts, she sold a large platter to her mother's ugly sinophile white boyfriend, who still holds out hope that she will talk to him one day. But his purchase of her work, she thinks, given the circumstances, was completely patronizing. She charged him full price for the thing. Says she couldn't look at it when she handed it over. It was like a child that had betrayed her.

I never expected to get so worked up about the Charles Ng thing. Here I am pregnant with the child of some guy I hardly know. I thought he was fine. He seemed pretty normal to you, right? But no girlfriend for nine years— it could be the sign of some really sick pathology. Unless he's had boyfriends but is totally in the closet. He and Ilene went to high school together. That's how Meg found him in the first place. I should ask her about him. Perhaps it will ease my anxiety.

I go down the rickety basement stairs, step around the washer and dryer, and bang on her door. There is a stumbling noise. I hear something crash to the floor. Ilene curses. She opens the door. Her hair is a mess. She wears a torn Take Back the Night T-shirt from some long-ago march, and a pair of ragged cut-offs. It's pretty clear she's been moping.

It might have been a mistake to come here. Ilene is pretty morose. She's been working at the wheel, if the grey blob of a ruined pot on the floor is any indication. Guess she hasn't got the touch today. She hurries me through the studio into the bedroom, which I guess, given the set up, doubles as a living room.

"Have you thought of a name for the baby?" she asks.

At least she wasn't completely drunk at the fundraiser

"I don't know," I say. "Depends on if it's a boy or a girl. Can you think of any good revolutionary heroes?"

Ilene smiles. She can if she puts her mind to it. "Are you going to give Garrett any say?"

"Well, that was what I wanted to ask you about."

The phone rings.

"I'm sorry. I have to get it," says Ilene. "My Dad hasn't been well, and he said he would call."

She gets the phone in the studio, half-closing the door. I can still sort of hear her side of the conversation, things like, "I don't have to do anything you say," and "What did you tell her, that I was a raving lunatic?" and "I can't believe you don't have the fucking guts say that in person." Must be Lewis on the other end of the line.

When she comes back into the bedroom, Ilene is fuming. "Lewis is such a control freak. He gets to do whatever he wants, and I'm the one that's supposed to be fucked up, go to therapy, go to China, whatever."

"Maybe this is a bad time," I say.

"There's no such thing as a good time," she snipes.

She's depressed and unpleasant. I think to myself that I don't really like her. "Maybe a trip's not a bad idea," I offer.

"Oh god. If you're here as a Lewis chorus girl, you can go now."

"Actually, I was hoping you could tell me a few things about Garrett."

"Garrett, sure I can. But there's something else I..."

I cut her off. I can't take it. "Garrett," I say. I'm pregnant. I need someone to take care of me, not the other way around. Soon, I'll have a child of my own, so who needs Ilene? But I need to know about Garrett, because I never even asked him about his father, or his grandfather, for that matter. What if he comes from a whole lineage of psychopaths? What if the family freezer is chocked to the hilt with frozen body parts, a woman's head here, a young guy's torso there, a frozen heart, a frozen hand, testicles in baggies, breasts frozen in boxes like chicken strips?

"He's a bit shy, but he's a nice person," she says, blandly. It isn't enough.

"That's it?"

"He's nice. He's boring. Listen..."

"No one is so boring that they don't have a story. And you've known him for seven years."

"Yeah. Hey, you know that sewing box of yours, the one in the upstairs foyer?"

"What about it? It was my Auntie Mo Ling Wing's."

"Did you know it has a false bottom?"

I didn't. But I don't really care right now. I stare at her.

She looks uncomfortable, like she doesn't know whether to continue or not. But she continues. "It has a false bottom. I discovered it by accident. I was just looking for more thread because I have this yellow shirt that lost a button."

I give her a does-this-look-like-a-face-that-cares expression.

She's squirming now. At least she isn't going on about her depression or whatever. "Anyway," she says, "it has a false bottom. There are letters. I wasn't going to read them, but..."

"You read them." This is why I don't like her.

"I'm sorry. I know it's wrong but I couldn't help myself. The handwriting is so beautiful, and they're tied with this brown velvet ribbon. I only read one." She stops.

I don't help her.

"You know, because I knew it was wrong."

"And?"

"Well, it's a suicide note."

"What?"

"Your aunt or whatever wrote it. It's dated August 17, 1943."

"August 17th..." I muse. "That's my parent's anniversary. And I think that's the year they were married." I do a bit of mental math. "Yes, 1943 seems about right."

"I remember your brother was visiting last year on that day. He was very sad. We talked about it. That's why..."

"That's why you felt you should tell me." Maybe she isn't as self-absorbed as I thought.

"Yes," she says. Her lips curl into a shy smile. I realize all the drama and bluster may just be cover-up for a person who feels very small. "So there's a mystery. It's very intriguing. And kind of romantic. I've been wanting to tell you, but I felt guilty about, you know... well... snooping."

She should feel guilty, the little minx. But I tell her, "It's okay. It is interesting. My mother was a complicated woman." I have quite forgotten about Garrett, at least for the moment. "Don't you want to know the whole story?" she says. "It would make such a great movie."

I laugh. Maybe Ilene isn't so bad after all. "Yes," I say. "Yes, I do."

Larissa Lai

Larissa Lai was born in La Jolla, California, grew up in Newfoundland, and lived and worked in Vancouver for many years as a writer, organizer, and editor. Her first novel, *When Fox Is a Thousand* (Press Gang 1995, Arsenal Pulp 2004) was shortlisted for the Chapters/Books in Canada First Novel Award. Her second novel, *Salt Fish Girl* (Thomas Allen Publishers 2002) was shortlisted for the Sunburst Award, the Tiptree Award, and the City of Calgary W. O. Mitchell Award. She has an MA in Creative Writing from the University of East Anglia in Norwich, England, and is currently completing a critical PhD at the University of Calgary. She is currently writer-in-residence at Simon Fraser University

Ann-Marie MacDonald
Writer Notes

Would anyone ever even ask another author, "How important is it for you to create heterosexual characters?"

The first lesbian moment I created was in *Goodnight Desdemona*. The lead character, Constance, this academic, goes into the worlds of Romeo and Juliet and Othello, and while she's in the world of Romeo and Juliet, both Romeo and Juliet fall in love with her, and she has hot little kissing scenes with both of them. And at first I thought, 'Well, how is this going to go down?' Because that was, what, 1987? And that play ended up touring, and all kinds of people enjoy that play. So I thought, 'okay, it's some kind of alchemical miracle—it's not that they didn't notice the two women kissing, it's that it didn't seem to make them too angry.' That was an early lesson for me, and an early confirmation of what I've always suspected, which is that the quote-unquote supposedly ordinary people, out in the burbs or in the hinterlands, are ahead of the curve—they're ahead of where a lot of people think they should be. People are always ready for more than they're given credit for.

I have respect for audiences in general. I learned that through theatre, so I have a respect for my readers. But my credo was, from the very beginning, that I want to take people to places they might not choose to go because they might find them offensive, or wrong, or frightening. How can I persuade them? Obviously, I have to commit myself to making a special invitation or to making the journey fun, or at least compelling in some way. Because why should I just come at them with, you know, a tablespoon of cod liver oil? They never asked me to. I'm going to invite them to a feast, and if I do my job, they'll stay with me. And it was only after I'd finished *Fall On Your Knees* that I realized I'd been kind of Machiavellian, in that I put all the hot lesbian stuff at the end. So it was too late for anyone to put the book down. If they had come that far, it meant they really needed to get to the end. I think people are more open-hearted than they are usually given credit for being.

And it was important for me to create a fully functional, real-life lesbian, and that was also hard. Madeleine doesn't have the operatic fate. It's not the thing that kills her; it's part and parcel of who she is and who she has been. I'm of the generation that had to still really read between the lines to find lesbian content anywhere. And it became a game. But for me, I just want to say, 'well, of course we're here, and there she is in the book. This is your principal character's point of view— you are actually seeing through the eyes of this lesbian, whether you ever thought you would or not, Dear Reader.'

—from an interview with Sara Cassidy published in *Herizons* Winter 2004

Ann-Marie MacDonald
excerpted from *Fall On Your Knees*

Before I got to her building I could hear Rose playing. It was coming from the church window, but church was not in session and this was definitely not church music, it was pure Rose. So this is where she practices. In exchange for playing on Sundays, I guess. I stayed under the window, sheltered by Rose's music, but I was soon disturbed by three women seated on kitchen chairs on the front stoop of her building. They didn't shoo me away, they gave me the low-down on Rose! They didn't know whether to feel sorry for her or to think she was nuts. I know the feeling. "Poor little girl," they were saying, "she bears her cross." "We all bear a cross." I wanted to say, "She's not a little girl," and I had to laugh because they went on, "And practising twenty-four hour a day, but never can learn a piece of music top to bottom no matter how hard she try."

"That's right, just wandering on the keyboard, lost to the world."

"'Cept Sunday, she plays like the angels come Sunday."

"That's the Lord's work."

"Thank you, Jesus."

Then one of them prayed that Rose would get some humility and they made jokes because they considered her too strange and—of all things—"homely" to get a husband, and what's the good of pride in a homely woman? I excused myself but the women didn't seem to notice, they just kept chatting as I picked my way past them up the steps and in through the front door for the first time.

The entrance has an echoey vaulted stone ceiling with turquoise and white tile mosaic. Maybe it was once a Turkish bath. I smelled a delicious stew. I followed a wide brass rail up marble steps worn to soft curves by a hundred years of footfalls, up to the second-floor landing, and was about to enter the church to surprise Rose when I had a flash. An evil one. I continued up to the third-floor landing and knocked at the door of what I knew must be her apartment. For a minute I thought there was no one home and I was halfway back down the stairs when a woman's voice stopped me.

"What can I do ya for, honey?"

I turned to the woman and said, "Sorry, wrong apartment."

"Who you lookin for?"

"Rose Lacroix."

"Rosie's downstairs practising."

"Okay, I'll just pop down and say hello."

"She doesn't like to be disturbed."

"It's all right, she knows me."

The woman smiled in a sly kind of way and said, "You don't know her too well though, do you? Come on in and wait, she'll be up for dinner in a few minutes."

"Oh. Thank you." I was confused. "I don't want to intrude on your dinner."

"You won't if you join us."

I followed the woman into the parlour. It was fancy and shabby at the same time. Like a rich lady who's slept in her clothes. Velvet everything. A plushy plum sofa with shiny patches. Dusty curtains drawn—burgundy with gold tassels. And a huge gilt mirror over the mantelpiece. The stew smell mixed with her perfume and made me feel a bit queer.

I said, "I'm Rose's friend from singing class, Kathleen Piper."

"Oh yeah? I didn't know Rosie had a little friend."

I felt she was being ironic, not to mention rude, but I couldn't figure out why, no more could I figure out who she was. Although she clearly knew Rose.

"I'm sorry, honey, I'm Rosie's mother, Jeanne. Do sit down."

I guess my chin must've dropped a mile but I couldn't help it, I was speechless. She lit a cigarette and laughed at me in a lazy way. She was wearing a full-length evening dress—dull red satin, slim and loose with skinny little straps and a deep V-neck, black sequin flowers. And obviously no underthings. I think that shocked me more than the fact that she was white, with straight yellow hair falling anyhow onto her shoulders, and thin blue eyes. Tiny lines, she must be close to forty, but it was so dim in there I couldn't tell. You could see she used to be pretty. No face paint, oddly enough. She was enjoying my amazement. She offered me a cigarette.

"No thank you."

"Good. Keep your voice clean. Drink?"

"Yes please."

She smiled that rudely familiar smile again, as if my accepting a drink made us lowly conspirators, for there was something low about her and yet she acted like bored royalty. I don't go in for drinking but I didn't want this woman calling me "Rosie's little friend" again. She gave me a whiskey and leaned back in the sofa across from me. Her left strap slipped down but she didn't seem to notice.

I said, "Thank you."

"I know you're surprised, honey, everybody is at first, my God you're pretty."

I hate myself that I blush so easily. She was making me madder by the second, I thought, so this is what Rose lives with, I'd go around like a hornet too if she were my mother. But I said, "Thank you, ma'am."

And she laughed at me again. The word "languid" is always used in books, but I finally found a use for it in real life. Mrs Lacroix was "languid".

"Call me Jeanne, baby."

I'm not your baby, I thought, but I said, "Jeanne."

And she chuckled again and looked me up and down and said, "Oh yes. Yes indeed."

She made me most uncomfortable, the way she lounged there scrutinizing me like a bird of prey that's too full with its recent meal to be bothered to eat what's in front of it.

Rose came in. She paused when she saw me. I couldn't

read her face, she just said, "Hi."

"Hi."

Jeanne grinned and said, "Rose, darling, your friend is simply charming. I insist you stay for dinner, Miss Piper."

"Please call me Kathleen, ma'am—Jeanne."

She winked at me. I blushed again. I looked at Rose, expecting her to be scowling at me, but she just said, "Want to see my room?"

I got up, relieved, although it crossed my mind that maybe Rose would murder me silently with a pillow once I got in there.

Her mother stopped us on our way. "Did you get my prescription, Rose?" she asked without turning around.

"Yes, Mother, I got it."

"Good. We'll wait till after dinner, I'm actually feeling quite spry today."

"Good."

"You girls have a little gossip, I'll call you when dinner is laid."

"Thank you, Mother."

This was the strangest thing of all. To find out that Rose has not a "Mumma" but a "Mother".

Rose's room is as different from the rest of the apartment as it can be. She has a single bed with an absolutely plain white cotton spread and no headboard. There's not even a rug on the floor. A wooden chair, a small desk with a pen and a blank sheet of paper and, of all things, the Holy Bible open at—but I didn't get a chance to see because she flipped it shut the moment I glanced at it. You'd think I'd caught her reading a racy novel. It looks like the nuns' rooms at Holy Angels. (I know because I snuck into their wing on the last day of school, hoping to find a long luscious wig in Sister Saint Monica's room but no such luck.) The only difference is, instead of a crucifix on the wall, there's a picture of

Beethoven. And do you believe this? She hasn't got a mirror!

Rose closed her door behind us and said, "So. Want to play Chinese checkers?"

"Why didn't you tell me she's white?"

"Why should I?"

"I told you about my mother."

"What about her?"

"You said she's not white."

"She got a year-round tan, that don't count for coloured."

"You said it did the other night."

"Yeah, well that's a moot point, isn't it, considering how you come out."

"I can't win, can I?"

"Oh yes you can, there ain't nothin stoppin you, girl."

"You hate me 'cause I'm white."

"I hate you 'cause you're so fuckin ignorant."

"Then enlighten me."

"Why should I bother?"

"Because I'm your friend."

"Friends don't spy."

"I'm sorry. You give me no alternative."

"There's an alternative. Leave me alone."

"No."

"Why not?"

"I like you."

"Why?"

"You're the smartest person I know, except for my father."

"Is that supposed to be a compliment?"

"And you're beautiful."

That shut her up. She looked at me as though I'd told her she had a year to live. So I added, "But your mother dresses you funny."

"It doesn't matter what I wear."

"You're right, you're so gorgeous it doesn't matter."

"Shutup."

"Come to Mecca with me tonight."

"I told you I can't."

"Do you do everything your mother tells you?"

She sat down on the bed, folded her hands in her lap and quoted scripture, "She has my best interests in mind."

"Oh really? What are those?"

"Getting out of this dump."

I sat down next to her, I tried to be delicate. "What's wrong with her?"

"Nothing. She does her best."

"You're the one who's ashamed."

Rose got quiet and looked at me as though she were holding a puppy and begging me not to hurt it. "You think, because she lives here, she's not a fine person. Well it's only because of me that she has to live here. Do you know what that's like for her? They treat her like trash, they don't know anything about her. Ignorant niggers."

I couldn't speak. Rose went on, "She's given up everything for my sake."

"She seems pretty satisfied to me."

"She's too polite to seem otherwise."

"I didn't think she was the slightest bit polite."

Rose really looked bewildered. How can she know so much about so many things yet know so little about her own mother? But I just said, "Where's your hat?"

I followed her out across the parlour and past the kitchen, where Jeanne was setting the table. That is, she was standing there with a fork in her hand, staring into space. Rose took me into Jeanne's bedroom—I should say boudoir. A mess of satin sheets in a huge mahogany bedstead with claw feet. A big oil painting over the bed of a fat white woman getting out of a tub. A vanity littered with silver brushes, pots of paint, and clumps of yellow hair—a crystal cocktail glass with lipstick smears, an ashtray crammed with red-tipped butts, a jumble of jewellery, tweezers, and an eyelash curler. Clothes strewn everywhere, and too many smells for one room. Rose opened a big wardrobe, rummaged through the top shelf and pulled down the charcoal fedora.

"Rosie!"

It was Jeanne from the kitchen. She sounded like she'd just hurt herself. Rose whipped the hat back onto the shelf and shot from the room. I got it down again and put it on, and went back out to the parlour. Rose's back was to me. But Jeanne was looking straight at me from the sofa where she lay. She looked like she was in pain, but somehow still slightly amused to see me in the hat. It gave me the creeps. Rose was reaching into her school bag. I could see the sheet music inside. She brought out a needle that she filled from a tiny bottle. Jeanne had her left arm flung out and she was pumping her fist. The vigour of that action didn't go with the swoon in her body. Her face was starting to tighten and go even paler, she was looking at the ceiling now. Rose injected her and Jeanne closed her eyes as though she were lost in prayer like the nuns. Her fist relaxed, she gave a little moan, reached up and stroked Rose's face. She murmured something then nodded off. Rose folded Jeanne's arm across her stomach, stood up and saw me.

"She suffers a lot of pain."

I felt embarrassed for Rose having to lie again.

"Did she see you in the hat?" she asked me.

"I think so."

"Please don't do that again. It upsets her."

"I'm sorry." I handed her the hat. "Do you have a picture of him?" I asked.

"No."

"Don't you have anything besides his hat?"

Rose looked at her mother on the sofa—out cold—and led me back into the boudoir. And disappeared into the wardrobe. I had this crazy idea that she might be gone for ever into another time and place. But she came out a moment later with a suit of men's clothes on a hanger.

Black and tan pinstripe trousers. Black waistcoat and tails. Tan cravat with black polka-dots. Starched white shirt with diamond studs.

"Goes with the hat," I said.

And she said, "Yeah."

And I said, "Try it on."

She didn't pretend to be shocked, which is how I know that in her heart of hearts it had occurred to her before. It's also how I knew that certain things between us were behind us now. Thank goodness. She just said, "I couldn't do that."

"Why not?"

"It would be like—sacrilege."

"He wasn't God, he was just some fella."

"He was my father!"

"And all he left you were his clothes."

She hesitated. So I started to undress.

"What are you doing?"

I didn't answer because I didn't know, I just pulled my dress over my head and got to work on my stockings and for some reason it worked, and she said, "All right, all right." And I put my dress back on as she undid the millions of buttons on hers and said, "Turn around."

I obliged. She took forever.

"Don't peek!"

"I'm not peeking."

Finally she said, "Okay. You can look now."

I turned around. Oh my.

She is a tall slim young man in a curious suit of black and tan. There is nothing to beat her leaning against the bricks of any building 'twixt here and Battery Park.

She said, "How do I look?"

"You're coming out with me."

"I—"

"Look at yourself."

She hesitated so I closed the closet door to expose the full-length mirror on the outside. I stood behind her as she looked at the beautiful young man with the fine-cut face between hat and cravat. She looked at herself for a long time.

And finally—"Do you think...?"

"Oh yeah."

She nodded to herself and turned sideways.

I said, "Your own mother wouldn't recognize you. Much less your mother's friends."

"Do you have any money on you?"

"Two dollars."

"I've got carfare."

"Let's go."

"No."

I thought, "Oh brother, she's got cold feet," but she offered me her arm with a smile and said, "Let's dine first."

Jeanne had somehow managed to lay the table. It was just a kitchen table between the sink and the icebox but it was covered with a snowy lace cloth and set with silverware engraved with "J.B." Rose lit the candles. She filled our crystal goblets with bubbly root beer and heaped the bone china plates with what we call boiled dinner down home. Potatoes, carrots, pork hocks (she calls them "pig's feet"), doughboys, but instead of cabbage there were green leaves of some kind. Daddy was right. There has come a time when I think it's the most delicious dish in the world. We sat across from each other and clinked our glasses, "To Mecca."

"To Mecca."

And drank. There was a place set for Jeanne too.

"She doesn't eat much anyhow," said Rose.

"It's good luck to set an extra place at table."

"Why?"

"In case your guardian angel wants to join you."

"Don't spook me."

"They're not spooky, they look after you."

"You don't believe that."

"Oh yes I do."

"Why, what's your guardian angel ever done for you?"

"Sent me to New York. Made me meet you."

"Lucky you."

"We're going to know each other for the rest of our lives."

After a moment she said, "I don't think I have a guardian angel. I think I'm on my own."

"You have one as long as I'm around."

She listened and I could tell she wanted to believe me, and I didn't think about what I was saying, I just said it, "And if I die before you, I'll come back."

She got tears in her eyes and so did I, it always happens when you talk about ghosts. I had two helpings of stew. Would you believe Jeanne cooked it? "She does all the cooking." So I guess she's not a completely useless mother after all.

"What does J.B. stand for?"

Rose hesitated, then said, "Julia Burgess."

"Who's that?"

"My grandmother."

"She alive?"

"Yuh."

"Where's she at?"

"Long Island."

"Do you visit her often?"

"I've never met her."

"I've never met my grandparents either."

"To hell with them all."

"I'll drink to that."

We toasted again, then I raised my goblet for the third time. "Let's drink to the twentieth century," I said. "Because it's ours."

"To the twentieth century."

Do you think it's possible to get drunk on root beer?

We quickly washed the dishes, then Rose fixed a silver tray with two glasses, an ice-bucket, a canister of soda and a bottle of whiskey, and put it on the coffee table next to the sofa where Jeanne lay. I was nervous that Jeanne would wake up and catch us but Rose said, "Don't worry. She won't wake up till her company comes." I didn't ask "What company?" because I didn't want to make Rose lie to me again. She led me to the door and opened it for me, *très galante*, saying, "Ladies first." As I stepped through the door, I turned my head to smile at Rose and caught sight of Jeanne in the mirror over the mantelpiece. She was lying perfectly still on the sofa, staring straight at me.

Do you think there's such a thing as a ghost who masquerades as a person? Do you believe that there are people whose bodies are still alive here on earth but whose souls are already in hell?

I didn't tell Rose that her mother had seen us.

What a feeling to walk arm in arm with Rose as a fella. People stared in a whole new way. I guess I've found the one thing that could make me look even more suspicious in this neighbourhood. It was a breezy evening. Rose had polished her old black lace-ups to a high shine and I wished like crazy I had my new dress on. Oh well, next time.

I had to force her through the door of Mecca as though at gunpoint. The great thing about the Mecca is that there's all kinds. I'd never soaked the place up like I did last night with Rose. I saw it all through her eyes and I was able to point out the regulars. It's mostly young coloured men and not that many women. The fellas are all slick dressers except for the holes in their pockets where the money's burnt through. They're earning more than miners, building tanks and artillery for "over there", I know because I been told by the guy in the silk tie called Aldridge. I've never seen guys preen and present themselves the way they do. They lean against the bar like honey-drenched stamens, waiting for the women to buzz around, and you just know they're all breaking their mothers' hearts. They wear secret smiles and chuckle a lot when they chat with the white guys.

There are a couple of middle-aged men too, a famous

jockey who eats five heads of lettuce a day, and a retired heavy-weight champion with a bald head from Halifax. They're the only ones who bring their wives, two very serious looking women of a certain age who spend the whole time with their heads glued together, chatting. There's a group of West Indian fellas who stick together and wear pencil-thin moustaches. One of them's a lawyer and another is my acquaintance Nico, a little live wire who has made a fortune in real estate and can't stop smiling. He calls me "*chérie*". There's a studious young man who always sits alone and writes in a notebook and there are two tables pushed together of motley individuals who are delighted with each other and everything else and who turn out to be actors. There's a Chinaman who holds court at the same table in the far corner every night.

Tonight I notice three or four other white girls sitting with their coloured boyfriends and I say to Rose that at least we're not the only mixed couple in the joint and she says, "Yes we are." I say, "They don't look coloured." And she says, "Say Negro."

As for the white denizens: a handful of tough-looking Irishmen in fifty-dollar suits with "dames" on their arms. A Jew who brings his barrel of hats into the club with him—he's a very formal older man who closes his eyes and nods slowly to the music no matter how wild the tune. Tonight there's also a high society table out for a low time—girls and boys who have no idea where they are and think themselves awfully clever for being there. They probably think the same thing of me.

There are also a few "working girls" of every shade who arrive alone and leave escorted several times throughout the evening under the watchful eye of the gamekeeper, who lounges in the corner consulting his solid gold watch. I some-times wonder, can it be any harder than washing floors? Or having seven babies?

Business must be booming because the management has installed a small stage, footlights, and a sparkly purple curtain with "MECCA" written *à la* Araby in gold sequins against a silhouette of minarets. Ten minutes after we sit down, a man in a tuxedo comes out from behind the curtain and announces, "Ladies and gentlemen, Club Mecca proudly presents 'Ali Baba and his Forty Follies!'"

The curtain parts on a harem. Light-skinned girls and a very fat dark sultan lounge on striped pillows. The girls dance the seven veils while he sings a song of illicit lust for one of them—the lightest one—and the band plays snaky music. The tent flaps part and handsome Prince Ahmed pokes his turbaned head through and kisses the heroine. Then bingo, you're in Gay Paree doing the cancan, and then the same young lovers flee the evil sultan all through the world's capitals while the chorus girls quick-change and outdance Ziegfield's. We went to Hawaii, Japan, Holland, and Canada, where they pretended to be Eskimos and Mounties! And although the girls changed costumes and countries every five seconds, they never wore more than half a dozen square inches, even when they were fur-clad in Canada's frozen wastes.

After the show the band played dance tunes but I couldn't for the life of me get Rose up on her feet. She did, however, graciously nod when other gentle and not so gentle men requested her permission to dance with me. I danced with the busted-nose Irishman, built like a tree stump but very light on his feet, boy. With the Jewish haberdasher, who made a waltz out of everything. With a lily-white boy from Long Island—I asked him if he was acquainted with the Burgesses and he answered importantly that they were his dear friends. I asked him if he knew Jeanne and he got a blank look—then said come to think of it there was a daughter years ago who "died tragically abroad." I laughed and he didn't ask for a second dance—just as well, he was like shifting sticks.

All the while, Rose slouched over her beer in that lovely suit. She didn't bat an eye until I danced with my pal Nico. It bothered her, I could tell, although why it should be any different than with the white fellas I don't know. Only difference I can see is, except for the stocky Irishman, the Negro men are the best on their feet. When I sat back down at the table while the band took a break, Rose said, "I'll dance with you if you teach me."

It was the first thing she'd said for an hour. I realized I had wanted to make her jealous. It bugged me that we had made it all the way to this club with her looking so gorgeous but all she wanted to do was sulk. I asked her how she liked the show.

"Irredeemably puerile."

"The dancing was great."

"The outfits are an outrage."

"Look who's talking."

"At least I'm fully clothed."

I made her take a sip of my whiskey, then I did something crazy—I kissed her on the lips. Just quickly, you know, but we both blushed. She didn't object, she simply raised her hand for the waiter and demanded two more drinks in a deep voice to make me laugh, then whispered desperately in my ear, "Do you have enough money?" I brushed my ear against her lips. She stayed perfectly still. I kissed her neck between the stiff white collar and her earlobe. I slipped my hand round the back of her head below her hat and stroked that gentle dip at the base of her skull. She turned slightly and kissed my mouth. So softly. I forgot where we were. That we were anywhere. We just looked at each other... so that's who you are.

The drinks came. And Rose looked away, shy again. What will happen to me if Rose ever ceases to be shy? I will have an attack of all the shyness I've been saving up.

Then something happened that I'd never seen before. The place flooded and turned overwhelmingly black, men and women both. I'll bet if I'd looked hard enough I'd've seen the ladies from Rose's front steps braving the Devil's music. The word must've spread since I'd been here. The house lights dimmed and the footlights shimmered on the minarets of Mecca. Silence fell over the whole joint and the impresario stepped up to invoke the Goddess of Blues, "Ladies and gentlemen, the star of our show: The Empress of the Blues.

Cleopatra of Jazz. The Lowest, the Highest, the Holiest, the Sweetest, Miss! Jessie! Hogan!"

Applause and shouts to outdo the *bravissimas* of a grand finale though the curtain has yet to open. It parts purple and gold to reveal: pearls and peacock-blue. Fourteen carats wink at every compass point. She starts off in a spotlight and emits a single moan. It goes on for minutes—growing, subsiding, exploding, until you're not sure if she's praying or cursing. She drags her voice over gravel, then soothes it with silk, she crucifies, dies, buries and rises, it will come again to save the living and the dead. People spontaneously applaud and shout, sometimes all together, sometimes singly. La Hogan is absolutely silent after the opening sacrament while God descends invisibly to investigate. Then, once He's split and the coast is clear, she spurts like a trumpet till the trumpet can't take it any more and hits her back—they fight blow for blow till she raises her arms and calls a truce. She takes a step off the stage. The audience yelps, the trombone belts a shocked comment, and she bursts into her song without words, quadruple time, strutting to the centre of the hall, dancing, the band following her like obedient treasure-bearers—except for piano—the drummer beats on every passing surface, people start clapping time as The Hogan somehow threads her stuff between the spindly tables and throngs of faithful. At the end of that first number she says, "Welcome and good evening," just as though she were an ordinary mortal. Sweat streams from her pearl headband and she flashes her ivory and gold smile. I guess she must weigh a good two hundred pounds.

I looked over at Rose. While everyone else in the place was swaying and rocking and beaming, she sat perfectly serious, listening and watching.

Afterwards, you know what she said about the music?

"Crude but compelling."

High praise indeed.

Under a smoky street lamp I stood face to face with my beloved and pricked my fingers against the diamond studs of her immaculate shirt front. Being tall, she slipped her hands naturally about my hips and pulled me close. And being bold, I put my mouth on hers and this time went inside and told her all the things I'd been longing to. Dark and sweet, the elixir of love is in her mouth. The more I drink, the more I remember all the things we've never done. I was a ghost until I touched you. Never swallowed mortal food until I tasted you, never understood the spoken word until I found your tongue. I've been a sleep-walker, sad somnambula, hands outstretched to strike the solid thing that could waken me to life at last. I have only ever stood here under this lamp, against your body; I've missed you all my life.

She kissed my face like fire. And it happened, I grew shy and could only give her the top of my head, which she kissed anyway. She said in a voice I'd never heard before, "I didn't think you had a scent, but you do." Which made me laugh because what a thing to say! But she explained, "No. Everyone has a scent and you either like it or you don't or you're indifferent. And you had no scent. And I thought that was spooky."

"You're easily spooked."

I love talking with our arms around each other.

"It made you seem not quite human," she said.

"I'm not—"

"Don't—"

"Scaredy-cat."

She kissed me again and we didn't stop for a long time, except to lean out of the light when we heard horses coming. We slipped into an alley and I pulled her shirt out from her pants. I pressed my centre into her and she sighed. It made me flood from inside, the sweetest music. We were finally dancing. I slid my hands under and up her smooth sides, I wanted to be slow to savour but we couldn't; she gripped me and moved under me. I felt her nipples under my palms and I think I died. Rose gasped as though I'd stabbed her and I felt like a savage robbing a sacred tree, her thigh between my legs. I found her hand and led it to a place I know, I kissed it with the mouth that I keep hidden, then took her inside and sucked her like the greedy tide that can't decide to swallow or disgorge. I lost track of everything. And even after I finally could stop, I knew that I would never be finished.

Oh Rose, it's not enough until I have all of you inside me, then give you back to the world fresh and new from my belly. She just said softly, "Oh," for the longest time.

Imagine, in an alley. It's not very romantic. But somehow it was. Terribly.

Crude but compelling.

Ann-Marie MacDonald

Ann-Marie MacDonald is a novelist, playwright, and actor, and author of the acclaimed play *Goodnight Desdemona (Good Morning Juliet)*. Her first novel *Fall On Your Knees*, became a much-loved international best-seller when it was published in 1996. Winner of the Commonwealth Prize for Best First Books as well as numerous other literary awards, it also became a selection of Oprah's Book Club. Ann-Marie MacDonald lives in Toronto.

Daphne Marlatt
Writer Notes as Interview

Is this a short story? It seems to be part fiction and part reading of Ethel Wilson's short story.

Fiction can be transformative, that's my starting point. It looks at how hope, dreams, fear, dread, all our various projections, shape what we live—often on an individual level but also on a collective level. I think lesbian fiction can offer a particular kind of transformative vision because it can see through or past the clichés of dominant culture. Of course it can also create its own clichés along the way. I'm interested in that in-between space where the clichés of the dominant can be read differently to create new possibilities for living within the larger culture, which is, after all, where we live.

Not entirely.

True, we live within overlapping circles of various community cultures—lesbian culture being one of them—all the way over to regional culture and national culture. History, that abstraction, constantly impinges on us in very large ways. Wilson, for instance, was writing in the shadow of WWII and its aftermath, the Cold War, and I think that shadow can be read in the blocked relationship her story recounts. Today we write in the shadow of corporate globalization and the terrorist outcome of a second war on Iraq. I'm not sure we fully see how this imprints on what we create. As a lesbian I stand both inside and outside my society, both complicit with its First World agendas and advantages, and, having been "othered" within it, critical of its endless replication of power-brokered binaries.

Why did you choose this story of Wilson's, "Til Death Us Do Part"?

Its opening phrase caught my ear, "*I have a friend...*" Not that I expect Ethel Wilson to have intended that lesbian resonance. She was raised in an all-female household in Vancouver's West End with the Victorian proprieties she describes so well in *The Innocent Traveller*. She was a dedicated doctor's wife who could also write a sarcastic story about the social niceties (read, hypocrisies) of a California medical convention and its gender separations. She wrote a lot about women and she wrote sensitively about the varied currents of liking and dislike between them.

But why bring a lesbian reading to her sad and rather conventional story about the blocked communication between two girls working in a wool shop?

I found it a moving depiction of how women complicit with the social mores of their time allow themselves to be trapped. Kate wants to hide the fact that she has an alcoholic mother. She's bound by the propriety, typical of the 1950s, that family life is private; you stick with family and you don't discuss your difficulties with people outside the family. So she keeps a solid wall between herself and Muriel, the narrator. Small-town Muriel has left her family and a lacklustre boyfriend behind on the Prairies. She's mystified by Kate's remote manner, which she reads as hostile. She alternates between trying to make friends with Kate and competing with her, but it's a stalemate. Finally, she tells Mrs. Physick, the absent shop-owner, that Kate's injured hand is badly infected. Then Mrs. Physick, who seems to know about Kate's predicament, takes action. Muriel is horrified by what she learns of Kate's home life—"*My belief is that bitch hit her on the hand with a bottle*"—and she decides that it might be *a comfort* to marry the not-very-inspiring boyfriend she'd left behind. Her last words, *what can you do* (with no question mark following), sound the basic motif of the narration. You can so vividly hear her shrug of resignation.

Shaped as I was by the remarkable openings and intense debates of the surge of feminism in the 80s and 90s, I felt I had to write against that shrug. I had to transform it. So now we have this "update" with a different ending, an "*up* date": El, a neophyte dyke just beginning to discover what she wants, and Kate—a Kate with hopes and dreams, who, when the moment comes, opens to it. At a time when so much seems to be shutting down, it seemed important to have a story about opening rather than closing.

Daphne Marlatt
Update

I have a friend,

it starts with I or she, rarely you. electric current I. or island I'll—surrounded by other islands equally unreachable. or else that one over there (she-cat). right away currents of competition come into play. even when he no longer owns the shop (well, he might, or at least the wholesale business, but she sees it differently). it being her story. as she turns on the tap to drench the rose-stems. shop-girl (that slight sneer) learning an art, taking it on

fiction, as if she hadn't grown up with it. history shadows fiction and she's grown in its shadow until fairly recently. or at least a shadowy past dogs her (Kate). that face she wants to forget, *sallow, almost yellow* floating up behind the roses she's cutting. *the sour smell of cheap whiskey*. a shabby eastside part of town. put behind her.

and then there's Muriel who comes from Portage la Prairie where the railroads cross, or crossed, where there wasn't much for a girl to do except get married (she's tired of Archie Edwards and the couplings of that life, already she knows that getting him will bore her). she's a long way from *My Summer of Love*—but there's something here, some glimmer that drove her west to Vancouver's boomtown edginess.

I have a friend….

a dream, a latch. to keep her company in the anonymous round of bus, work, bus, home—which isn't home, not yet. she ghosts herself, I-ing other young women she passes, unsure whether their laughter together excludes her. eyeing the fleshy rise a camisole reveals, or the low-slung line of a studded belt, blue butterfly surprise in the delicate spinal cleft. she's just beginning.

for Kate, it's the fragile immediacy of flowers, their colour, shape. their not lasting. she has dreams, but they don't involve anyone real. nightmares do. mother's a maw to forget. she concentrates on this sink, this one in the back of an uptown florist shop, this long table littered with leaves and stems. buckets of water on concrete with standing blooms, fragrant, cool, a fiction, almost flagrant in the dead heat of summer.

July 17. July 25. July 29. Muriel doesn't know much about fiction but the city inspires her. it doesn't take her long to explore, now that she's updated her name to Myrrh, something cool like that. or maybe just El. in reverse, it's Kate who's aware of all that *le* could mean—not *Elle* so much, she's perused its pages often enough at the library, determined to shake the under-smell of poverty, determined to attract someone moneyed, like him in the vermouth ad, Venice canal in the distance. it's El without the *le*, El from the grid of a dusty prairie town who, in this city infiltrated by water, senses where bridges might lead

I have a friend, well I should say...

someone i know, i mean she works at the shop and she's sort of interesting because she never says much, not to me anyhow. she's nice enough with the customers, but with me she's snippy or quiet, irritated maybe, or maybe she's just defensive about something, i don't know. the thing is she's really good-looking, in that spiky-hair diamond-in-the-navel kind of way. hey, she has a fabulous body, talk about slim—not that Gloria would let either of us come to work with what she calls "a bare midriff"—i figure Gloria's about my mom's age. but Kate, she wears these cool clothes and when she smiles—well, not to me... *I wish she would respond a bit.*

you smile, reading the current. thinking how queerly unconscious desire wells in this update of a woman's words half a
century ago. now are you reading in? given how history shadows fiction. dykes on bikes, Stonewall, fisting. words that
Ethel Wilson never knew, though she writes about that subtle
in-between space women touch in each other. its rapid about-
face currents.

how they well up in pseudo-domestic sinks—wool shop with
its tea kettle rituals. flower shop with its coffee runs. (Kate,
i'm going for a latte—want me to get you one?) all those fading (prim) roses (labial). Kate doesn't respond and El, new to
the city, is up to her elbows in dreamy water.

it wasn't warm for Kate, that maternal water she's trying to
leave behind. crystal meth in the kitchen sink and no Ms.
Physique to pry her gently out of self-contained hate. hands
busy under the tap, Kate's washing the dirt off.

separate histories. in Ethel's story of the 50s, they glance off
each other. glance away...

reading/ the writing on the wall/ of a face—how history shadows us in the act. rewrite that story locked in the isolation of
the 50s, that fiction of the private hell of a domesticity it
would never, never do to breach. now that we're plugged in by
netblog, palmcorder.

El's staring at the bouquet she's just made. it needs something,
what do you think, Kate? long moment of assessment. Kate
turning with an abrupt nod, try that—points at white tips of
tails (cattails, thinks El, cat got your tongue?) what is it then?
Gloria calls it Betty. Betty? well, Veronica's purple (stupid). oh,
i get it, Betty and Veronica. then she takes the plunge: without Archie, yes. let's just do without Archie for once.

Kate's rare for-once smile.

El/le

beginning to write a different end, reverse the current, break through Muriel's powerless imagination, *but what can you do?* which didn't or couldn't knock down walls. it takes (Ms. Physique) the nerve to just wade in.

they've always left the shop in opposite directions. where do you live? it doesn't matter. (what doesn't matter? and why is she so secretive?)

Gloria's away and now they're short-handed. El's making up the slack, with worried glances at Kate who seems harried, impatient. at closing-time, in tension's rush to be gone, Kate fumbles the last bucket, skids in its wake. a long crash. Kate in her cool little mini-skirt crumpled on flower-water on a concrete floor. El kneeling with her, a welter of breakage, flowerheads (no bonehead here)... let me help. Kate's white face a sudden flood of tears.

i'll never make it. yes you will.

after Emergency and the cast on her hand. after a long walk to Robson, trees ruffling heat-breeze through the stilted bits and pieces of their stories. after Thai noodles that Kate introduces El to, El urging a beer or two to dull the pain, Kate trusting enough to agree. they end up at the Lotus, dancing to Abba, dancing each other's dream. it's only the beginning of historied adjustments that will take them months, perhaps years. pasts don't fit together easily. if the fit unravels they will blame fiction.

blame flower buckets and bridges. or you, dear reader, making the connection.

Notes:

My Summer of Love. Pawel Pawlikowski's 2004 film.

Ethel Wilson, 1888-1980. Vancouver fiction writer. this story is a considerably free reading, a contemporary update let's say, of the situation in her story "Till Death Us Do Part" in her 1961 collection, *Mrs. Golightly and Other Stories*. except for the title of Pawlikowski's film, all phrases in italics are quotes from Wilson's story. My thanks to Lydia Kwa for her suggestions, especially the inspired "Ms. Physique" for Wilson's "Mrs. Physick."

Daphne Marlatt

In 2004-05 Daphne Marlatt was Simon Fraser University's inaugural Writer-in-Residence in their newly resurrected program. She has published two novels (*Taken* and *Ana Historic*), a collection of essays and letters, and numerous poetry titles including *This Tremor Love Is, Steveston,* and *Salvage*. Her contemporary Noh play, *The Gull*, with music by composer Richard Emmert, is scheduled for production in May 2006 by Pangaea Arts (Vancouver) as a bilingual Japan-Canada project.

Shani Mootoo
Writer Notes

How can my point of view not be queer? Harry is the protagonist of my most recent novel, *He Drown She in the Sea*. Even though Harry's desire is for a woman, he's been told his entire life that this particular desire isn't normal or valid. This, to me, reads as very queer.

A book reviewer in the US wrote (of me writing *He Drowns She in the Sea*), that "His greatest achievement is the portrayal of Harry." It's interesting that the reviewer assumed I was a man, and I assume that this was because he could relate to Harry. In creating Harry, I wanted to paint the picture of a straight man through this queer person's eyes, one whom I would feel comfortable, happy, and safe to be in the same world with. It's my way of writing the straight world. My vision, or hope.

Whether I write a story that has an obviously lesbian or gay theme, or one that deals with a mainly heterosexual world, the lens through which these stories are envisioned is a predominantly queer one, a valuable lens, I think, on worlds, particularly the heterosexual one, in which we must exist.

Shani Mootoo
The Upside-downness of the World as it Unfolds

1.

I was just about to type the word with which I would launch
into my story, but that word has a way of evoking a memory
of the attack of a slender 18" x 1" length of wood sprung
thwaaaack! Against a thinly covered row of bones, and my
knuckles remember the ache as if the pronouncement had
come down only seconds ago, decommissioning my fingers. A
simple, overused word. Not one, however, that is overused in
my back-home, but overused here, in this country of english-
es (but not so many English folk as they themselves might
like). The first time I used that word was some twenty-five
years ago, in front of Mrs. Dora Ramsey, the ancient retired
British tutor my parents hired to push, no, shove us through
the Common Entrance exam. And ever since that usage, so
many years back, I have had trouble even thinking the word.

Tdrrrrrring! a little bell rings, taking us back into the past.
There it is again: tdrrrrrring! A glass of cow's milk and a plate
of currant rolls ("dead fly cemetery," they are called, flaky pas-
try triangles studded with hundreds of dark reddish brown
shrivelled currants) and the unpeeled cheeks of ripe Julie mangoes sit on a kitchen table. Two girls, my sister Sharda and I,
nine and ten years old, ignore the dead fly cemetery and grab
the mangoes first, each cheek held up to the mouth, teeth
sunk into the golden flesh, yellow creamy juice slipping down
the corner of a mouth and running in a crooked egg-yellow
rivulet down the finger, down the palm, down the arm to drip
off the elbow. Sweet satisfaction and then the two girls grow
sullen, sticky yellow elbows digging defiantly into the table, as
they prop their chins into their sweet-smelling palms. Their
mother snaps, "Stop lahayin and drink up that milk. If you
weren't such dodo-heads you wouldn't have to go to private

lessons. And you have no choice. Take that sulk off your face this minute!"

"But Mummy...."

"Don't but with me. You are going if I have to drag you there myself!"

She didn't drag us there herself, Boyie the chauffeur did. He drove us (our reluctance made the car sluggish) three blocks and around the corner to a house set far back in a cul-de-sac where, without our having to announce ourselves, the tall wrought-iron gates rumbled and parted at their centre seam. Boyie never crossed the gate; he was afraid that it would close behind him, trapping him, subjecting him to synonyms, antonyms, onomatopoeia, and other words he heard us hurling at each other as if they were ultimate insults.

"You synonym!"

"Do you want to get subjunctived?"

"Onomatopoeia sme-ell, onomatopoeia sme-ell."

"No they don't. You do. You smell."

So Sharda and I walked from the bottom of the driveway, with our exercise books, vocabulary and usage texts, and finely sharpened yellow pencils, up a long and winding asphalt path, whispering encouragement to each other through motionless lips. We looked hard through the jacaranda and bougainvillea shrubs scattered missionary-style all over the lawn, trying to spot the clammy cold white English hand and lordly eyes of the controller of the gates groaning shut behind us.

We always entered the house through the kitchen. Widowed Mrs. Ramsey, living out her days and thawing out her marrow in the colonies, would stand at the top stair waiting by the back door, watching us mount each step as if we were carrying sacks of mangoes on our backs. She would make us wipe our shoes on the husk mat at the top stair outside the kitchen and push us through the kitchen where Rommel, the Rhodesian Ridgeback, lay on the cool terrazzo with his hind legs sprawled straight out behind him, guarding his pot of rice, bones, and leftovers melting down under a bubbling froth to dog-food mush on the stove-top.

Following Mrs. Ramsey's spreading frame, we meandered through the house of curios commemorating the coronation of Queen Elizabeth in 1952. We slid our hands along our upside-down reflections, clear like a still lake's, on the 200-year-old colonial-style mahogany dining table and chairs, to the verandah with purple, yellow, and white hanging orchids, potted pink anthuriums, and a wall of purple bougainvillaea. Shading the patio was an S-shaped avocado tree, with S-shaped branches weighed down by ripe avocadoes hanging like Mrs. Ramsey's heavy breasts (which Sharda and I were always trying to see more of, to know what secrets their Britishness held), and as big, the length from an elbow to one's outstretched middle finger. Nothing in Mrs. Ramsey's garden was mongrel, everything was trophy- and certificate-winning, deeper in colour, bigger, contorted or striped or variegated hybrids; everything was straightened and tied with plant wire and trained with trellises. On the edge of all this, in the cool evening breeze, is where we sat and were taught to behave like the well-brought-up young ladies in *her* back-home where she had once long, long ago been the principal of a private high school for girls only.

New words were fitted in our mouths and we were taught how to use them. Word: pagan (pā'gən), *n.* 1. one who is not a Christian, Moslem, or Jew; heathen. 2. one who has no religion. 3. a non-Christian. Sentence: The pagans of Indian ancestry pray to images of a dancing Shiva, a blue Krishna, or the cow.

Top marks.

We recited multiplication tables from the back cover of our exercise book, and often when time permitted we were given a complimentary lesson in flower arrangement or table etiquette. How, with knife and fork, to eat roti and curried châtaigne, which her Afro-Indo-Trinidadian half-day maid cooked. Soup and cereal, to tip or not to tip, when and how. And how to eat a mango correctly. Never ripping with hands and teeth, or slurping off the edge of a cheek; always cutting with a knife and fork. Slice off cheeks, grid the inside with a knife, then slide knife under the sections and release with fork.

One night Mrs. Ramsey tried to slice up and grid my family. My parents, my sister, and I were invited for supper; Mrs. Ramsey served plump, perfumed, and runny mangoes for dessert. My parents ate their cheeks the way mangoes have always been enjoyed in Trinidad, cupped in one hand and sucked and slurped, the meat dragged off the skin with happy grinning teeth. Mrs. Ramsey sat straight-backed as she gridded her mango cheeks and proceeded with knife and fork to deal with one manageable square at a time. Without a word to each other, Sharda and I weighed the wisdom of choosing one mango-eating method over the other and decided to decline dessert.

That night when our Ahji, Daddy's mother, came to put us to bed with her childhood textbook of the Hindi alphabet and wanted us to learn her mother's language, we both said that we didn't care about India and didn't want to learn a language that only old and backward people spoke. That night Ahji gasped and died a little.

Oh! The word I began this preamble with, or rather without (you see, this is still the preamble, not yet the story!)... Well, days later, again in the cul-de-sac, I answered some command or other with the word—are you ready for it?—with the word *okay*, and Sharda and I watched Mrs. Ramsey catch a fit, hopping and squealing.

"I beg your pardon! Did I hear correctly? What was that you answered me with?"

And I meekly repeated my word, thinking it inoffensive and not warranting comment: *okay*. She again hopped, scowled and made her eyes beady tight, and brought out Rudyard, the wooden ruler. She let me have it over my knuckles until I felt a hot wet ooze slipping out from between my knotted legs, and then she explained through clenched teeth, "*Okay* is slang. Abbreviation of *oll korrect*—itself a re-spelling (read mis-spelling) of *all correct*. Slang. Do you understand *slang*? Look it up!"

I fumbled through my dog-eared navy blue pocket dictionary and was too confused to read full phrases but several words leapt out from under the heading *slang* and left an indelible impression:... *nonstandard... subculture... arbitrary... ephemeral coinages... spontaneity... peculiar... raciness.*

And then she squealed, "*Okay* is not simply slang; above all it is an Americanism, that history-less upstart, a further butchering of our Oxford! Never, (pause for emphasis, and close-up on mouth pursed anus-tight) never let me hear that ... that... that meaningless utterance again!"

nation

On that evening I did not simply learn about slang; a revelation occurred to me, a shift as vivid as when one's sinuses suddenly quake and move around behind one's face as the passages clear. I realized that White (I assumed that America was White [from TV and *Time Magazine*] and I assumed that England was White [from my first history book, and the second, and the third; from *Coronation Street*, *The Avengers*, *Women's Weekly*]) ... I realized that White is not all the same. Mrs. Ramsey's upturned chin and haughty reserve appealed to my parents, whose propensity to supplicate was well served, but the American families who were in Trinidad to govern our oil fields were reviewed as Whites who had gone to seed. They flaunted their lack of gentility with their leisurely patio barbecues (imagine serving guests on paper plates and with plastic utensils!) and pot lucks (imagine a hostess expecting her guests to bring their own food!). It went unchallenged for me that in the hierarchy of Whites, British was Queen and American was peasant.

Early in life I already displayed the trait of championing the underdog, and so much better if the underdog were also "Other." India was not "Other" enough for me. India was at home in Trinidad. Ahji did not bring out her alphabet book again but she quietly, subversively, and obstinately brought India into our house by intensifying her wearing of saris,

hierarchy w/in one place → marginalization of Americans in Trinidad

singing of bhajans, and performing of conspicuous evening poojas by herself. The house filled up every evening with smoke from camphor squares and the radio no longer played calypsos or the American Top 40, only music from Indian films and Hindu religious music. North America became the "Other" underdog for me. When it came time for me to go abroad for further education, this is where I ended up, to the veritable irritation of my parents.

Tdrrrrrring! Tdrrrrrring! And we (you and I, not the cast of the preamble; you and I have left them all behind now) find ourselves feeling cold, hugging our shoulders, and bouncing from foot to foot, even though we are indoors. Tdrrrrrring! and we look outside and see tall buildings, low grey sky, a couple of scraggly pine trees, and some exhaust-greyed flowerless shrubs here and there. We have arrived in North America, Canada to be precise, downtown Vancouver to be razor sharp. And the word *okay* is no longer italicized, even though there is a faint ringing in my knuckles still.

2.

Okay! So now that I want to know about India, Ahji has died, and I can't afford to go there. And White friends, unlike my White childhood tutor, no longer want to whiten me but rather they want to be brown and sugary like me, so much so that two of them in particular have embarked on a mission to rub back in the brown that Mrs. Ramsey tried so hard to bleach out. It was my taste for "Other" music (now that I live in North America "Otherness" is elsewhere) that bumped me into those two, whose interest was in "Other" cultures.

Ever since I saw Zahara, my ex-sweetie, walking hand-in-hand with another woman, I have been crying to the music of lovesick Sudanese musicians. Of course I debated questions of exoticization and exploitation by the World Beat craze, but always I assuaged my conscience with the thought that Zahara is Muslim and from Zaire, close enough to Sudan, and since I had bedded with her I had some right to this music as a balm for my sick heart. I was misguided perhaps, but those who are losers in love usually are.

Ever since she left me I found myself lured daily to the music store that specializes in World Beat music. With a good dose of contempt curling a sneer in my upper lip, I would, nevertheless, buy up every piece of mournful beseeching coming out of Muslim Africa. When my mother found out (a story in itself) that I preferred the company of women, she said that I had put a knife in her heart, but when she heard that the object of this preference was Muslim, she said that I had shoved the knife deeper and twisted it in her Hindu heart. I hope that she does not have the opportunity to see, let alone hear, my CD collection: Nusrat, Hamza, Abdel Aziz, Abdel Gadir, etc.

The blond, stringy-haired man at the counter was trying to get me interested in a CD by Mohamed Gubara from Sudan. With my eyes closed, I leaned against the glass case that displayed harmonicas and guitar strings, and listened to the Sudanese musician bleating tabanca songs and strumming the tambour.

I imagined his face, his eyes shut also, and his tambour caressed at his chest like a lover he was embracing and singing to. The chimes above the doorway to the store tinkled under Mohamed Gubara's voice and a hint of men's cologne underneath the flowery scent of a woman announced a presence more arresting than Mohamed Gubara's music. I opened my eyes and recognized the shortness of the hair, the breastlessness of the shirt, the Birkenstocks and grey socks. I thought that she recognized similar things in my appearance, but I learned later that she had had no idea that I might be "family." The reason she stared and smiled and then came over to talk was that she frequently visited India. Meet Meghan.

—Did I want to go for a cup of chai next door?

—I don't drink tea.

—A glass of lassi, perhaps?

—I'd prefer a cappuccino.

And so over cappuccinos and an attraction to her, I wiggled my way into hinting of my sexual persuasion, which I had correctly assumed was the same as hers. We exchanged phone numbers and for the next forty-eight hours I leapt to answer every phone call, hoping that it would be her. Her call came after seventy-two hours.

—Did I remember her?

—Uh, yes, how was she enjoying her new CDs?

—Oh, they're just wonderful. How about dinner? At an Indian restaurant that she frequents?

—Uh, sure, okay. Why not. (Yes! Yes! Yes! Even though a <u>too-long absence from home has created in me an intense intolerance of Indian food</u>.)

All but wrapped and tied up with a bow (I cut my own blend of men's and women's scent, blow-dried my hair twice— the first time I was a little too intense and one side was bouffant-ish and the other not), I arrived at the restaurant to find that she and another woman were seated waiting for me. Enter Virginia, her partner for the last five years, of whom she had not hinted before.

No need to have made my bed and washed the dishes.

3.

Meghan and Virginia turned out to be peace-seekers to a fault. Quietly, with no heroism whatsoever, they retreated from everything remotely resembling indulgence. Their desire for peace, harmony and one big happy world was not, to my relief, accompanied by incense-burning and patchouli fragrances! Nor had they fallen into the crystal craze. And one other thing: they had a good-natured contempt for tissue-thin Indian skirts with little claustrophobia-inducing mango-seed paisleys and hemlines with frayed tassels. Thank the powers that be! They picked a safe, simple lifestyle.

They had, however, made one big-time purchase: a hot-off-the-press, pristine, four-door Mazda 626. It was a little expensive, but undeniably a sensible buy—not what one could call excessive (not one of those limited edition types). After all, who expects reliability and safety to come without a price tag attached?

In all the time that I have known them I have never once heard either one raise her voice, in vexation or jubilation. So I can't really say that I minded when they spoke about Peace and Oneness with an accent or in the singsong tone of the fumbling-bumbling Indian stereotype in Peter Sellers's movies. They didn't mean to mock or be malicious. Take my word for it. In fact, they were both genuine in their desire to be Indian. Meghan could slide her neck horizontally from shoulder to shoulder like the small vibrantly coloured paper mâché Indian dancer that used to sit on our windowsill, around the corner and down the street from Mrs. Ramsey's, its head dangling sideways in the wind. (To my shame, to this day I am still unable to slide my neck, or give a convincing imitation of an Indian accent.) Sliding her neck, Meghan would say in an accent thick and syrupy as a jilebi, "All we want is peace and happiness in this world. I am wishing you these this very morning!"

Around her neck she wore a little pendant, a brass globe the size of a "jacks" ball, with the world in bas relief on it, hanging from a shiny black satin cord. A sadhu she bumped into in Bangalore, years ago, had given it to her. After giving her blessings, she would grasp the world and give it a little shake. The world would tinkle brilliantly, the sound slowly fading as if it were moving outward into some other consciousness. Tdrrrrring! And again, Tdrrrrring!

Meghan and Virginia had been to India travelling around several times, separately, before they knew each other. In fact, that is where they met; Meghan was heading south from Calcutta to Madras, ashram-hopping, and Virginia was making the opposite trip, from Mysore in the south to Varanasi up north. They met on a hustle-and-bustle street somewhere in between, intuitively yanked together like magnets: two white Canadian women searching, searching, for what they did not quite know, until, that is, they found each other. Destiny. Mission. Karma. They realized that they both had Ukrainian roots (they have since found out that they are distantly related), another magnet for them. They quickly discovered that they had much more than that in common, too. On the day that they met, Meghan did a string of pirouettes, one after the other, until she faced north, and she headed in that direction, accompanying Virginia. But that is a story in itself, and they can tell their own story. I am tired of telling other people's romantic stories.

At some point they came back home to Canada, and a couple of months later left the hustle, bustle, and overall coldness of Toronto to head for Vancouver, which is a lot closer to India. They say that when they go down to English Bay and dip their toes in the water they can feel a current of seductive tassa drumming vibrating all the way from the heart of India, encircling their feet and rising up in them. Sometimes lying in bed at night in their North Van home, nestled in the quiet, forested uplands, they hear chanting from the ashram in Calcutta.

It is from them that I learned about Varanasi, the river Ganga, and Calcutta in such grassroots, earthy detail that I can smell and feel particles of dusty heat collecting in my nostrils. They can decode my ancestors' ceremonies for me, when what I know of them is mostly from the colourful coffee-table picture books that are always on sale at the Book Warehouse for $4.95.

The first time I met them I heard Meghan say "acha" at some point in our conversation, and I left it go, thinking it was a Ukrainian expression. Later, when she said "chalo" and then "nahi," I had to cock my head sideways and ask if those were the same Hindi words that I had heard Ahji use. They came naturally to Meghan. She often exclaimed in longer Hindi sentences, catching me off guard, making me feel ignorant and like a charlatan. Ahji would have been baffled by the upside-downness of the world as it unfolds.

The only Indian words I know are those on the menus of Indian restaurants and in my very own *Indian Cookery by Mrs. Balbir Singh*. From the first day when I arrived in Canada people would say, "Oh, great! You can teach me how to cook Indian food, and that tea, what is it called? Masala tea? Chai? You know, the one with the spices." But I didn't know, hadn't heard of such a tea until I came up here. Instead of disappointing people before I even got a chance to make any friends, I went out and bought that cookbook, which has just about saved my face more than a few times. Mrs. Singh taught me words like vindaloo, mulligatawny, bhuna, matar, pullao, and gosht, and of course, roti in some of its varities: chapati, puri, naan, and so on.

It was inevitable that Meghan and Virginia would one day invite me to go with them to the Hare Krishna temple out in Ferrinbridge. "Come learn about your culture!" they suggested in the jovial manner of those enlightened to such absurdities of life. Feeling like a cultural orphan, I decided to go. I was only a little surprised to find out that they were Krishna followers. You see, it is not that I was surprised that two white women would belong to that movement. In fact, I was always under the impression that Hare Krishnas were, indeed, white, having been introduced to the movement by the Beatles, and then having seen with my own eyes only white folk chanting the names of Hindu gods and beating Indian tassa drums at airports in Miami, New York, and London. It is only recently, at the Peace March downtown, that I've seen among the Krishna contingency a handful—well, less than that, really— of browns awkwardly partaking in the clapping, swaying, chanting, drumming, and tinkling amidst a sea of white men wearing orange kurtas and white dotis, and white women wearing thin heaven-white cotton saris, the women so emaciated and long-limbed that their saris, which were tightly wrapped instead of draped, looked like some type of garment other than a sari (perhaps a mummy's outer encasement, with an ohrni thrown over the head). It made me wonder who came first, the white followers or the Indian ones. Who converted whom.

What surprised me was that these two women, who were a lot closer to my living room than the Beatles or fleeting orange kurtas and nameless chanting faces in airports, these acquaintances of mine were Krishna followers. These two very ordinary, well-heeled (suede Birks) and responsible people! Well, what I really mean to say is "these good-looking white dykes!"

I readily decided to swallow my shame that these two were better Indians than I, and to go ingest some of the sounds, smells, colours, and tastes (everyone talks of the free vegetarian meal after a prayer meeting) of my foreparents' homeland.

Sunday evening, the evening I was to learn a little about my culture, the pristine Mazda 626 sidled up to the curb in front of my apartment building. The inside of the car was ablaze with colour: Virginia's grinning face peeped out from under the cherdo of a brilliant red silk sari, her face framed by a navy blue border with discriminating flecks of silver paisleys. Meghan's cherdo hung around her neck, leaving her sandy-coloured head hovering in that dangerous place where one cannot pin her down to being female or male. Boyish one minute, unmistakable woman the next. And then boyish again.

Meghan was immensely pleased with herself. Her silk sari was forest green, with tiny gold paisleys all over and a thick, heavily-embroidered border of silver and gold. My own plain white T-shirt, dark blue rayon slacks, Dr. Martens' brogues, and white socks (I guessed, correctly, that we would have to remove our shoes, so I wore a pair of brand-new dressy socks that I had been saving for a special occasion) made me feel like a party-pooper going to a costume party. "Wow! You guys look great!" and other exclamations came out of my mouth, but the thoughts in my head flipped back and forth between "God, do I ever feel underdressed, shabby, shown-up as a cultural ignoramus" and "What the heck do you want with dressing up in saris and praying to Indian gods? What business do you have showing me what I have lost? Go check out your own ancestry!" A string of unprintable thoughts and expletives surprised me. Would have turned Mrs. Ramsey blue.

Meghan pulled the car away from the curb and Virginia turned back to talk to me. When I saw her blue satin blouse I realized that I had unconsciously harboured the thought that they would be wearing T-shirts instead of sari blouses. After a few minutes I became aware that I had overdone the "Gosh! They're sooo beautiful" sentiments, and I felt quite awkward. When we got out of the car I saw their full saris, faultlessly wrapped. The pleats of the patli were equally spaced, perfectly placed. I was in the mood to bet that they had had the patli arranged and then permanently sewn in place.

I was not the only South Asian at the ashram, as I had expected to be. In fact, a good half of the modest gathering was brown-skinned. None of the brown men wore the orange and white of the Krishnas, though. They wore quiet, polite Western suits. The brown women all wore modest day saris. Dressed as I was, the only female browny in Western wear, I understood, as if it were a revelation, Ahji's panic and distress at the unravelling of her culture right before her eyes.

Virginia and Meghan, with eyes closed, clapped and swayed to the chaotic drumming and the tuneless chanting of the all-white leaders. I stood as stiffly as an old piece of dried toast, with my hands clasped behind my back. The other brown folk, on the periphery of the room, not at all central to the goings-on, clapped discreetly, without their bodies exhibiting their spiritual jubilance.

In a temple of Krishna and Rama, surrounded by murals depicting scenes from the Bhagavad Gita, among peace-desiring people full of benevolence, my temperature—temper, actually—rose. The sermon on a particular chapter of the Gita was delivered by His Holiness, a white man in orange, with a head shaved except for a thin tail of hair emanating from the upper back of his head. He sat on a throne surrounded by his entourage of white devotees. He had just returned from India full of inspiration and energy and was passing out stories of the work being done there to complete the building of a city and centre of Krishna devotion. "Go to India," he said repeatedly, grinning impishly with the privilege of having done so himself several times.

The men sat closest to him, in front, and the women sat at the back. The brown women fell into their places at the very back, against the wall. Midway through the sermon a young man came to fetch women, who were needed in the kitchen to serve the food. He crossed over and meandered among the congregation of white women who were nearest to him, heading for the brown ones. They dutifully rose and followed him into the kitchen, missing the ending of the sermon.

I wondered what wisdom it was (if that is what it was) that kept people from committing crimes right there and then. A familiar burning touched my knuckles, but this time it was from too tight a fist wanting to impact with history. An urgent rage buzzed around my head and ears like a swarm of crazed mosquitoes. I unfisted my hands and flayed them around my head, brushing away the swarming past and present.

I looked over at my two friends sitting at my side. Meghan and Virginia, genuine in their desire to find that point where all division ceases and we unite as one, shone radiantly. Meghan followed my eyes as I watched the brown women walking singlefile to the kitchen. In her favourite accent, full of empathy, she said, "Pretty sexist, eh! That's a problem for us too."

Tdrrrrring! Oh! There's my doorbell!

A letter from back home, from my mother. In the unfamiliar tone of her written English she writes, "...She gave me her prized potted scorpion orchid just days before she passed away. As if she had a premonition! She had asked your Papa, quite some time back, to be the executor of her will. Her wish was that he contact her stepson, George Arthur Ramsey, in Surrey, England, and have her body flown back to him for burial among their kin. We did our best for our good friend, to whom Sharda and you owe thanks for your skills in the English language. After several telegrams back and forth, Papa found George living in Philadelphia, U.S.A., with his new bride, an Indian woman from East Africa. (I automatically wonder if she is Muslim.) So her body was sent to him there, where he held a funeral for her. We sincerely hope that this arrangement was okay...."

Shani Mootoo

Shani Mootoo was born in Ireland and grew up in Trinidad. She has lived in Canada since the early 1980s. Her acclaimed first novel *Cereus Blooms at Night*, was published in fourteen countries and was a finalist for The Giller Prize, the Ethel Wilson Fiction Prize, and the Amazon/Books in Canada First Novel Award. Her book of poetry is entitled *The Predicament of Or*, and "The Upside-downness of the World as it Unfolds" comes from her collection of short fiction, *Out on Main Street and Other Stories*. An accomplished visual and video artist, Shani Mootoo's novel *He Drown She in the Sea* was published in 2005.

Elizabeth Ruth
Writer Notes

Writing fiction is really just the elusive, impossible process of chasing one's soul, catching it for a moment, and then translating it onto a page. It's hard for any writer, but perhaps especially hard for writers who live on the margins where their vantage point onto the wider world is often discounted or ignored, and where they may see that little in life is static, fixed, unchanging—including sexual "orientation," gender, sex itself. Indeed for writers who don't sit comfortably within the mainstream, or worse, those who don't try to, the soul—that unknowable, unproven entity—is probably also fluid and in flux. It can't actually be caught, and yet we go on trying...

Am I a lesbian writer or a writer who happens to be lesbian? How, if at all, does my life intersect with my writing? Do I believe there's a distinct lesbian literary "voice"? The answers to these and other questions depend on the day, the moment, the company I'm keeping, even my mood. The answers will also depend on you, the reader, on whether you believe I chose to write, chose to have my most intimate intellectual, emotional, and sexual relations with women, or whether you believe these things chose me.

Perhaps beginnings are key:

I was born to an unmarried mother in 1968, when there was still enough stigma around illegitimacy that most women of the day were coerced or actively pressured into back-alley abortions or putting their babies up for adoption. I was born in a Catholic hospital to a Protestant mother who was shamed and encouraged to give me up for adoption. The birth control pill was new in Canada and women finally had some degree of control over their reproductive lives. This meant fewer unwanted pregnancies, and so fewer babies available for adoption. My mother—brave, defiant woman that she is, kept me.

I was raised without a father. Ontologically speaking—not

merely practically speaking. When people say that they were raised by a single mother, they usually mean something entirely different. There is no father's name on my birth certificate, no photo in my drawer of some man dead or long gone, no child support payments or custody battles, no negative storyline of rejection for me to hang my hat on. He doesn't even know I exist. I didn't think to ask about my biological father until I was almost twelve years old when someone in the schoolyard forced the issue. In our home, the social role of father and the biological fact of paternity were separate concepts, as they remain for me. My biological father was, in some ways, like the anonymous sperm donors of today.

My childhood was wonderful chaos and glorious change. It was creatively stimulating and by most people's standards, then and now, dramatic. My mother worked more than full time, so we always had food and a place to live. She slept in the living-room and I was given the one bedroom in our many apartments, or once, the closet of our bachelor apartment. (My bed just fit and I loved the cosiness and the dark.) I moved schools almost annually and in one year—grade three—changed schools three times. People came into my life and disappeared like phantoms, but from each I learned a new story. I kept on the outside of social circles; there was no point in becoming too attached. Psychologists have a field day with childhoods like mine—and I grew up hearing their predictions from teachers and guidance counsellors and neighbours about how I would surely end up pregnant at sixteen, a high school dropout, a drug addict. I would self-destruct. I suppose, in part, I later studied psychology to prove them wrong.

We spent two years in Bogotá, Colombia, where I was educated in Spanish and in the brutal realities of a class system that supports the rich by squashing the poor. Living in South America was the single biggest defining experience of my young life. It shaped who I would become. It gave me a different language to love, showing me first-hand how language creates thought, and how I could be a different person in a different tongue. Life abroad exposed me to places and people I'd never known existed, informed my understanding of systemic violence, oppression, and the need for active, global resistance.

I was never sheltered from my mother's day-to-day struggle to pay rent and find affordable housing, or taught to be ashamed of our family, where visiting relatives in psychiatric facilities and hanging out with relatives between prison stints was (and is) a fact of life. I was allowed to know gays, lesbians, and a couple of very sexy transsexual working girls, who populated the landscape of my childhood. In short, I was never prevented from knowing the full, ugly, sublime human experience. I was encouraged to embrace it.

How could I become any kind of writer other than the kind for whom people and issues on the margins are the central preoccupation? How could I not somehow subvert the canon and challenge literary convention? Outlaws and outsiders are my people, those I come from and those I choose to love, and they interest me in life and in the fictional world of my imagination. I must write them into being. I must write the world as I need it to be. To write anything else would be to write myself out of existence. Does that make me a lesbian writer or just an honest writer? How, if at all, does my sexuality intersect with my writing? Do I believe there's a distinct lesbian literary "voice"? My answer is yes. And no. And maybe. You decide.

"tiny insurmountable hills" is the title story in a linked collection I'm developing. It deals with moments in our lives that get minimized—are deemed small and insignificant by our culture or communities or by ourselves—when they are actually monumental defining moments that shape us. With this story I explore the nebulous concept of "free choice" as it relates to women's reproduction, and the relative privilege and powerlessness different women experience in terms of motherhood. "Tiny" was inspired by a news story from 2003 when a newborn was abandoned on the steps of Toronto's City Hall. Little information was given about her biological mother, except that she'd been living in a shelter for homeless women.

Elizabeth Ruth
tiny insurmountable hills

"Cross me off," I told that snot-nosed skinny new social work-er at the shelter.

"But it's winter," she said, like I couldn't judge that for myself. "It's fifteen below outside."

I smiled but not a real one. Not the kind I stored for Momma before she died or my brother Jimmy. No, I flashed the other kind, all toothy and wide, pulled it up out of the pit of me, like I was pulling a rabbit from a hat, and sat it on my face for the professional. It makes them feel good about them-selves thinking we're co-operating, thinking we like them. And when they feel good about themselves, they feel a whole lot better about helping us.

"Cross me off," I repeated.

She shook her head.

"I can't do that, Pauline. Not when you're so close to final-ly being housed." Her cheeks got all spotty like she was a baby with a face rash. She rolled her chair across the clear plastic mat and reached into the oak desk drawer where they kept our meds. She fished through the pile and found a plastic bag with a strip of yellow masking tape on it. The name "Pauline" was written in black marker. She thought that was my real name. She rattled one small pill bottle after another like she was rattling her granddaddy's teeth in a jar. When she was sat-isfied that I hadn't skipped my meds, she shut the drawer. "Oh," she said. "You're right. You're all caught up." She swiv-elled and rolled over to me in that queen-shit chair. Her tune changed then, softened like rancid butter. "Why don't you tell me what's *really* going on. You've been on the priority list for a year and now, when you're so close, you want off?"

Her words stuck like Elmer's glue fastened them. I thought about Christopher, about when he was born all jittery and crack addicted, how I got to hold him a whole five minutes before he started wailing, and the nurse came and took him from me. "Your kind always wants off easy," that nurse said. "Excuses. Special treatment. If it was up to me, you'd all be sterilized." Truth be told, I was relieved to have Christopher gone. You're not supposed to say that about your own baby, but I was pretty sure he took one good look at his sorry excuse for a mother, got a sweet whiff of the crack sweating up through my skin, and knew enough to register protest. It was better he be gone to someone else; still I felt my bones coming apart from their joints, and it hurt bad. No one to talk to and nothing to say; I held my breath until I passed out in that clean, white hospital bed.

In the shelter with little Miss BSW staring back at me, same blue eyes as that nurse long ago, I couldn't hold the plastic smile any longer. My face went slack and I felt a sickness coming upon me—through me—from the inside out.

"I'll take my chances in the streets," I said.

She stood up, letting the chair roll away behind her.

"I'm sorry, Pauline, I can't stop you from leaving but I'm not taking you off the housing list."

I shoved her. Not hard, mind you, just hard enough that she'd know what I'd known since long before she was even born: every sorry son-of-a-bitch has a choice in this life, and the last thing you want is to be the one who takes it away.

She regained her footing and pressed the button on the underside of the desk to call for the other staff on shift. The buzzer rang throughout the house. Big fat Janet-the-planet came clomping down the front hall in her steel-toed boots, probably forgot to lock the kitchen door behind her again. My belly started tumbling like it was full of soft pebbles, and I should've known it was a girl I was carrying this time. No boulder, all stubborn and fixed like Christopher, but flexible, resourceful. I'd been polishing them pebbles inside me like little pieces of granite, polishing them to fine gemstones. For a split second I thought I might be different with this baby, I'd be good and stay clean, but guess what? All the mother-fucking goodwill in the world don't change shit. Hooked is hooked, baby or no.

"Fuck you!" I hollered at the staff as Janet waddled into the office. "Fuck you, you little muffin. What do you know about me? It's my life and if I want to live it in the big beautiful outdoors, I will. Take me off the list!"

"Pauline!" Janet used her firm voice, the one she reserved for what staff called "crisis situations." I turned to her, ballooned out like she was, her fingers as yellowed at the tips from smoking as mine, and I thought how most of the time I didn't mind Janet-the-planet. She was my age at least, fortysomething, and occasionally she'd sneak me a smoke when I ran out. But she wouldn't know a real crisis if one fell at her feet and gave birth to a new moon.

"Janet," I said in the same tone of voice as she'd used on me. "This girl here don't know my situation. You two don't even know my real fucking name!"

§ § §

Lisa lay with her feet in stirrups covered in green paisley oven mitts. A poem that her aunt had pinned to her refrigerator with a Jesus magnet was stuck on the opposite wall: "Desiderata." On the counter, beside the microscope, sat a beige file folder with her first initial and her surname printed in thick black ink and next to her name the words "high risk." Janet, Lisa's lover of five years, winked at Lisa while Dr. M. opened the cap on the sperm vile and, with a long, thin syringe, extracted a tiny amount. He dripped sperm onto a microscope slide, switched on the microscope's light, and leaned forward to inspect. "Motility is good," he said. "These fellas are raring to go. Have a look."

Janet smiled and moved to see for herself. Some sperm swam fast, others slow. Some were fatter, had bigger heads, longer tails, one spun in circles. Another jerked backwards. For an instant Janet wondered whether they were making the right decision in using an anonymous donor.

Lisa was glad that she couldn't see the sperm moving, alive. The more she knew about the donor, the more real he became in her mind, and she knew he had to remain a distant, perfunctory moment in time or else the child that resulted might one day pick up on lingering information and want the whole story. The secret to raising a healthy child without a biological father, she had decided, was to teach it that it cannot miss what it has never known.

Lisa flinched when Dr. M. inserted a cold metal speculum into her vagina. She took a deep breath and tried to visualize her open cervix, a wide, pink donut glistening with mucus that would help the sperm to stay alive. As the doctor drew the rest of the sperm into his syringe and released it, Lisa played with the ring she had worn for good luck. It was her grandmother's wedding band. Her grandmother had given birth to seven children. Lisa closed her eyes and imagined the sperm swimming hard up to her uterus and her egg rolling down strong to meet it in the fallopian tubes. She was a tree with ripe fruit, peaches, apricots. She was fertile. After Dr. M. left, and despite reassurance that it would make no difference, she remained on her back with her legs up in the air for twenty minutes.

Janet was cautious about becoming invested at this stage—she'd prepared herself for a lengthy process. When Lisa insisted that she'd conceived immediately, Janet dismissed the claim as justifiable, albeit mistaken, enthusiasm and went about her days nonplussed. They would discover that Lisa was correct two weeks later when they returned to the clinic for blood work. The doctor's confirmation would, after so many abstract, hypothetical conversations about having children, strike Janet as wonderfully concrete. Her chest would swell and a wish, as fine and untouched as a blank canvas, would rise up.

§ § §

I packed all my belongings in a single bag and left the shelter. I doubled up my clothes so I was wearing two layers under my winter coat, which saved me from carrying too much and left my arms free—important when you're wandering the streets alone. Got to be ready for anything. I used up my daily government money to pay for the streetcar; it was too damn cold to walk. Guess I wouldn't be buying any smokes.

That day it was colder than any other I could remember. Colder than when Momma was buried or when Jimmy was sent up to jail in Penetang. Colder than the first winter I had spent wondering who was mothering my little Christopher, or if he survived me. I had the sweats though, water pouring down my sides, under my arms, like a strange fever had come on. When I stood at the corner waiting on the streetcar my face was flushed from heat but my short hair froze to my scalp.

The streetcar turned south on Broadview and ran west along Queen. I watched Regent Park creak by, my old stomping ground, and clenched my jaw. They say government housing is better than no housing, they do, but none of them's ever lived in a place anywhere near to that hole. I don't care what fancy educated lady wants to tell me different; even when the drug running and the guns aren't a problem, opportunities are cut down like trees. No child growing up in those projects escapes getting pinned as going nowhere fast. Teachers pin him. Neighbours pin him. Even the poor little bastard comes to stain himself with hopelessness. I sat back in my seat, stretched my cold, swollen feet in my boots, and when we angled up the road a bit farther and left all that madness behind, I grinned silly.

I got off at City Hall. Had the idea of marching straight up the cement walkway, straight on inside to where the squat little mayor sat, and demand he take me off that goddamned housing list once and for all. It was a joke; making us wait three, four, five years for a home we could hardly afford and didn't want, and when we did manage it, stacking us like dominoes into tiny brick ghettos, jamming us together with all our crack and booze and hustling, until there's nothing else and no way to see beyond. Why did I want to be on that list, waiting desperate, when I could cut loose and at least hold my dignity? Was no way I was having my baby in a shelter or in one of those infested boxes they called subsidized apartments. Making the whole thing start over again, making another me. No thank you.

Children were bundled in their winter coats and hats and gloves, skating on the rink at Nathan Phillips Square. They laughed and fell over on wobbly ankles, got up again and chased each other, inhaling thin needles of ice and loving it, I could tell. The parents of the youngest ones shouted encouragement and waved from the sidelines. A few even laced up and went skating themselves. I've never been on a pair of ice skates. Can't imagine I'd be good at balancing, trying to move without falling over on my ass. No, I don't imagine I would be any good at that.

I smelled the strong odour of grease from the hamburger and french fry truck mixed with the sweet, watery smell of hot chocolate with miniature marshmallows, and I wanted to toss my lunch.

§ § §

Nine week Obstetrical Ultrasound.

Lisa and Janet held hands while Dr. M. interpreted the ultrasound report for them:

Gestational age:	8 weeks.
Gestation:	single, intrauterine.
Yolk sac:	0.78cm
Gestational sac:	1.06cm
Crown Rump Length:	0.2cm
Foetal Heart Beat:	Yes. 109 bpm.

The pregnancy was viable, the technician had registered a heartbeat, but the embryo appeared to be only eight weeks when it should have been developed to nine. Lisa had a fifty-fifty chance of miscarrying. "There's nothing to do but wait and see," said Dr. M. marking an X through the report with his pen. "Women over thirty-five. You know the stats."

That night Lisa dreamt of death, of Janet's and of her own. She woke the next morning, after Janet had left for the shelter, and called in sick to work. Her class would just have to make-do with a substitute. She returned to bed and lay with her hands crossed over her belly, trying to visualize the heartbeat, her second one. She conjured positive words to teach the life inside that it was wanted. She walked around talking to herself, to the embryo, though she knew it was only the size of her longest eyelash. She ate canned plums because her grandmother had said that plums, with their red fleshy meat, were good for fertility. Within a week of receiving the ultrasound Lisa had told the guppy floating inside of her that they each had to pull their weight, that it was up to them both now. She ran all the yellow lights along Bloor Street when driving to school, as if tempting fate was taking back control. You want to defeat me, she thought. You want what's mine? Catch me first.

Janet took the phone calls and warned the few friends and family members they'd prematurely told of the pregnancy. She chastised herself for not having followed her instinct, which was to wait until they were clear of the first trimester before sharing the news with anyone. But it had been exciting and had simply pressed out of them uncontrollably. If something did go wrong, Lisa had said, it would be good to have support. Now, Lisa had begun to spot blood and Janet was sure she was watching the beginning of the end. She kept this sentiment to herself.

Janet didn't understand how Lisa could stand not knowing whether the baby had ceased growing, whether its heartbeat was waning. The thought of Lisa carrying death around inside gave Janet a sinister feeling, and she avoided Lisa at home, avoided touching her as they squeezed past one another in the bathroom to brush their teeth before bed and in the kitchen when making meals. They no longer made love. Janet moved through those interminable weeks leading up to the second ultrasound in a slow motion daze. Routine daily life became absurd, grotesque. Women on the sidewalk with pregnant bellies and baby strollers jumped out at her from every corner like strange advancing and retreating clowns. She felt as though she were trapped inside the Salvador Dali reproduction hanging in the office at the shelter. Dr. M's last words rang in her ears like funeral bells. "I don't mean to be gruesome," he'd said. "But I want to reassure you. If it happens, you won't see body parts."

§ § §

I sat on a cement bench to gather my thoughts. My ass was numb. My stomach rolled and complained. I could feel all six pounds shifting inside my belly—I'd done it again. Got myself knocked up. Seemed any man so much as even gawked at me and I was pregnant. Before long people at the rink were packing up their children, frozen and tired, and workers were funnelling out of City Hall. The rink lights came on, all different colours. Against the grey-white backdrop of the evening sky and the pale grey concrete and ice, I must've looked to God like nothing but a tiny speck of dirt.

It was close to ten when I took myself around the side of the building, searching out somewhere to hide and be safe while the pains tore through me. I felt like a dog who'd been hit by a car and was hunting for a quiet place by the side of the road to curl up and die. I didn't remember it hurting so bad with Christopher. I buckled onto my knees on the hard grey concrete near an empty staircase. Nobody saw or heard. The concrete was terrible cold. I pulled the only blanket I had, a pink one I'd nabbed from the shelter's donations room, and rolled myself onto it. I loosened my buttons and zippers, and slid out of my two pairs of pants but not my coat.

I rolled around on the hard ground, breathing and heaving

and trying not to push. What in hell I was I gonna do? I couldn't have the baby; I wasn't ready. We didn't have a place to live and my money was all gone. Plus, even though I'd known in some ways—when I could admit it to myself—that I was carrying again, in other ways I swear on my own sweet Momma's grave, I didn't know it. Couldn't accept it. Those months leading up to my leaving the shelter were like a watery vision, a dream you want to wake from but don't. At fortysomething, I was too old for baby-making, wasn't I? I hadn't visited any doctor, unless you count the shrink who prescribed my meds, and he never asked why I was growing bigger, must've thought I was bloating out on the pills like the others. I guess I figured that if a doctor don't see it, and the staff at the shelter don't notice it, maybe it simply ain't there. So, like I said, I knew but I didn't, and that's the way it was, right up until she ripped out of me and slid onto that dirty pink blanket on the concrete like a shiny wet plum slipping from its skin.

She let out a high-pitched wail, but I didn't touch her, except for reaching down and digging through the sticky umbilical cord with my thumbnail until we were separated. I knew she didn't want me any more than Christopher had and touching her would've left me imprinted on her skin for good. Better she make it on her own or not at all. I lay there another few minutes, maybe five or ten, I couldn't say, and pushed some more until the guts came pouring out of me. Once the cramps faded I rolled away, stood upright, and stuffed myself back into all those layers. Blood ran from me like a faucet and I smelled sour and tangy. When I wiped my nose, my hand smeared fresh red blood across my cheek. I walked away and then I ran as fast as I could into the city night, and I gave no more thought to her. She was done with me. She was clean clear of me and living on her own now. Lucky her.

§ § §

Lisa walked west along Queen Street looking in decorated

store windows. When her hands and toes grew cold, she decided to continue on to the Eaton Centre a few blocks away. She hurried along the slushy sidewalk, past University Avenue and City Hall, where children were skating. Inside the mall, she tried to distract herself by scanning the sales racks for new winter clothes. She had made it three more weeks, almost to the critical twelve week threshold, and each approaching hour made her more anxious. Time was no longer an intangible with endless possibilities stretching out ahead, it was something she dreaded, a unit of measurement she wished she could reach out and clasp in her fist, like a firefly, and seal away in a jar. The foetus was fully formed though small.

Lisa soon lost herself in the noise of the crowds and the dizzying reds and greens and golds of the holiday displays. When she passed the food court on the bottom level of the mall she smelled smoked meats and grease, odours that had begun to render her nauseous. She desperately wanted a can of pop but instead sat on a bench and ate a single scoop of vanilla ice cream, reassured that ice cream counted as one helping of dairy and dairy was good for the baby. When she was done, she stood and felt pain rip across her lower abdomen. The pain was sharp, like teeth biting down. She scanned the mall for a public washroom.

Lisa leaned forward on the toilet and held her abdomen. She breathed heavily, but made no noise—others using the washroom might think she was doing something strange in the cubicle, like vomiting or masturbating. When she pulled down her underwear she saw that she'd begun to bleed. She tried not to be alarmed or jump to conclusions. After all, spotting during early pregnancy wasn't necessarily a sign of miscarriage, and the blood on her white cotton underpants was faint and brown. She would not allow herself to consider the possibility of loss. She would refuse. If she sat motionless, the baby would settle and her cramps would cease. Maybe if she prayed, bargained with a god she was no longer sure she believed in. If only she could wish it away. But the longer she sat—and she couldn't rise anymore because the contractions were severe—the heavier and redder the flow became. Finally, she gasped.

"Excuse me," said a woman in the adjacent stall. "Are you all right in there?"

Lisa stared at the bright red blood in the toilet bowl.

"I'm fine. Just having bad cramps."

"Oh, mine are bad too," said the woman. "Take two Advil, that always helps."

"I will. Thank you."

After a moment the woman flushed her toilet, moved to run water at the sink, activated the hand dryer, and squished across the tile floor in wet boots. Lisa was by herself again, more alone than she'd ever known was possible.

Later, Lisa wished that she could have answered all of Janet's questions accurately, described what it had felt like, and what she'd witnessed laying in the toilet bowl between her legs. She would've liked to say that she'd thought of Janet because it was their shared experience, a shared loss. But she could not. This loss was hers alone and she knew it.

What she remembers, she remembers vividly: the blood streaming down between her legs in a pulsing fashion, painting the white bowl in a surprisingly beautiful display. The tissue floating, softly as air, and each new fold pushing out to the rhythm of the cramps, to the contractions of her cervix.

Lisa hadn't wanted to read about miscarriage in advance and she hadn't, believing that the mere thought could provoke one. But Janet, she knew, had been reading everything she could lay her hands on, as if the more knowledge she acquired, the better armed she would be. Once, Janet had left a book face down on the kitchen table and Lisa had absent-mindedly turned it over while eating her breakfast. Her eyes had scanned the page and locked onto a sentence explaining that for many women miscarriage began and ended fast, but for others the bleeding continued for days, even weeks, leaving a partially expelled gestational sac and embryo inside the mother.

In the washroom stall she tried to picture it, the heartbeat, and that's when she felt a mass pressing out between her legs, not very big, not solid like a stone, but firm enough and heavy enough to push out of her all at once, intact, and to cause a plopping sound when it hit the water. She gazed down and there it was: purple, black, and deep, deep red, the membrane, diaphanous as chiffon, waving. She tried to discern a shape and found the loose outline of a miniature alien figure, more shadow than definition—paddles, head, giant eye sockets. She wanted to touch it, feel what she'd made, almost made. She forced herself to reach down into the water, afraid of having the sensation it left permanently stuck to her fingertips, and gently poked a flattened plum mass, the tiny insurmountable hill. All at once the automatic toilet bowl flushed and before she could say goodbye, her baby—or the rudimentary parts that would have been her baby—were swept away for good.

"I wasn't ready," Lisa told Janet when she got home and burst into tears on the couch. Janet had thought she meant the miscarriage, but Lisa had meant that she wasn't ready to be one of those women who are marked as barren or broken, or simply unnatural. She wasn't ready to be powerless. If it had been up to her, she would've sat there all afternoon, watched it, stroked it, tried to get to know it a little and then in her own good time, let it go.

Elizabeth Ruth

Elizabeth Ruth's debut novel, *Ten Good Seconds of Silence*, was published in 2001 and named a finalist for the Rogers Writers' Trust of Canada Fiction Prize, the Amazon.ca/Books in Canada First Novel Award, and the City of Toronto Book Award. In 2005, her second novel, *Smoke*, was published to critical acclaim. Elizabeth Ruth was the founder and curator of Clit Lit, a monthly queer literary series that ran from 1998 to 2002. Over 400 writers read at the series, and in 2002 Elizabeth compiled and edited some of their most memorable pieces for an anthology entitled, *Bent On Writing: contemporary queer tales*. Elizabeth Ruth teaches creative writing at the University of Toronto. She may be reached via www.elizabeth ruth.com.

Karen X. Tulchinsky
Writer Notes

Place

Everything we experience informs an artist's work. "Write what you know," we tell emerging writers. What we know is a mixture of personal and collective experience, history, and collective unconscious. I grew up in Toronto and moved to Vancouver where I now live. Most of my work has been set in Toronto and San Francisco, a place I have only visited but adore. I am most comfortable on the west coast, where I can smell the salt of the ocean, feel the pull of the tides, and experience greenery all year round. The rhythms of the place are slower than in the east. It's interesting that the place I left, Toronto, features most prominently (to date) in my writing. Sometimes it's easier to evoke a place when you are not actually living there.

Living in Canada completely informs my work, especially since much of my work is set in the United States. Whether we honour our national cultural identity or not, it is crucial to our well-being to see reflections of our lives in fiction. Canada is inundated with books, films, and television from the US, which distorts our identity and is hard for Canadian writers to compete with. If you walk into a bookstore in the US, I'd guess that ninety-nine percent of the books on the shelf are homegrown, whereas if you walk into a Canadian bookstore, it's a miracle if ten percent of the books on the shelf are written by Canadian authors.

Identity

Being a lesbian and part of the queer community shapes the content of my writing as much as being a Jew and part of the Jewish community does, as does my experience in a biracial relationship, as does my identity as a butch dyke. I don't know if there is a discernable lesbian voice or perspective.

Certainly, there is a distinct queer point of view—that of the outsider, because of who we love, which is different than being an outsider because of your race or heritage. For example, as a Jew, I am outside dominant WASP culture (i.e. Christmas and other statutory holidays that are Christian-based), but this experience doesn't separate me from my parents or sisters. Being Jewish bonds me more closely to my family. My outside of the "norm" experience as a lesbian bonds me to my friends in the queer community but separates me from my blood family. I write about this—sometimes in all its tragedy, other times in all its comedy.

Creative Process

It's more mysterious than we like to think. Although most of my previous work has been set in the gay and lesbian community (I'm one of the lesbian writers who writes about gay *men* as well as gay women), my latest book, *The Five Books of Moses Lapinsky*, is set in the 1930s and 40s in Toronto's Jewish community. The main character is a boy who grows up to become a world champion boxer. In the book, I wrote extensively about boxing, war, and violence amongst men. There are few female characters in my book, and those who are there are strong, but in the background. This was not intentional. Sometimes a book and its characters will lead the way, and there's nothing the writer can do but follow. Sonny Lapinsky, my main character, emerged as a boxer. In early drafts I fought this idea, simply because I knew nothing about boxing, and what I did know, I didn't approve of or enjoy. But my character would not back down. He needed to be a boxer no matter what I thought of it. So I gave in, and conducted extensive research on boxing and soldiers in the Canadian Armed Forces during World War II, so that I could write about these boys and men. It was an amazing experience, both personally and as an artist, to push myself to explore the world of men.

Audience

My first audience has been the lesbian, and then gay, bisexual, and trans communities, and our allies. My second audience has been the Jewish community. With my latest book, my audience has broadened. All Canadians, except for First Nations people, came here from somewhere else, either recently or generations ago. The immigrant experience is vast in Canada. I have had an amazing response to *The Five Books of Moses Lapinsky* from a diverse audience who have gone on to discover my earlier books set in the queer community. I wish I could say that lesbian writers are shaping Canadian fiction in spite of homophobia, but I don't really think there are very many out lesbian writers who are writing about the queer experience. I know that I will continue to write about the life I see before me, and that other times I will be drawn into writing about experiences I have not had, and be led by my story and my characters into territory both known and unfamiliar.

Karen X. Tulchinsky
Ruined by Love

The sun is desperately trying to burn off a cold, grey fog that settled over the beauty of San Francisco early this morning. The sky is pale grey and wet. The usual bright purple, red and orange of the flowering shrubs are vague and shrouded by the thick fog. The air is humid and damp. I'm rushing around my best friend Betty's one bedroom flat on the top floor of a modest house in Bernal Heights, madly stuffing the last of my things into the huge duffle bag I borrowed from another friend, Chester. This is no ordinary packing job. This is for real. It's breaking my heart to say this, but I'm leaving San Francisco.

At least I'm not getting thrown out, deported by the immigration department, as I have feared for the last three years. I've somehow managed to elude them, working under the table at a neighbourhood pub called Patty's Place, as the best damned bartender Patty's ever had. You can't get a green card to be a bartender. To legally work in the US you have to have a skill that nobody who already lives here has. Pretty much anyone can bartend, as long as you can take the pressure. I got the job because Patty is also an expat Canadian and she felt a kinship with me when she heard I couldn't find a job and wanted to stay. No, it's not because I got caught working under the table that I'm going. I'm leaving of my own free will. I guess you could call it that. I'm leaving for love. And free will sometimes gets a bit mucked up when love is involved. That's been my experience anyway.

"That's mine," Betty grabs from my grasp, a small black comb I got free from the Osento Bathhouse for Women.

"Pretty sure this one is mine," I counter, snatching it back. "See?" I show her a broken tooth at one end of the comb.

She studies it closely, then relents, hands it back. Betty is far too fussy to hang onto a comb with a broken tooth.

Especially a comb you can get free just for having a sauna at Osento. Betty's been in a bad mood ever since I broke the news to her that I'm returning to Canada. My long distance lover Julie and I are tired of the distance. We met eighteen months ago, when I travelled to Toronto for my mother's wedding. Since then, Julie has been in Toronto, where she works at the Asian Community AIDS Service. I've been back here in San Francisco, tending bar at Patty's, and having my usual interesting life the rest of the time, living with Betty.

We're a pretty interesting combo as roomies—Betty and I. Originally from Philadelphia, Betty drives a van for SuperShuttle, but really she's a poet and (lately) a political activist. A few years ago she cut off her dreadlocks, shaved her head right down to the scalp. But recently, she decided to grow her hair. It looks pretty cute right now—tight little black curls, close to her scalp—but then, everything looks good on Betty.

I'm Jewish and Canadian and not nearly as cute if you ask me—but I have had some good reviews from some of the girls I've dated. I would never shave my head right down to the scalp. Too scared I'd look like an alien I guess, but my hair is pretty short. Brown, a quarter inch long. I keep the bangs a bit longer, but only because I'm insecure. I'm not as butch as some of my friends, but I do get called "sir" a lot, in stores and restaurants. I'm not sure what you'd call my style. Maybe lesbo-hip-hop-retro-punk-butch. Is that a category?

I don't recommend long distance relationships, like the one I'm having with Julie. The long distance phone bills alone will kill you. And if that doesn't get you, the intensity will. It's kind of exciting really—the ups and downs. But the downs can be a little too low and the ups are sometimes so manic they fool you. It's like having a pretend relationship, like you're forever on a first date, on your best behavior to make a good impression, but you never get to really relax. It takes a lot longer for the hard issues to surface. Julie and I only see each other once every two months for a weekend, or if we're lucky, a week. Then it's goodbye and back to the phones for a while. When we're together, there's not much point in fighting, because our time together is so precious, why waste any of it being in a bad space?

It was Julie's idea to move to Vancouver. We'd gone back and forth, been over every possibility. Should she move to San Francisco? Too hard. Then we'd both be illegal aliens. Should I move to Toronto? Could, but after three years on the west coast, I'm pretty much set on leaving winter behind. We were at a stalemate for a while, then she got offered a job in Vancouver and everything fell suddenly into place.

It was one of those life-changing phone calls that was over before I had a chance to realize what I'd done. It went something like this:

"Nomi I miss you."

"I miss you too."

There was a beat of silence. I think she was smiling a huge smile. "Well, you're not going to have to anymore."

"Really?"

"I've been offered a job. Program coordinator for AIDS Vancouver. Isn't that great?"

"Wonderful." I felt so proud of her. Sounded like a big important job, the kind you have to dress up for, carry a cellphone and a laptop, attend board meetings and liaise with the media; nothing at all like my work—pouring draft and mixing margaritas, cleaning ashtrays and sweeping peanut shells from an old hardwood floor. Cashing out at the end of the night and hoping like hell that everything balances and I've made a few bucks in tips.

"It starts in two weeks," Julie was saying. "We can stay with Josh and George. You remember I mentioned them? It'll take us a month at least to find a place."

I just about dropped the phone. Josh and George. Vancouver. Right. We'd talked about this. Our previous phone call had been all about how hard it was to be apart. And as soon as Julie could get a job in Vancouver we'd both move there and set up house. Why did I feel so taken aback then? Like the air had just been sucked right out of me. My head felt light. I was having trouble breathing.

"Nomi?"

"Great." I managed.

Silence.

"What's wrong Nomi. I thought you'd be happy."

"Happy. Yes. I am. It just, took me by surprise is all. It's great."

"You don't want to live with me."

Just what I needed. Femme tricks over the phone. I could hear a quiver in her voice. Any second now the tears would flow and I'd end up the bad guy, the evil one, whose sole purpose in life was to hurt Julie. "Of course I want to live with you baby. We've been talking about it." I just didn't think it would be so soon. Was she right? Was I afraid to live with her? Or just sad to leave San Francisco? "It's great. It's really really great. Great. Great, great, great," I said over and over. Like a moron.

It's been three weeks since that call. Julie flew out to Vancouver a week ago and set up our temporary home in the extra bedroom at Josh and George's place. I was supposed to be there when Julie arrived, but Patty wasn't happy about me quitting so suddenly and kicked up a fuss. Patty's Place is a small pub on Cortland Avenue, up in Bernal Heights, a working-class neighbourhood, residential, with small bungalows, Irish pubs, single mothers, Asian and black families and lesbians. Patty is a collector of old memorabilia. She scours garage sales and flea markets for kitsch, then displays her finds in the pub. On the walls of Patty's Place there's a poster of Bette Midler when she was in *Jinxed*, one of Janet Jackson's earliest albums, an old wooden toilet seat, a No Parking sign, a 1988 gay freedom day t-shirt, a poster from Harvey Milk's 1977 bid for City Supervisor, a birdfeeder, cuckoo clock and her latest find, a boxing glove autographed by Mike Tyson (before he got into all that trouble for biting another boxer's ear off).

The clientele at Patty's place are mostly locals: lesbians, queens, trannys, bisexuals and straight retro-hippie dudes. There's an old long oak bar that runs the length, with stools. The cash register is from the 1920s. You punch in the amount and little paper numbers pop up—the height of technology at the time. It's beautiful and ornate and timeless. Patty serves free peanuts in the shell. People toss the shells on the floor as if this was the wild west and we didn't know any better. Patty is old-school butch, in her fifties, with short slicked-back hair, tough as nails but a total mush ball inside.

"Who the hell else am I going to get on such short notice?" Patty barked at me when I told her I had to quit.

"Lots of people would work for you Patty," I pointed out.

"Yeah, but I'd have to pay them more than I pay you," she grumbled.

"Thanks a lot."

"You sure you know what you're doing Rabinovitch?" She looked me straight in the eye.

"Course I do," I insisted, although the truth is, I haven't a clue. The last lover I lived with was Sapphire, the girl who dumped me for a guy, just before I met Julie. With Sapphire, it was always her way or the highway. I don't think Julie is like that. But you never really know until you live with a person. Especially femmes, who, let's face it, are generally hysterical. I've gotten kind of used to living with Betty. It's easy. We hardly ever fight. Neither of us is a neat freak or ridiculously messy. Our work hours are completely different so we don't need the shower at the same time and we both get plenty of time alone in the apartment. It's uncomplicated and we're used to it. I don't know what she's going to do without me.

Betty insisted on driving me at least as far as Sacramento, where I can catch a bus up the coast to Vancouver. When our other friends—Chester, a mild-mannered librarian in her mid-thirties, Patty, my boss, AJ, recently single, Gore-Tex and , fleece-wearing, nature loving lesbo, and Guido, leather clad motorcycle dyke—heard that Betty was driving me to Sacramento, they all decided to come for the ride. I have my own personal entourage out of the Bay Area. Looks like I'm going to need it. As much as I want to live with Julie, I'm sad to leave San Francisco. For the first time in my life I have community. I have friends. And the city itself has wedged itself deep in my heart. The bay, the hills, even the fog.

"You leave anything and I'm just going to toss it," Betty threatens as I struggle to close the zipper on the duffle bag.

"Why can't you mail it to me?"

"I'm remodelling after you go," she says.

"What?"

"A new look. Everything's going out the door. I'm painting and only bringing back in the essentials. It's like a cleansing. You know what they say Nomi. If you want new things in your life you gotta get rid of the old."

"Are you calling me old?" I am offended by her choice of words, and feel as expendable as an old broom you'd just toss out when it's time for a new one.

"Aren't you ready yet?" She slips into her leather jacket and waits by the door.

Chester arrives first, as usual. She hugs me, which is not usual. Then in her habitual manner, she smooths back her salt and pepper hair with one hand. Lately the salt has been taking over the pepper, but on Chester it looks good, in a Richard Gere kind of way. It makes her look distinguished and responsible. Like someone you'd trust with your tax return. Or your daughter. On the street, two young guys in loose pants, slung way below their butts, walk by with a huge boom box, blaring rap. Another man shouts something in Spanish. The fog is beginning to burn off. It might turn out to be a nice day.

"Here Nomi, I brought you a present." Chester hands me a tiny American flag.

"What would I want this for?"

"You can hang it at your new place."

"I'm not so sure an American flag's gonna go over big in Vancouver," Betty, who is more politically astute, suggests.

Chester looks crushed.

"It's great," I lie and jam it in the front pocket of my bag.

"Why wouldn't it go over big?" Chester is completely clued out.

Betty snorts. "Because everyone outside of America knows that George W. Bush is nothing short of a war criminal. That his pre-emptive strike on Iraq is no more justified than Hitler's invasion of Poland, that Homeland Security is a euphemism for 'now we can do whatever the fuck we want to anyone who disagrees with us.' And if the national export of Iraq had been broccoli instead of oil, the Republicans could give a fuck about the oppression of the Iraqi people."

"Wow," says Chester, "don't they eat broccoli in Iraq?"

Betty just stares at Chester. Where would she start?

Betty became political only recently. Last month she dated Kiesha Valdarez, director of the Bay Area State Committee on International Human Rights. Betty was so taken with Kiesha that, at first, she faked her political commitment (just to get her into bed) but the more Betty hung around Kiesha's crowd, the more enlightened she became. Now, they're just friends, but Betty's commitment has remained. Right now, she's trying to get signatures on a petition to recall Governor Arnold Schwarzenegger.

There is a horrifying racket outside, sounding like a broken chainsaw cutting through thick metal. Chester opens the door and we see Guido ride up on her reconditioned Harley. She picked it up from the *Buy & Sell* for a thousand bucks. You can imagine what terrible shape it's in—a Harley for that price. Right now, it's being held together by paper clips and duct tape but Guido swears she's been fixing it up. Guido's been offering rides, but everyone keeps turning her down, afraid the damn thing's going to fall apart when she turns a corner. We watch, as with great butch gusto, she adjusts her leather jacket and swings her leg to the pavement, smoothing her leather chaps into place. Guido's under five feet tall, but she's got moxie. She's the smallest, toughest butch in town. Rather than come inside, she stands out on the sidewalk admiring her bike, polishing the chrome with her red bandana.

A bus stops a block past Betty's and AJ hops off, out of breath, her red fleece sweatshirt inside-out.

"Sorry I'm late. I was worried I'd miss you guys." AJ yells as she rushes toward us.

"Let's hit the road," Betty grabs my duffle bag and walks down the porch steps to the van. Chester was going to drive her Honda Civic, but since everyone's coming, Betty's taking her work van. Betty is a SuperShuttle driver, taxiing a ten-seat passenger van from the airport and back all day long. She's supposed to be working right now, but she struck a deal with the dispatcher to conveniently forget about her for a while, so she can drive us to Sacramento. Just in case anyone spots us, she's wearing her uniform—black pants, crisp white shirt, tie, and SuperShuttle windbreaker. We're pretending to be customers, asking Betty to carry my bags and for information on tourist attractions. Betty, of course, is ignoring us.

"Patty's not here yet," I point out. Betty's in the driver's seat. I ride shotgun. Guido, AJ, and Chester jump in the back.

"We're picking her up at the pub." Betty puts the van in gear and makes a tight three-point turn, driving up over the sidewalk, scraping the muffler, with a loud crunching, screeching sound.

Patty's waiting for us outside. She marches up, opens the passenger door.

"Get out Rabinovitch. That's my seat," Patty barks.

Used to taking orders from her, I obey, I slide out of the front seat and ducking my head, scoot all the way to the back of the van, beside AJ.

Betty points the vehicle in the direction of the Bay Bridge.

"Shouldn't we have a ritual or something? To send Nomi back to Canada." AJ asks. Ever since AJ's long-term lover Martha broke up with her, AJ's been clinging to one crutch or another to get through. Right now, she's joined a coven of Wiccans. Those girls have rituals for everything.

"You're not burning any sage grass in the van," Betty yells. "They'll think I've been smoking pot."

"Maybe we should just tie Nomi up and refuse to let her leave," Guido suggests.

"She'll just escape," Chester points out.

"I mean a ritual to say goodbye." AJ says. "We could go around the room and everyone says a little something to Nomi."

"You could stuff your ritual in your sage grass pouch," Patty tells AJ. "I ain't participating in any witchy woo crap. Besides, we're in a van, not a room."

"You don't have to be unpleasant," AJ snaps back.

"I'm too old to change," Patty counters. Patty's not really too old to change. She's fifty-five, maybe fifty-six. There's still time to change. She just thinks she's too old.

Betty turns on the stereo, finds a hip hop station, and cranks the volume. On the highway with the windows rolled down, wind rushing in, and the music blaring, no one talks. Traffic is heavy, drivers are aggressive but Betty drives for a living. She could do it in her sleep. She barely notices when the SUV in front of us slams on his brakes and stops in the middle of the bridge. Betty just hits the brakes purposefully and scoots into the next lane, nice and easy, like she was planning it all along. She ignores it when the guy in the Hummer beside us gives her the finger.

Driving down Interstate 80, we're all in our own little bubble, watching the city disappear behind us. On the Bay Bridge, I turn to look out the back window. My heart sinks. I'm happy to be embarking on this new adventure in my life, thrilled that a woman like Julie loves me, but San Francisco gets under your skin. It's the beauty of the place: deep red bottlebrush trees along sidewalks; vibrant purple wisterias climbing up the sides of Victorian houses, which are painted lovingly in complementary colours; giant white bearded irises; rambling rose bushes; the scent of seawater and wind. One of the most tolerant cities on earth, where a transgendered guy can get a decent job, gay couples can hold hands in the streets, SM dykes can stroll down the Castro in full leathers, and diversity is the norm. My heart is splitting in two at the sight of the city growing smaller. I wonder when I'll be back. And know that when I do come back, nothing will be the same. Everything will be different. I won't be a person who lives here anymore.

We get to Sacramento in record time. The temperature is five degrees hotter, but with the sun blazing down, and being inland and away from the ocean breeze, it feels thirty degrees hotter. We all strip down to tank tops. Betty pulls over beside a pub, "Let's go get a drink. One for the road. To send Nomi off properly."

Inside the pub, Betty orders me a vodka martini. Everyone else copies her. Not our usual drink. We mostly drink beer. But this is a special occasion. While we wait for our drinks, Betty looks around.

"Are we already in Canada?" She seems uneasy.

"What do you mean?" I ask.

"No black people. Look around."

She's right. Other than Betty, everyone in the pub is white. "Should we go?" I make a move to get up.

Betty shrugs. "Not like I ain't been here before. It's cool. Just weird."

"So what the hell are you going to do in Canada, Rabinovitch?" Patty asks as the waiter returns with our drinks. "Work in a bar?"

"Could, but I think I'll try something else."

"What else are you qualified for?" AJ asks.

Good question and one that depresses the hell out of me. Not much, is the answer. Before I moved to San Francisco and got the job at Patty's, I was a bicycle courier in Toronto. You can make good money once you get fast enough, and you stay in great shape, but it would be great to work with my mind instead of my hands.

"Maybe you should go back to school." Chester suggests. She should know. She went back to school part time last year to upgrade her skills. She'd been a librarian for years. There's a limit to how much money a librarian can make. Now she's developing education programs for the City, getting paid a decent buck. She's always trying to get the rest of us to go back to school. It's worked out so well for her.

"Yeah." I don't know. I was never really a good student. "But gotta get a job first. Can't let Julie support both of us."

"Yeah," agrees Guido, "you know what happens if you let your femme support you." She shakes her head at the horrifying thought. "No sex."

"Says who?" AJ doesn't like this because it's true. She was with Martha for twelve years. A chartered accountant, Martha always made at least twice as much money as AJ and they hardly ever had sex.

"It's a rule. Look it up," Guido insists, taking a big slug of her martini. "Think I like Scotch better."

Betty declines, since she's driving, but everyone else follows Guido's lead and tries a Scotch next.

On the way to the washroom, I figure I should call Julie. I stop by the pay phone.

"Nomi." She sounds so happy to hear from me. "Where are you? I miss you."

"Uh, Sacramento."

"What? I thought you'd be closer by now." The disappointment is clear in her voice. "Josh and George are making dinner. A Welcome to Vancouver Dinner."

"Tonight? We'll never make it by tonight. Even if I jumped

right on a bus, from here, by bus it's about twenty-four hours."

"You have to get here tonight Nomi. The party's for you. I thought you were leaving first thing in the morning."

"Took a bit longer. Betty and the gang drove me this far, to Sacramento. I'm heading to the bus station after this."

"Don't be late Nomi, please. What am I going to tell Josh and George? They're being so nice, letting us stay here."

"Okay, don't worry. I'll be there." What am I nuts? It's impossible. But Julie has that effect on me. Anything she wants is all hers. I'm completely powerless to be sensible when Julie's in the picture. We kiss over the phone. I hang up and return to my table. Someone's ordered a second round of Scotch. Betty's sipping a Saratoga cream soda.

"Let's go," I say. "I just promised Julie I'd be in Vancouver by dinner."

"Are you crazy!" Betty stares at me like I'm insane. Which is probably the truth.

"Couldn't be helped. Come on. You have to drive me further. I'll never make it on the bus. Drink up." Miraculously, everyone obeys and downs their drink.

"I gotta get the van back Nom. I can't be driving you all the way to fucking Canada." Betty screams.

"Just to Oregon. I'll get the bus from there."

"For fuck's sake," Betty says, but she grabs her wallet and dashes outside anyway and has the van started up by the time the rest of us pile in.

"Cool," says Guido, "I didn't want to go to work tonight anyway." Guido's working as a bouncer at The Lumberjack, a popular fag bar. You wouldn't think to look at her five-foot frame that she'd be much of a bouncer, but Guido is strong and, more importantly, she's got the psychology all worked out. There's never any problems on her shift, so smooth is she at talking down the crazies. "It's military night. Can't stand the sight of all those fags in army fatigues."

"We'll be back by morning?" Chester took the day off, but needs to work tomorrow.

"Damn right we will," Betty says, as she squeals out of the parking lot and heads back toward the highway.

The drive from Sacramento is reasonably smooth, as we head north into the mountainous terrain of northern California. Until we have to stop for gas. Betty pulls up to the self-serve pump. Guido pumps the gas, while the rest of us hit the restroom, five butch dykes from San Francisco, dressed in a combination of leather, denim and T-shirts, short hair, and shaved heads. I guess to the store clerk we look like teenage boys, out for trouble. He grabs a baseball bat and leaps out from behind the cash to prevent us from entering the ladies room.

"Whoa, down boy." Betty tries, but you see in the clerk's face that he's a redneck racist and if anyone's going to feel the brunt of his bat first, it's going to be Betty. I step in front of her.

"Can I help you sir?" I ask politely.

He looks a bit confused at the sound of my voice, but I can see his eye registering something. Maybe he thinks I'm a *younger* teenaged boy than he originally thought. "That's the ladies room," he manages.

I lower my voice and lean in. "Sir, we don't want any trouble. We just need to pee."

"And we're not boys," AJ adds.

The clerk stares at each of us, in turn, trying to decipher this last bit of information. "You're girls?"

"Women, actually," Chester clarifies.

This new information seems to have diffused our foe enough that, one by one, we slip into the bathroom. I don't think it's a good idea to leave Guido all alone outside, so I wait with her until the others are back in the van.

"That's why I never leave the city," Betty says, back inside the safety of the van. "You see the look in his eye?"

"It's even worse in Oregon," I say. "It's pretty much a Bush-loving wasteland from Sacramento all the way to Portland. If we go much further, we should buy a porta-potty."

"That's right Rabinovitch, but we're dropping you at the border to Oregon, then we're going home."

feeling
(freeloaded

"Fine by me," I say, although I'm hoping they'll take me further.

At the Oregon border, Betty pulls over. It's kind of deserted. There's a ranch on one side of the highway, horses grazing on an open field of brown grass and hydro power lines on the other. Nothing much else as far as the eye can see except highway, cars and fields. I stare at Betty. She's not really going to dump me here, is she?

"Well Nom, guess this is it," Betty says solemnly.

"Yep," Guido agrees. "That's the border."

"About time. I'm getting sick of driving," Patty complains.

"Getting hungry too," AJ adds.

I'm a little scared, but it's what we agreed to. I grab my duffle bag and hop out. "Well, thanks guys. Guess I'll be seeing you." I must look completely pathetic. A lone dyke standing by the side of the road with my duffle bag. I'm hoping they'll reconsider, but they just wave and drive off. And I'm alone. Nothing but cars speeding by, while I stand on the gravel shoulder of the Interstate 5.

What a stupid plan, I realize suddenly. Should have at least gotten a ride to the bus station. Nobody picks up hitchhikers these days. Nobody except for serial killers. I can either walk to Vancouver and get there in about a week. Or stick out my thumb and end up in a car with a psychopath. He'll take me to some deserted shack in the back hills of Oregon and murder me, after sodomizing me for three days, probably after first jailing me in a hand-dug cellar with nothing to eat but water and whatever bugs I can catch. On the walls I'll see names scratched into the dirt by fingernails. Candy was raped here. Or Bobby died here in 98.

No one but Julie will miss me. And she'll be furious that I didn't make my Welcome to Vancouver Dinner party. Then she'll swear to break up with me if I ever turn up alive. But when I haven't arrived for two days, she'll call the police. And first my picture will end up on milk cartons: *Missing: 30-some-thing butch dyke. Last seen by the side of the road in Oregon.* Later my body will be found in a dumpster outside a 7-11 in Portland, and a whole team of forensic scientists will be sent out to determine how I died. Betty will go nuts with the guilt and end up in a psychiatric institution. Patty will go on as before. She has no shame. Chester will start drinking heavily, AJ will join a cult, and Guido will be so messed up, she'll have a motorcycle accident and end up a quadriplegic. All of our lives will be in the toilet. These are the thoughts I am having when I am startled by the sound of a van pulling over behind me, its horn honking.

"Get in, you fool," Patty pokes her head out the window. I have the door open and my body inside the van in seconds.

"You think we'd really leave you in the middle of fucking nowhere?" Betty asks.

"You have to wonder," I say, so relieved I just sit on the floor behind Betty, and lean my head against the seat. "I was already on milk cartons," I say.

"See?" says Chester. "Told you it was a cruel joke. She's already gone round the bend."

"We were only gone five minutes," justifies Guido.

Felt like five hours.

"How far did you say Canada was?" Betty asks, hitting the accelerator a little bit harder.

"From here? About twelve hours. Ten if you drive real fast," I estimate.

"Then we'll burn rubber." Betty says and with a flourish, she steps even harder on the gas.

We make it to the border in just under eleven hours. There's a line up.

"Does everyone have ID?" I realize what we are about to do.

"Does a library card count?" Chester asks.

"Oh boy." I don't want to even guess what kind of treatment we are going to get at the border.

Forty-five minutes later, it's our turn to talk to the customs official. He leans his head to one side, trying to peer into the dark van. "Citizenship," he asks Betty, the driver.

"American." She answers.

"The rest?" he tries to see all of us.

"US, American, Yep, Landed immigrant, Canadian, " I say.

Our mixture does not sit well with the guard. He gets out of his booth and peers right inside the car. "Where you going?" he asks Betty. She looks at me.

"Vancouver," I answer.

"What for?"

"I'm moving, I live there." I catch myself.

"Well which is it?"

"I live there."

"Where?"

Oh shit. I don't even have an address. The plan was to call Julie when I get into town. "Main Street," I try. I know they have a Main Street.

"Whereabouts?"

"Broadway," I say, hoping like hell Broadway meets Main.

He seems satisfied. "What about the rest of you?"

"Just giving her a ride, sir."

He stares hard at Betty. "How long you planning on staying?"

"Few minutes." Betty says.

"Hours," Chester clarifies. "We'll probably have some dinner, then hit the road."

He thinks about it for a minute. "Please pull in over there and speak to the officials. " He hands a card with something scrawled on it to Betty. "Give them this."

"Shit," I say, as Betty pulls into the parking space outside the Canada Customs building.

"What?" Betty asks.

"This ain't good," Patty says. "Knew we shoulda left her in

Oregon." Patty shoots a look at me. Actually the only person who's done anything illegal is me. I lived in San Francisco for three years as an illegal alien. Everyone else is perfectly clean. Doesn't mean they won't be taken for a ride though. Customs officials have much more power than they ethically should.

Inside the building they question us each in great detail. Chester gets off relatively easy. Maybe it's the grey hair or the fact that she's a librarian and special educator for the City of San Francisco. AJ gets similar treatment, although the officer doesn't like the way AJ stutters. He thinks she's got something to hide. But really it's just nerves. They bend over backwards to be nice to Betty—the officer in charge, a white man, keeps talking about the diversity training he recently underwent and how everybody, regardless of race, gets treated the same on his watch. I bet deep down he's a complete racist and was forced to take the training or lose his job. The officer doesn't like Patty's story. She produces her green card, tells him she moved to San Francisco twenty-five years ago and owns her own place, a neighbourhood pub.

"You mean a gay bar?" He asks, somewhat antagonistically.

"Everyone is welcome," Patty says, very diplomatically for her.

They save me and Guido for the end, hustling the two of us into a private room,

"Strip," they tell Guido.

"Excuse me?"

"We think you might be hiding something. You heard the officer."

We stare at them, stunned. I think Guido has just confused them is all. If you didn't know better you'd swear Guido was a guy. She's not transitioning. She's not on hormones, has had no gender assignment surgery or anything. It's more of an attitude with Guido.

"I think we'd like to talk to a lawyer." I say. This can't be happening. Are they planning to rape us with their batons

after we've stripped? Or maybe they'll toss us in jail, call us terrorists and hold us for weeks before giving us access to legal
counsel, all in the name of National Security.

"It's okay," Guido says. She's holding it together but I can
hear the shakiness in her voice. "Let's just get this over with."

Then I look at the officers' uniforms and remember they
are with Canada Customs. Thankfully, Canada hasn't gone
nuts over national security the way America has. But if not
terrorists, then who do they think we are? I start unbuttoning
my shirt.

"Not you," the officer says. "We just have some questions
for you."

Guido quickly strips down to her boxer shorts and t-shirt.
The guards seem fascinated. "You wear men's underwear?"

"Is that illegal in Canada?" Guido is astonished.

"You can get dressed," the nicer of the two guards says.

"You." The meaner one points to me. "Come with us."

As they lead me off, I make eye contact with Guido. "I
think you better call me a lawyer."

"You don't need a lawyer." The nice guard says.

"Not yet anyway." The other adds.

They drag me into an interrogation room, make me sit on
a hard plastic chair, that has gum under the seat. They sit
opposite me in similar chairs, around a cheap folding, board
room table. They study my driver's license and birth certificate for a long moment. I wait, and worry about what will happen to me next.

"So you're moving to Vancouver?" The mean one asks.

"Yes. Well, I live there."

"Look, which is it?"

"I live there."

"Yeah, for how long?"

"Recently. I moved from Toronto." I lie.

"Look we're Canadians too. We're not going to turn you
over to the Americans." The nice guy starts.

"But we could. In fact, we should." The other guy leans

over the table menacingly. "You've been living in California, haven't you? As an illegal."

I say nothing.

"Are you planning to go back there?"

"I don't know what you're talking about."

He bangs the table with a fist. "We can just turn you in to the Americans. I can guarantee you, they won't be as kind."

"I'd like to speak to a lawyer." I repeat. I figure at this point, anything I say can and will be used against me in a court of law. I've seen enough cop shows. I know the score. So the less I say the better. I'm hoping I'm right about the lawyer thing. I'm thinking that they are required to allow me legal counsel if requested or their whole case would be thrown out. I have no idea if I'm right, but it's the only card I've got, so I keep playing it. "I'd like legal counsel present," I repeat.

The officers get up and go into the corner where they whisper to one another. I hear, "let her go," "not worth it," "my lunch break is in ten minutes." And "you're too soft on them." They stop whispering and return to the table, where they proceed to stare me down for five full minutes.

"Go on. Get outta here," the mean guy says.

I scramble to my feet.

"But you better watch your ass crossing the border in future." He glances at my ID, "Nomi Rabinovitch." He tosses back my ID. I'm outta there before they can change their minds and inside the van in seconds.

"Go," I scream to Betty. "Go. Hurry."

She hits the gas.

"Don't speed." I shout, worried now about everything.

It's when I look through the windshield and see the North Shore Mountains, illuminated by the ski lights, rising above Vancouver, that I realize I'm home. It hits me right in the middle of my belly. I've never lived in Vancouver before. San Francisco's felt like home for the last few years, and before that Toronto. I'm not sure if it's just relief over getting out of customs alive, or if it's a deeper spiritual connection to this new place. Or if I've just finally lost my mind from the strain. But the feeling begins in my belly and spreads. I am home.

"Okay," Betty says, "Where's Julie? We'll drop you off, and get the fuck outta Canada. Seems like they don't want us here anyway."

"Don't be crazy," I say. "You have to spend the night. As long as you're here."

Betty looks around the van at the others who seem to silently agree.

We pull up to a two-story heritage house with wraparound porch in the east end of Vancouver, just off Commercial Drive. Julie's sitting on the porch. When she sees the van, she runs out to us. I'm out the door and into her arms in a flash.

"Nomi," she kisses me all over. "You drove all the way?"

"Yeah. It just kinda happened." I kiss her back.

My friends wait patiently in the van. They know Julie and I haven't seen each other in over five weeks. We have a lot of kissing to catch up on.

Two men slip out of the house and wait behind Julie. She stops kissing me and turns to them. "Nomi, this is Josh and George." The guys surround me in a hug.

"We've heard everything about you. Every little thing."

"Come on inside. We'll start with an aperitif. And move on to the asparagus dip."

I turn my attention to my buddies. "Come on, you guys. Dinner."

They tumble out of the van and introductions are made. Josh and George gather us up—a motley crew of recently harassed dykes—and into the safety of their house. The sweet warmth of brandy slips down my throat, easing the last few hours, erasing the memory of the customs guards' unnecessary harassment. It feels strange to be here, in this new place, surrounded by my lover and my best friends. A deep pain begins to gnaw at my gut, because I know that in the morning, Betty and the gang will be hitting the road. It's only a sixteen-hour drive from Vancouver to San Francisco and I know I'll see my friends, but I won't be living with them. We won't be sharing our daily lives the way we have for the last few years. I'll be moving on. And the next time I see them, everything will be entirely different.

Betty sidles up beside me. "You're ruined," she says. "Aren't you?"

"Absolutely ruined," I agree.

"Here's to love," she holds her drink high and in the air we clink glasses.

"To love," I say to the room. I scan the faces, stop on Julie, who smiles at me. I'm here. We made it. Julie is a beautiful woman and she loves me. There is so much love in this room, it's almost hard to breathe. But I do. I take a deep breath, smile at Betty, and start getting ready for whatever happens next.

Karen X. Tulchinsky

Karen X. Tulchinsky is the award-winning author of *The Five Books of Moses Lapinsky*, which was a finalist for the Toronto Book Award and a Lambda Literary Award. *B. BookWorld* said of the novel, "Karen X. Tulchinsky does for Toronto what Mordecai Richler did for Montreal." Since its release, Tulchinsky has read from the novel across North America, and has appeared on *Imprint* for TV Ontario, CBC Radio's *Sounds Like Canada* with Shelagh Rogers, and *Writers and Company* with Eleanor Wachtel. Tulchinsky's screenplay adaptation of *The Five Books of Moses Lapinsky* was recently optioned by Ocular Productions and is currently in development with support from Telefilm Canada.

Tulchinsky is a recent graduate of the prestigious Canadian Film Centre, where she wrote two feature-length screenplays and a short film, *Straight in the Face*, which debuted at the Toronto International Film Festival. She wrote an episode of *Robson Arms*, a new drama series, for CTV and co-wrote *Floored by Love*, an episode for Citytv's anthology series, *Stories About Love*.

She is the author of *Love Ruins Everything*, which was named one of the top ten books of 1998 by the *Bay Area Reporter*, and *In her Nature* which won the VanCity Book Prize—BC's largest literary award. Karen X. Tulchinsky was born in Toronto, but makes her home in Vancouver, BC.

Marnie Woodrow
Writer Notes

Is the geography of where you live important to your writing? Are you interested in conferring literary status on a particular place?

My immediate geography, by which I mean my neighbourhood, my home environment, and my proximity to a body of water, is essential to my work. Places I've travelled to influence me even more.

I'm interested in having Canada recognized as a location for plot developments that are more exciting than a good snowstorm or feminist awakening. That said, writers are still fighting about whether it's "okay" to use the names of Canadian towns in fiction because [gasp] American readers might not recognize the name.

How does living in Canada inform your work?

In terms of what I write and how I express myself publicly, it frees me. I feel lucky to not live in an oppressive society where any of my published works and interview responses would have easily landed me in prison. In geographical terms, it has little real influence at this time, except that I live in one of the most expensive cities in the nation.

To what extent does being a lesbian or part of a queer community shape the content of your writing?

The only way in which I'm truly conscious of it at this stage in my life is when a young, queer person writes to me asking for advice about their creative dreams, or for help with an English assignment, which shows they are advancing the quality of this world by being themselves, too. That's when I know that it's important for me to continue mentioning that I identify as lesbian, even if my imagination is, of necessity, bisexual.

Is there a discernable lesbian voice, style, or perspective?

I really don't think so... unless you count the delayed first kiss technique used by so many of us in our fiction.

Are there particular queer writers whose work has moved or influenced you?

The queer writers who influenced my choice to become a writer were James Baldwin, Timothy Findley, Tennessee Williams, and Marie-Claire Blais, all of whom addressed queer themes and concerns in various direct and indirect ways. I'm a huge fan of Helen Humphreys's work and remember reading *Leaving Earth* and cheering because I was sick of coming out novels and poorly written lesbian romances. I also think that a number of writers (gay and straight) who deal with the themes of loneliness, escape, and yearning, speak to my imagination.

Are there particular works of queer literature to which your work has responded?

The only one I can think of is Tennessee Williams's play, *A Streetcar Named Desire*, which had an important literal and metaphorical role in the creation of my novel, *Spelling Mississippi*.

Is there an intersection of perspective between being an artist and identifying as lesbian?

I don't think so. My whole identity has been formed via my creativity and what is required to place it first in my life in spiritual, economic, and temporal terms.

Is there an intersection of perspective between Canadian and lesbian?

Not that I know of.

Diasporic writers in Canada often place their novels in their cultural origins and create protagonists who speak from those socio-cul-

tural experiences. Yet gay male authors often create novels with a heterosexual female protagonist and it's not uncommon for lesbian authors to write books with no lesbian content whatsoever. Do you agree with this observation, and if so, what do you consider to be the reason for these differences?

All writers write what they want to write, what comes to them easily. Today, I don't think anyone needs to hide behind a "palatable" character: they write what works for them creatively. Some people work best with a certain kind of sublimation as the driving energy. And subterfuge and observing others is second nature to queer writers, so maybe we're just interested in writing down all that we've watched all along, the whole pageant, not just what happened at the potluck last night.

Who do you perceive as your primary audience?

If attendance at events and emails are any indication, I have a very diverse audience—women, men, gays, straights, teens, and readers over 65. It's thrilling and incredibly gratifying to reach so many different readers. I love it.

Are lesbian writers shaping Canadian fiction in spite of homophobia or has Canadian fiction become more inclusive?

I think we have some very open, strong women and men writing in this country from all angles, and I think the world is becoming more inclusive.

Do you encounter homophobia when submitting work for publication?

If I do, it must be the silent variety, which is probably worse in the long run, because the overt kind can at least be addressed with an open and insistent nature. I actually think there's much more literary prejudice against writing that's comical in tone, to be honest. That's the battle I'm concerned about.

Lesbian content disrupts and challenges traditional heterosexual narratives but the most popular types of lesbian writing in the United States, namely romances, mysteries, and the coming out novel, are conservative in form. Are you interested in writing in a manner that challenges these conventional aesthetics?

I think I do this just by writing the characters I write. But I never sit down to write anything with an awareness of aesthetics and expectations or genres or notions of conservative versus challenging. My partner always laughs because I have zero interest in what the Joneses of the literary kingdom are up to. It's possibly a form of arrogance, or maybe a real need to stay hibernated creatively so my projects can unfold the way I like them to. I think it's for the same reason I never chose to hide who I am when I began to publish: I don't honestly care what everyone else is doing or what they think of me. It might also be why I had to leave university and why I refuse to weigh myself.

Marnie Woodrow
Body Doubles

Four-thirty comes and they gather. They can't help it: the clock urges them down Sunset to the place that is cool enough and dark enough to blur the sharp edges of their troubles. It used to be a real hangout for the Hollywood crowd, the grips and gaffers, the people whose names you see in the credits if you stay till the very end of the reel. Now it's a cool, dark bar run by the same man, but it is not what it was. He knows it, but Victor still keeps polishing glasses, shrugging at the whims of time. As far as he's concerned, there are bodies in the bar, it doesn't matter what they do. Or rather, what they did, because most of his customers are inclined to place the word "former" in front of their professional titles. He watches them, but he doesn't listen to what they say. Their rants and sorrows don't make a difference to Victor's life; he's a stoic, formerly an optimist.

Sheila arrives first. She's been watching the clock since noon, wishing she could have a drink. Her doctor told her never drink at home, never alone, because then she'd have a real problem. So when the clock hands edge toward four, she runs to her battered Mustang and puts the pedal to the floor. the Victory Bar is the one place she's expected nowadays, and she isn't about to worry Nan by failing to show. Nan needs her and Sheila might even need Nan back. Sheila guns her car and comes at Sunset from behind, screaming out of her apartment block, the Virgin Mary air freshener swinging in time with the gearshift. She has to arrive before Nan because her friend has an anxiety problem that causes her to eat cocktail napkins to calm herself. Sheila knows this habit that could lead to serious digestive problems in a woman of Nan's age. When she pulls up in front of the bar, she sees Jack loping toward the door. He's one of the men she sees every day at The Victory Bar and knows the least about. His name and a few details because he usually sits too far down the bar from her for her to eavesdrop on him. Maybe today I'll ask him what he was, she thinks. Maybe today I'll ask everyone what they wanted to be when they grew up.

Soon the Victory Bar is full of bodies with glasses in front of them. Sheila and Nan are at one end of the bar, Jack and Henry at the other. At a nearby table, Ginger and Lou sit together, and standing beside the jukebox, looking lost, is Seth. He's the only regular at the Victory Bar who hasn't found a drinking buddy. He was a food stylist, and when you've spent your life primping lettuce heads and varnishing half-cooked lobsters, there aren't many people to talk to. No one wants to know that the food in cooking magazines isn't real, or that when it is real, it's covered in paint, raw on the inside and far from edible. Not even the people at the Victory Bar. Many times he has been brushed off, like someone whispering prophecies that nobody wants to face. So now he simply stares at the jukebox, wondering whose job it is to put the records inside. Some former DJ, he thinks, some guy who was fired from a radio station for saying controversial things about beef. Seth knows better than anyone how touchy people are about food. You can't tell them the truth about what they eat or they become hysterical. He rolls his glass of vodka between his palms and tries to memorize the song titles, knowing that someday, this jukebox will be obsolete, too. That, instead of taking quarters, it'll accept VISA.

Ginger and Lou found each other because of their related professions. Ginger was a chicken-sexer in Northern California; Lou a livestock photographer. What are they doing in LA? Well, what is anyone doing in LA? The whole androgyny trend put Ginger out of business, and Lou lost out to digital cameras—so simple to operate that even a farmer can take pictures of his own pigs and cows. After a brief stint photographing pit bulls for a calendar company, Lou retired. Now he sits and drinks dark rum and quietly sings the lyrics to "Get Off My Land!" or "Old MacDonald Had A Farm" 'til his lady friend arrives. Ginger keeps his mind off what used to be, what might have been, and all the rest of those torturous phrases that remind a person that he lost his nerve and gave up. He finds her former profession mildly erotic and wonders if they should get married, move to New York where there are few painful reminders of Nature. She's smoking a cigarillo and explaining the failure-proof techniques she once used to determine the gender of chickens. She explains it every single day, yet she has this way of telling it that makes it seem new and exciting each time. Maybe it's the way she jerks her hands violently apart to demonstrate what she's saying, or the way her voice deepens when she describes what happens to male chickens once they've been found out. When she's finished, she'll turn to comfort Lou. She'll insist that photographing pigs and cows makes him qualified to shoot portraits of actors. "They're all, basically, cattle of a kind," she says, waving for more drinks. Lou isn't convinced, but he nods and promises to call an agent in the morning. He promises this every afternoon, but by morning he doesn't remember what he was supposed to do. He'll look at his telephone and know that there was someone he was supposed to call but when it doesn't come to him, he heads off to the pool and swims away his hangover.

Nan is especially ragged today, and Sheila buys her a shot of Jack Daniels to soothe her nerves. There's no consoling her some days, though Sheila is probably more equipped than anyone to manage Nan's grief. It's six o'clock and Nan is getting that look. Her brown, leathery face is puckering, and she's staring into her drink and yep, sure enough, she screams, only today she screams actual words: "For god's sake, I was Faye Dunaway's FUCKING TORSO in Chinatown!" Then she buries her head in her hands and sobs, oblivious to Sheila's cooed words of comfort. You can tell by looking at Nan that she was a pretty hot number in her youth. In fact, she still is a pretty hot number, only now she's busy shattering herself with liquor and cigarettes. Her face was never much to look at, but her body reminds you of why she did so well in her profession. Nan was a body double for twenty-two years, the substitute corpus for actresses too shy, flabby, or conveniently religious, to show any skin. Her specialty was stomach-shots, though early on her breasts had been her primary meal ticket. In those days, actresses were still nervous about nude scenes. Now they can't wait to strip down and show it all off, even the old ones. Every one of them working out at fancy gyms, waxing themselves Brazilian style, and eating low-fat diets; why, it put Nan right out of commission. Her last role was for the movie *Barfly*, and she can't seem to get over the pain. She was the "After" girl, and suddenly she was told she was only suitable for "Before."

Sheila asks Victor for a dish of peanuts and waits for Nan to calm down. Like Nan, Sheila wanted to be an actress. She came to LA from a small town in Ohio, full of dreams and hopes. One tampon commercial and it was all over. She'd done Shakespeare in her home town, for god's sake, and Ionesco, and then, presented with what she thought was the golden key to the door of television stardom, she blew it. Once the tampon ad was in heavy rotation, once she became known for flogging feminine products, the only offers Sheila got in the world of TV involved other embarrassing products: deodorants, yeast-infection kits, hemorrhoid creams. The key bent in the locked door to television stardom, and she became a receptionist. Even then, people would come into the dental office where she worked and say, "Hey! Can you still horseback ride and swim during your period?" They all thought it was very funny, but eventually Sheila had a small breakdown. They got to her. So she knows what Nan is feeling, even though their stories aren't exactly the same. She's a lot luckier than Nan because her small breakdown was just big enough to qualify her for a psychiatric pension. She keeps trying to tell Nan that all she has to do is check herself into a hospital for a few weeks, but Nan is stubborn, and consequently, broke. Once Nan is calm, they'll do what they always do, which is to study a copy of *Cosmopolitan* and try to guess which models are computer-generated.

Jack would be perfect for Nan, but he hasn't introduced himself to her. The only person he talks to is Henry. Yet, when he hears Nan scream her agony, he considers going over to her end of the bar and buying her a drink. He knows the pain she's feeling, feels it himself. In some ways Jack's plight is worse because every so often someone will recognize him and shout out "Hey, it's LONG DONG!" How they manage to recognize him after all this time is beyond Jack. He underestimated the devotion of porn-hogs. He's done everything he can to look like a whole different person, short of having plastic surgery. His hair is silver now, and he's let his belly bloat out in front of him. He wears baggy, wool pants and long shirts, untucked so that his crotch is hidden. But there are some fans whose knowledge of the porn industry is so vast and so sentimental that Jack is never going to be completely safe from them.

Henry sees his best friend Jack eyeing Nan and begins to worry. Henry once thought a woman could offer him comfort, share his grief. Getting tangled up with that one broad taught him otherwise. Francine was his biggest mistake, next to the career he chose. She had been a company mascot for Jiffy peanut butter, toured around the whole country hugging kids and dancing in supermarkets, dressed in a foam-rubber costume shaped like a jar. Henry had just been fired from the Beverly Hills Lawn Bowling Association when he met her. He'd been a team mascot for twenty-five years, but when he developed a limp, they replaced him with some young kid. Henry's loyalty and dedication to the sport counted for nothing. Yes, Francine got him when he was weak, but like all else in his life, it didn't last. One afternoon a guy walked into the Victory Bar wearing a dolphin suit, just off work at some big aquarium opening and looking for a drink. Francine was materialistic; seeing this guy, still employed and possibly well-connected in the world of costumed characters, won her over. Henry was history, and he didn't need to feel any worse. Seeing

Jack with his eyes on Nan, Henry feels a cold shiver run through his body.

Seth whirls away from his post at the jukebox and shouts, "I know! Let's play a game! 'Who's The Biggest Loser In This Joint?' " He storms over to Nan and slaps her on the back, a bad idea.

"Hey asshole! Bobby De Niro licked this back!" screams Nan. She spins around and hauls up a fist to punch Seth right in the mouth.

Sheila catches Nan's fist before it lands, then shakes her head. She can see that Seth is one of those skinny, nervous men that will litigate at any opportunity. He's backing off now, but into the arms of Jack who is twice his size and looks very unhappy.

"Leave the ladies alone!" he growls, shoving Seth away with a swipe of one of his giant arms. Sheila is turned on. Nan is oblivious to the chaos around her. She's lost in remembering how many takes it took to get De Niro's tongue to look "artful" sliding up her spine. It was the only time Nan didn't mind staying late at a shoot. She could smell the coffee on his breath, and she hadn't wanted to shower afterward, but she had another gig the next day that necessitated washing up.

"Folks," Victor is now ambling down the bar. "Free shot for anyone who can sort this out without drawing blood, okay?" He jerks his head in Seth's direction and makes a motion across his throat that says, "You're cut off, mister." Seth is panting in the corner of the room, checking his spindly arms for bruises. Lou and Ginger watch with vague interest while Henry, knowing Jack is done for, checks his wallet for cab fare. Sheila, still turned on by Jack's intervention, reapplies her lipstick and smiles coyly into her compact mirror.

Nan coughs and shakes her head in her signature half-hysterical way. The memory of De Niro's tongue dissolves, and she remembers that she was asked to sub in for Katharine Hepburn's hands for a made-for-TV movie. She meant to call her agent back this morning but forgot. Then, out of the corner of her eye, she notices Sheila eye-balling Jack. Actually she sees two of Sheila in this peripheral moment, and so it is twice as enraging.

"Watch it, sister!" snaps Nan, "We won't MENTION your career as a tampon-huckster, will we? I'm sure this man would be real interested in your bloody, and I say that with great emphasis, pathetic career!" Her brows arrow down on her crooked nose, and she looks a little crazier than usual.

Sheila snaps her compact shut and orders another Sling to keep from smacking Nan. She makes a mental note to be late arriving tomorrow: let her eat napkins for all I care.

Jack extends his hand to Nan and says, "I'm Jack. Some people know me as Long Dong."

Hearing this, Ginger and Lou break into fits of laughter while Henry stands up, moving protectively towards Jack. Nan grins at both versions of Jack, the solid one and the one wavering just to the left of him. Lou whispers loudly about donkeys with less to offer than Jack and Ginger cackles, punching his arm to make him stop. But Jack doesn't care, he has his eyes pinned to Nan, and he feels his heart beating in a way it hasn't in a long time.

"Buy you a drink?" Jack ventures, ignoring Sheila's tongue-cluck and everyone else's manic intrusions. "You're kind of lucky nobody can recognize you."

"Am I?" Nan purrs, perking up and trying to make the two of Jack become one. She wants to tell him how her calves used to be the talk of the town, how her breasts were written up in the Hollywood Reporter once upon a time. Instead, she accepts his offer of a drink she doesn't need and motions for him to move closer.

"Victor, turn that goddamned air conditioner down, would you?" barks Sheila, rubbing her bare, plump arms. She can smell Jack's cologne and while she wants to be happy for Nan, she can't find it in her heart after the tampon remark. She glances over at Henry and sees potential, then changes her mind and concentrates on her drink.

Observing her unsolicited dismissal, Henry bridles and returns to his original seat. Seth sits down next to him, and Henry groans into his beer.

"It's a sad day when the outcasts turn on each other," Seth says, gazing up at the DRINK CUERVO sign that flashes above the rows of bottles.

Misery loves company, Henry thinks, fiddling with a paper umbrella.

Was a time when I was the King of The Garnishes, Seth thinks, but he doesn't say it aloud because Henry is obviously one of those arrogant pricks who thinks every queer man in the world is coming on to him. Please, Seth thinks, don't you know who I am? Was a time when the best magazines called me just to arrange a slice of orange in a supermodel's drink. *Vogue, Elle*, all of them banging down his door, offering easy money: he should have saved some. Then, one day, somebody decides women weren't supposed to be photographed within twenty feet of food, and Seth was back to sculpting butter into swans for weddings and commitment ceremonies.

"Downsizing," Henry mutters. "Think you're special, then BLAM. My mother told me, Henry, specialize, narrow your focus, go with your gift. So what do I do? I drop out of college and dress up like a goddamned grasshopper, and everything seems great, right? I'm living large, I'm strutting my stuff in all the best stadiums. But you can feel it slipping away, and it always does, nowadays. Nothing sticks, nothing lasts."

Seth, breathless at the fact that someone has spoken to him, even near him, is silent in case Henry wants to keep sharing. But Henry remains mute, stroking his beer bottle and glancing in the direction of Nan and Jack. Seth straightens up on his stool and elbows Henry gently, making him look at Ginger and Lou, now deep in conversation, touching hands and giggling.

"Love does," says Seth, pointing at Ginger and Lou. "Love can work out." Henry looks unconvinced, but now Seth has gained courage. "You want to go down to the ocean and talk some more?"

Henry glares at Seth, but then, for the first time, he notices how gentle this skinny guy looks, how genuinely kind and interested he is in what Henry has to say. Hell, he thinks, why not? Why not go to the ocean? Like most people in LA, Henry knows where the ocean is but never goes. He shouldn't have sold his car but he had to. Rent money was due, he hadn't yet managed to get his job at the car wash where the memory of his lost Trans Am now haunts him. He shudders, thinking of all those beautiful people in their glamorous cars, their smug faces when they emerge from the tunnel of beating sponges and spraying water.

"Maybe we should ask Sheila along," Henry suggests, adding, "The tampon chick, you know, she looks like she's being ignored or something." Seth nods and hops down from his chair and goes over to Sheila.

"You know, I really loved your comic timing in that Gyna-Wipe commercial," Seth says, placing his hand on Sheila's shoulder. "Me and Henry are going down to the beach, you want to come along? See the moon and the stars, have a bonfire?"

Sheila looks over Seth's shoulder at Henry who is smiling and waving. She thinks, Maybe I'll ask him what he used to be. Maybe, just for once, I'll ask him what he'd like to do next. To Seth, she says, "How you getting there?"

"Your car?" Seth asks, hopeful. He hadn't thought of how to actually GET to the ocean, only knows that's where he wants to be.

In the parking lot outside the bar, Henry feels a new sense of possibility. He points to the night sky and turns to grin at his new companions. "I want you two to just remember one thing: they can never downsize the moon."

"Amen to that," says Sheila, unlocking the car. "You should write greeting cards, Henry. You'd make a killing, baby."

Marnie Woodrow

Marnie Woodrow is the author of two short fiction collections and the novel, *Spelling Mississippi*, short-listed for the Amazon.ca/Books In Canada First Novel Award in 2003. She is currently at work on a collection of new short fiction and a novel. A writing instructor at the University of Toronto School of Continuing Studies, she also works with queer youth whenever possible.

Bibliographer Notes

The "Annotated Bibliography of Canadian Literature with Lesbian Content" arose when James Miller, the Director of the Pride Library at the University of Western Ontario, invited me to do some collection development work, which is the process of planning and selecting a balanced collection of library materials. I was aware that the Canadian Lesbian and Gay Archives did not collect fiction and I noted that the Pride Library had rather more gay male than lesbian content, so I proposed to James that the Pride Library should devote some of its resources to the acquisition of Canadian literature with lesbian themes. Finding the books, however, turned out to be a challenge.

Developing a list of non-fiction materials on lesbian and gay topics was a simple matter of using Library of Congress Subject Headings to search the Canadian National Library Catalogue. But literature is often not assigned subject headings, or given quite general ones, or given ones that fail to acknowledge queer content. For example, in the Canadian National Library Catalogue entry for Ann-Marie MacDonald's *The Way the Crow Flies*, the subject headings provided are Girls—Fiction, Cold War—Fiction, Military Bases—Fiction, and Families of Military Personnel—Fiction. Reviews of MacDonald's novels rarely, if ever, mention the lesbian content despite its socio-cultural importance.

Since I had no readers' advisory guide to Canadian lesbian literature, I decided to develop one. In the United States, most lesbian fiction has been put out by lesbian publishers while the number of lesbian-themed books put out by mainstream publishers or even small presses is scant. Of course, this limits the careers of lesbian authors. However, for readers, buying lesbian-themed books is a straightforward process of consulting the catalogues of lesbian and gay publishers. Canada, in contrast, has never had an exclusively lesbian publishing house, although there have been several lesbian-positive feminist presses such as Press Gang, Gynergy, Women's Press, Sister Vision, Second Story, and Polestar. Looking through the books published by these presses led me to a number of lesbian-themed books, but many of Canada's literary presses have also managed to publish a lesbian title or two. And in Quebec, the majority of lesbian-themed work has been put out by literary and mainstream presses, beginning in 1963 with Louise Maheux-Forcier's *Amadou*, Canada's first lesbian novel.

I initially titled my bibliography "An Annotated Bibliography of Canadian Lesbian and Bisexual Women Authors," but this created several problems. There were authors who no longer identified as lesbian or bisexual or even female. There were lesbian authors whose work has never addressed lesbian themes or included any lesbian content whatsoever. There were authors who resented being listed on the bibliography as they considered it an attempt to ghettoize their books. So I decided to change my focus to lesbian-themed work. My criterion for inclusion is "significant lesbian content," which is necessarily subjective. The personal lives of authors, however, and their reasons for writing particular books is neither my interest nor my concern: satisfying the needs and desires of readers is.

Nairne Holtz

Selective Annotated Bibliography of Canadian Literature with Lesbian Content
Nairne Holtz

Alguire, Judith

Iced. Women's Press, 1995. In *Iced*, protagonist Alison Gutherie, a former hockey star, accepts a position coaching a Toronto team playing in the premier season of Canada's first women's professional hockey league. She soon learns that coaching the team to peak performance on the ice is a much simpler task than helping them cope with issues in their personal lives. These include stalker ex-husbands, coming out, drug use, and inter-team romances and rivalries. Another difficult challenge for Alison is Phil Tweddell, the lacklustre franchise owner, who regards the team as a mere stepping stone for his own ambitions. Finally, Alison must deal with her attractions to both a suave, sexy coach on an opposing team, and to a troubled member of her own team. As Canada's first lesbian hockey novel, *Iced* is an entertaining sports soap opera and romance that succeeds beyond its genre. Alguire addresses issues of gender equality, sexism, and homophobia in sports with both intelligence and humour.

Armstrong, Luanne

Bordering. Gynergy, 1995. *Bordering* is a gentle, quiet novel about place and community written in ordinary language. Set in rural British Columbia, *Bordering* tells the story of Louise McDonald, an unsophisticated farmer from a small town who is coping with the aftermath of her first affair with a woman. Paralyzed by her inability to shape her own life, Louise takes action when her best friend's daughter is caught smuggling drugs. As she explores the town's open but unacknowledged secrets, Louise begins to create a new life for herself.

Armstrong won the Canadian Children's Book Centre Award in 1995-1996.

Banerji, Anurima

Night Artillery. TSAR, 2000. Banerji weaves personal experience and identity politics with Hindu mythology and Persian mysticism to create romantic poems grounded in lavish, potent imagery. Her poems focus on loss and nostalgia for people and places. She renders her experiences and feelings with an attention to detail that is both feminine and South Asian. In "Raga Malkauns," Bannerji follows the sequence of a raga, a classical form of Indian music. She writes, "alap. / her skin unfurls like a scroll of papyrus / intimately she whispers her prayers into my skin / inscribing the secrets of sanskrit on my hips / and there is the calligraphy of her tongue / this woman's ink brushed into every pore." When Bannerji addresses politics, however, her work has more of a sting. In "Summer, or, I Want the Rage of Poets to Bleed Guns Speechless with Words," she writes, "It has been this way for a long time, since they put a restraining order against my breasts and called it a bra."

Blackbridge, Persimmon

Prozac Highway. Press Gang, 1997. *Prozac Highway* is a wry, sad, engrossing novel written in a realist style. The title is a nod to Elizabeth Wurtzel's 1994 memoir, *Prozac Nation: Young and Depressed in America*, and both works feature a female protagonist coping with chronic depressive disorder. In *Prozac Highway*, a fortysomething lesbian performance artist and sometime cleaning lady has a destructive affair with a young academic, retreats from what she calls the "meat" world, and spends her time online corresponding with other people diagnosed with mental illnesses. The engaging and amusing protagonist is not particularly introspective but in the end allows people to reach out to her.

Blackbridge won a Ferro-Grumley Award in 1997.

Blais, Marie-Claire

Nights in the Underground: an exploration of love. Translated by Ray Ellenwood. Musson, 1979. Translation of: *Les nuits de l'Underground*. Stanké, 1978. In one of the first lesbian novels published in Canada, internationally recognized author Marie-Claire Blais explores the relationship between art and love and the dangerous necessity for lesbians to create an open place for themselves in both their own hearts and in the world. The season is winter and the setting is the Underground, a lesbian bar where an eclectic group of women play out the dramas of their lives. At the centre is Blais' protagonist, Geneviève, a sculptor who conflates her lovers with paintings, her desire with art, and who, in the process of various literal and metaphorical journeys, recreates herself. She travels from Montreal to Paris, from heterosexuality to lesbianism, and from a sexual obsession with Lali, an alcoholic doctor who has an immense capacity to both seduce and wound, to a more mature love with Françoise, an aristocratic, closeted older woman who proves herself up to the task of assuming an alarming but essential risk. Blais, a widely acclaimed Quebeçois writer, has written a darkly humorous novel in a language both raw and evocative, moving seamlessly from the interior mind of an artist to the exterior world of a wild, noisy bar filled with patrons from all walks of life.

Blais won the Governor General's Literary Award for fiction in 1996, 1979, and 1969.

Brand, Dionne

In Another Place, Not Here. Vintage Canada, 1997. From the very first page of this novel, Brand mesmerizes readers with her provocative and poetic language. Elizete, an uneducated worker on a sugar cane plantation, falls in love with Verlia, a Toronto woman who has returned to her Caribbean home to join the revolution: "The four o'clock light thinning she dress, she back good and strong, the sweat raining off in that moment when I look and she snap she head around, that wide mouth blowing a wave of tiredness away, pulling in one big breath of air, them big white teeth, she, falling to the work again, she, falling into the four o'clock sunlight. I see she. Hot, cool and wet." Thus begins a bittersweet romance between two women who are both lovers and foils to one another. Elizete, who is convinced that Verlia is her grace, conjures a luxuriant dream world capable of propelling her to and through Toronto's mean streets, surviving as an illegal immigrant. Verlia, a woman in constant flight from her dreams and emotions, came to Toronto as a middle-class teenager in the 1970s looking for the Black Power Movement as a place to redirect her anger into meaningful change. Writing in both Caribbean dialect and Canadian English, Brand skilfully explores place, culture, and belonging in relation to race and sexuality.

Brand won the Governor General's Award for poetry in 1997.

Brossard, Nicole

Baroque at Dawn. Translated by Patricia Claxton. McClelland & Stewart, 1997. Translation of *Baroque d'aube*. L'Hexagone, 1995. Brossard is a critically acclaimed avant-garde writer who was part of the first wave of lesbian-feminist writing that emerged in the late 1970s and early 1980s in Canada, mostly from Quebec. Brossard is an innovative formalist who typically blends poetry and theory. She uses techniques such as puns and experiments with syntax and grammar as a way of challenging notions of subjectivity and meaning. *L'amèr* (Quinze, 1977), *Le sens apparent* (Flammarion, 1980), and *Amantes* (Quinze, 1980) each address feminism, sexuality, and desire, but Brossard's method of destabilizing narrative often obscures the lesbian content of these works. *Baroque at Dawn* emphasizes character, thus allowing for a more explicit treatment of lesbianism. The novel is framed throughout with images of water, as Brossard thematically explores connections between physical and sensory experiences of immersion, particularly the immersive states of virtual reality, language, and the act of creation. The novel's protagonist, Cybil Noland, is a writer whose efforts to write are not always successful. The novel begins with Noland immersed in a state of desire for a young, female stranger who picks her up in a hotel bar. Following their erotic encounter, Noland is invited by a female oceanographer, Occident, to come aboard a ship with a somewhat sinister all-male crew in order to participate in an unusual creative project. Noland, along with a female photographer, is to take advantage of virtual reality technology to experience and later write about life under water. Noland rejects the virtual reality technology created by the three male programmers who also use it to incorporate and produce their fantasies of women. Virtual reality, it seems, replicates a patriarchal discourse even when experienced by a lesbian feminist. Brossard then disrupts her own narrative to introduce herself as a character who has written the book that we find ourselves reading, and who is assisting the translator with its translation. She uses these techniques to involve the reader in the act of creating the text, making *Baroque at Dawn* create in essence a virtual reality for her audience

Brossard won the Governor General's Award for poetry in 1984 and in 1974.

Butler, Audrey (now Alec)

Radical Perversions: Two Dyke Plays. Women's Press, 1990. *Radical Perversions* includes the plays "Black Friday" and "Claposis." "Black Friday" is a play about family secrets and loyalty. Drawing upon her Cape Breton roots, Butler creates a lesbian protagonist, Terry, who travels back to her hometown with her black lover, Spike. Terry's purpose in making the trip is to come out to her family and to discover the truth about her father, an alcoholic unionist who may have been unjustly blamed for the shutdown of the mining company with devastating economic effects on the town. Terry's mother and aunt have their own secrets as well, and in the process of revelation stronger bonds and new definitions of family are created. In "Claposis," Butler writes of three women who become romantically involved with one another. Butler opts to tell her story in reverse chronological order, a device she uses to express the shifting nature of love, intimacy, and power in romantic relationships. "Claposis" allegedly means "two waves meeting" and is an apt metaphor for her portrayal of the cyclical emotional dynamics among the women. Although both plays succeed in engaging the reader with their humour and affectionately drawn characters, "Black Friday" is the weightier of the two works.

Callaghan, Morley, 1903-1990

No Man's Meat. E. W. Titus, 1931. One of Canada's best known and most prolific writers, Callaghan made literary history when he squared off with Ernest Hemmingway in a boxing ring in 1929 and knocked him to the ground. Callaghan went to Paris in 1929 where he spent a few years hanging out in the Left Bank with a veritable who's who of writers that included F. Scott Fitzgerald, James Joyce, and Gertrude Stein. One can only speculate whether his encounters with the famous expatriate community of literary and artistic lesbians influenced his work in this novel. In *No Man's Meat*, the unruffled existence of the Beddoes, wealthy artists living in the idyllic northern Ontario countryside, is disrupted by the arrival of their friend Jean Allen, a reckless gambler. Like the sun on the face of the rock that the Beddoes watch each day, Jean brings colour and excitement to their lives. But when she gambles away her virtue to Mr. Beddoes in a game of craps, Mrs. Beddoes responds in an unexpected manner. Callaghan, known for his tales of men trapped in personal and moral dilemnas, has written a strange and at times comic tale, rich in descriptions of Canadian geography.

Callaghan won the City of Toronto Book Award in 1986, and the Governor General's Award for fiction in 1951.

Dempsey, Shawna

Lesbian National Parks and Services Field Guide to North America. By Shawna Dempsey and Lorri Millan. Illustrations by Daniel Barrow. Pedlar Press, 2002. The fun began as a performance art piece at the Banff Centre for the Arts where long time collaborators Shawna Dempsey and Lorri Millan dressed in uniform as "lesbian rangers" to interact with the public. This experience was developed into a series of multimedia projects, including this satirical field guide. Dedicated with a nod and a wink to Anne Murray, the *Lesbian National Parks and Services Field Guide to North America* covers survival skills, descriptions of flora and fauna, and information on the ersatz Lesbian National Parks and Services. Much of the charm of this guide lies in its packaging. Beautifully designed and illustrated by Daniel Barrow and Zab, this book evokes a 1950s field guide with its hand-drawn illustrations, tan font, and rounded cover. However, this nostalgia for the past is subverted by the content that satirizes traditional homophobic attitudes,. Dempsey and Millan appropriate the language and imagery of scouting and armed forces recruitment ads to create the spiffily dressed, well-prepared Junior Lesbian Ranger whose mandate is the stewardship of the "fragile lesbian ecosystem." This association of lesbianism with the natural world is also a gentle mocking of essentialist lesbian feminist politics. Using double entendres and tongue-in-cheek earnestness, Dempsey and Millan celebrate sexuality and diversity while criticizing heterosexist assumptions of so-called natural sexuality and gender roles, as well as internalized homophobia within the lesbian community. The book, clocking in at 264 pages, is long for what is basically a joke, and the relentless faux quotes attributed to their actual friends may annoy anyone out of the loop. Nonetheless, Dempsey and Millan's work is certainly a unique piece of lesbian Canadiana.

Donoghue, Emma

Hood. Hamish Hamilton, 1995. Donoghue, an Irish writer now settled in London, Ontario, spins a witty, bittersweet, and very accomplished tale of a contemporary Irish school teacher mourning the accidental death of her female lover while living in a climate in which their relationship was at best, tacitly acknowledged. *Hood* is both a meditation on loss and a literary love story, told by flashback, of the attraction between an adventurous, unconventional, and not entirely faithful woman and her more withdrawn and constant lover.

Donoghue won a Ferro-Grumley award in 2002 and the American Library Association's Gay, Lesbian and Bisexual Book Award in 1997.

Douglas, Marion

Magic Eight Ball. Polestar, 2000. Calgary writer Marion Douglas' strength is her ability to observe the ordinary lives of her characters with thoughtful detachment and compassion, expressed in deadpan humour throughout. *Magic Eight Ball* is a quirky, delectable literary novel about a young girl growing up in Southwestern Ontario in the imaginary farming town of Flax. The story is more an examination of the protagonist's anxiety about intimacy than a traditional coming out story. As an adult, she studies sociology in university, becomes pregnant after a single, fleeting encounter with a man whose name she can't really recall with any accuracy, leaves Ontario for Alberta to live with an elderly aunt, and finally, painstakingly, falls in love with another woman. Douglas' protagonist views the world with a thoroughly entertaining hyper self-consciousness, including amusing references to how her personal life would be classified in sociological terms.

Douglas won the Writers Guild of Alberta / George Bugnet award in 1995.

Dunnion, Kristyn

Mosh Pit. Red Deer, 2004. Dunnion's *Mosh Pit* harkens back to "social problem" young adult novels of the 1970s in which the youth of the protagonist did not compromise the seriousness of the themes or the grace of the writing. Dunnion successfully updates the genre with blogging, crack cocaine, and a heroine who identifies as a lesbian from the opening page. Simone is a teenage dyke torn between loyalty to her destructive best friend and her own need to carve out a different kind of life for herself as she navigates her way through a grungy urban landscape of punk bars, booze cans, crack houses, and the sex trade. The plot is far from original, but Dunnion manages to adroitly twist stock characters and situations into fresh configurations. She focuses on Simone's budding identity as a young butch rather than her coming out and does not relegate Cherry, the wayward best friend, to either victim or mean girl status. Instead, Cherry's irreverent blogs show her to be simultaneously vulnerable, exploited, and a frighteningly resourceful criminal. Simone is rescued, naturally, but her support comes from young queer sex workers and punk musicians. Sexy Carol, the love interest, comes perilously close to the hooker with a heart of gold stereotype but her refusal to offer Simone an easy ride into the sunset provides necessary complexity for both the character and the novel. *Mosh Pit* is not a short novel but there is enough plot to sustain interest, and Dunnion effectively captures the sassy argot of modern teenagers.

Elwin, Rosamund

Asha's Mums. Rosamund Elwin and Michele Paulse; illustrated by Dawn Lee. Women's Press, 1990. *Asha's Mums* is written for the four to six year old age group in language that kids can use and easily understand, and is attractively illustrated with watercolours. The book tells the story of Asha, a young black girl who is going on a school trip to the Science Centre. Asha is afraid she will not be able to go with her classmates because her teacher insists that Asha did not fill out the permission form correctly when she listed two mothers as her parents. Asha describes her family during show and tell, and the children in her class argue about whether a person can have two mothers. Fortunately, some children think you can, and Asha's lesbian mothers, both of whom are women of colour, show up at the school to convince the remaining students, not to mention the clueless teacher. This rather low-key book, which reflects a not uncommon dilemma for same-sex parents as well as the multiracial demographics of the city of Toronto, has been the subject of controversy in recent years. The Surrey, British Columbia, School Board of Trustees passed a resolution stating that *Asha's Mums* and other books depicting children with same-sex parents are not appropriate as learning resources for young students. This resolution was challenged in court and in 2002, the Supreme Court of Canada ruled against the school board on the grounds that provincial legislation in British Columbia states that the public school system is secular and non-sectarian.

Fleming, Anne

Pool-hopping and Other Stories. Polestar, 1998. Fleming has written a series of stories capturing pivotal moments when circumstances compel people to take decisive action to change the course of their lives in ways dramatic or ordinary, but always compelling. A child takes her albino sister to show and tell, a woman musician reveals the betrayal of her lover and bandmate, teenagers dare each other to plunge into neighbours' pools on hot summer nights, and an older man robs a bank to win the love of his estranged gay son. Fleming's characters, be they members of suburban families or urban lesbians, are well drawn with intelligence and self-deprecating humour. The characters' lives are engaging and their personalities tend to linger in the mind of the reader for some time after the volume has been read and put aside.

Franson, Leanne

Assume Nothing: Evolution of a Bi-Dyke: Comics. Slab-O-Concrete, 1997. In what started as an effort to woo a particular woman, Franson self-published mini comics about her life as represented by her alter ego, Liliane, and in the process, developed an underground following. *Assume Nothing* is a selection of these comics with stories ranging from the inexplicable occurrences of everyday life, such as finding a patch of skin on a shelf in a new apartment, to the unpredictable terrain of sexual discovery as Lilliane makes the transition from fag hag to bisexual dyke. In the unlikely event that Franson's loose, expressive drawing style fails to beguile, the intelligence, self-deprecating humour, and loving depiction of "la belle province" will succeed in captivating readers with both the dramatic and quieter moments in the life of the well-intentioned protagonist.

Gibb, Camilla

The Petty Details of So-and-So's Life. Doubleday Canada, 2002. In her second novel, celebrated award-winning author Camilla Gibb leaves behind her grim humour and experimental style in favour of a more subdued realism. *The Petty Details of So-and-so's Life* nonetheless triumphs as a subtle, stylishly written exploration of a dysfunctional family. The burden of contending with a sadistic, mentally ill father and an alcoholic, barely capable mother leads siblings Emma and Blue Taylor to choose aggressively different life paths. Emma seemingly plays the role of good girl to Blue's bad boy—she heads off to university while he drops out of school. They are both engaged, however, in the same act of escape. Emma's ability to daydream, to imagine alternate possibilities for herself, leads her to try on identities as if they are disguises: Russian princess, academic, archaeologist, ice cream shop worker, straight girl, and lesbian. Blue, as his name suggests, is a depressive living a precarious blue collar existence as a drug-dealing skin and ink artist. Neither Emma nor Blue succeed in leaving their past behind; their work metaphorically reflects their need to dig beneath surfaces, which in turn leads to their most damaging personal disasters. Gibb rejects therapeutic notions of closure in favour of acceptance: acceptance of love, of failure, and of one's self, thereby offering her characters hope in place of anger and culpability.

Gibb won the City of Toronto Book Award in 2000.

Gidlow, Elsa, 1898-1986

Elsa: I Come with My Songs. Booklegger Press, 1986. Elsa Gidlow may have been the first woman in North America to publish literature with lesbian content. In 1923, a small American press published *On a Grey Thread*, her debut collection of love poetry addressed to women. Gidlow was then twenty-five years old and had just moved to New York City from Quebec. Gidlow never returned to Canada, but her autobiography is nonetheless of interest to Canadians because of her description of her early life as a lesbian poet living in Montreal.

Gidlow was born in England, but her family moved to a village on the outskirts of Montreal when she was five. She grew up with her six brothers and sisters in a three-room house that did not include plumbing. From a young age, Gidlow was fascinated with books and had a rich interior life, but she received little formal education and began doing clerical work in Montreal at the age of sixteen. Around this time, she met a woman at a business course and fell in love. Their intense friendship ended when her girlfriend met a man. This prompted Gidlow to organize a writers' group as a way to meet other "outsiders," which turned out to be wildly successful. Elsa Gidlow became part of a bohemian group of men and women, some of whom were gay, who introduced her to literature, aesthetics, theosophy, and pacifism. Inspired by writers in New York who published their own newspapers and magazines, Gidlow, along with one of the gay men, Roswell Mills, created *Les Mouches Fantastiques*, what might now be called a 'zine but was then a mimeographed paper. It included poetry, translations of Verlaine, articles on "the intermediate sex," and one-act plays sympathetically depicting same-sex love along with editorials condemning World War I. Gidlow had a romantic relationship or two with a few bisexual women but in 1920, bored with the "provincialism" of Montreal, she moved to New York to try to earn a living as a writer and to meet lesbians.

Gidlow never became a successful writer of literature. Her chap-books of poetry were mostly self-published or published by the community in which she lived, but she managed to support herself financially as an editor and freelance journalist for much of her life. Her writing style and themes were conventional but her engaging autobiography reveals a woman whose politics were way ahead of her time (in California, she was to become part of an early back-to-the-land commune). Elsa Gidlow was a passionate woman who lived her life on her own terms even at the price of poverty and rejection.

Hamilton, Jane Eaton

Hunger. Oberon, 2002. In *Hunger*, Hamilton explores themes of longing and loss in the lives of lesbians, heterosexual men, and women. What would otherwise be rather conventional storylines of infidelity, illness, and children leaving home are executed in a marvelously idiosyncratic manner. Hamilton successfully marries humour with pathos in a lean, accomplished style reminiscent of short stories in the *New Yorker*.

Holbrook, Susan

Misled. Red Deer, 1999. Holbrook blends autobiographical anecdotes, philosophy, and poetry in an exhilarating maze of word play. She strings together word associations, naughty puns, twisted clichés, and reworked fairy tales while she explores the multiple, mistaken, and shifting meanings of language and experience. In "Crush," a searing examination of her youthful queer crushes, she writes: "Crush. That's a tame one. That's a word you can have over for Sunday dinner. A blushing teeny-bopper and a puppy with a leather shoe: Aw, you say, she's got a crush. What about all the hearts that have been garbage compacted, steel-toe ground, 18-wheeler run over; grand piano dropped, record pressed, rockslide into bloody rubble?" Holbrook pursues forms that challenge her audience yet her lively sense of humour offers entertainment.

Hopkinson, Nalo

The Salt Roads. Warner Brothers, 2003. In *The Salt Roads*, Hopkinson departs from her critically acclaimed science fiction to create a novel that is a hybrid of historical fiction and magical realism. Politically sophisticated yet stylistically uneven, Hopkinson's novel addresses the theme of black women's bid for sexual, spiritual, and economic freedom as she unravels a tale of the lives of three women and a goddess. Mer, a midwife and healer, is an African slave on a sugar plantation on Santa Domingue (later known as Haiti). Jeanne Duval is a bisexual Afro-French dancer and mistress to nineteenth century poet Charles Baudelaire who shocked his contemporaries with his morbidity and explicit sexual poems on lesbians and vampires. Thais is a Greek-Nubian prostitute living in fourth century Egypt who makes a pilgrimage to the desert.

When Mer and two other women on the plantation bury a stillborn child, their prayer unleashes Ezili, a goddess or loa of love in the voodoo pantheon who moves through time and space to possess humans in order to interact in the natural world. As she comes into consciousness by occupying the bodies, passions, and histories of her hosts, Duval, Mer and Thais, Ezili represents the diasporic history of black women scattered across continents yet bound together by their experiences of grief, labour, and sexuality. Hopkinson sprinkles the characteristics ascribed to the Haitian goddess among her female characters who are in turn possessed by the loa. In matching the women's dissimilar stories, the author creates a brilliant literary conceit of possession in all its facets: sexual, economic, and spiritual. Hopkinson fearlessly honours female sexual pleasure and creates strong female characters, but unfortunately equal attention is not given to the women's stories, with the bulk of the story concentrating on Duval and Baudelaire at the expense of Mer's romantic relationship with another woman and her conflicts with Makandal, a shape-shifting slave who is fomenting a revolution.

Hopkinson won the Sunburst Award in 2003 and the World Fantasy Award in 2002.

Humphreys, Helen

Afterimage. HarperFlamingo, 2000. Inspired by a series of works by Victorian photographer Julia Margaret Cameron, the exquisitely written *After Image* tells the story of a love triangle between Annie Phelan, an impoverished Irish-born maid who arrives to work at the estate of Isabelle Dashell, a single-minded photographer struggling to break into the late nineteenth century male-dominated art world, and her dreamy husband Eldon, a cartographer whose health prevents him from exploring the world he charts. By shifting interior monologue from the female artist to her muse, from the privileged man with liberal ideals to his servant, Humphreys delves into themes of subjectivity, class, the oppression of women, and the silencing of lesbianism. The reader is left with the task of distinguishing between that which art merely objectively records and that which it leaves to the subjective imagination. Humphreys' background as an award winning poet is evident in the seamless manner in which she weaves metaphor and simile throughout her text, providing the reader with a vibrant portrait of Victorian-era England. Humphreys won the Writer's Trust of Canada Fiction Award in 2001 and the Toronto Book Award in 1998.

Jones, Lizard

Two Ends of Sleep: A Novel. Press Gang, 1997. Witty, entertaining, and thoughtful may not seem like the most appropriate words to describe a novel about a downwardly-mobile lesbian activist recently diagnosed with Multiple Sclerosis, but *Two Ends of Sleep* eschews drama and sentimentality. The effect of MS on the protagonist, Rusty, is to place her in a perpetually drowsy state between waking and sleeping. As her sense of what is real and what is fantasy begins to blur, Jones creates a similar ambiguity in the text itself. The reader is left to decide the reality of infidelities and criminal behaviour in this affectionate portrayal of lesbian love, desire, and community.

Jutras, Jeanne-d'Arc, 1927-1992

Délira cannelle. Éditions Québec/Amérique, 1983. Jutras has written a series of autobiographical novels featuring her alter-ego, Georgie. In *Délira cannelle*, Georgie is working as a grocery store clerk, and her recent public coming out has caused many of her customers to shun her. One rainy day, she falls into conversation with one of the last remaining friendly clients, Mme Lalande, who decides to wait out the storm and chat. Mme Lalande reveals her own past—the story of a troubled marriage to a gay man and their scandal-ridden split—and that of her neighbours: Délira Cannelle is an obese woman obsessed with winning the church bingo and travelling to the Vatican, and her husband is a grumpy, wheelchair-bound war vet who spends his time filling in crossword puzzles. Georgie herself reminisces about her teenage beer-bottle runs to pay for dates with her sweetheart, Irène, when they could escape from Irène's mother's watchful eye. The stories of these three women are only minimally intertwined but each is facing the realization that life hasn't turned out as they would have expected, with the storm serving as a metaphor for troubled endings and new beginnings. The true pleasure of reading *Délira cannelle* arises less from the characters, however, than from immersing oneself in Jutras' vibrant and evocative writing style—a perfect rendition of working-class Québécois slang, peppered with colourful expressions and beautifully misspelled to convey accurate pronunciation. Partly a rich and meandering triple portrait of *la petite vie*, partly a tale of unlikely connection across the heavily drawn lines of sexual orientation in early '80s Quebec, Jutras' simple story is full of humour and hope. *Andrea Zanin.*

Kwa, Lydia

This Place Called Absence. Turnstone, 2000. Kwa deftly explores themes of grief, hope, risk, and desire through the interwoven voices of four women living in different places and times. Wu Lan, who lives in Vancouver and grew up in Singapore, has taken a leave of absence from work to cope with her father's suicide and her female lover leaving her for a male colleague. Mahmee, Wu Lan's mother, still lives in Singapore and is haunted by the ghost of her dead husband. Lee Ah Choi and Chow Chat Mui, young women living harsh lives in brothels in early twentieth century Singapore, have found comfort in each other's arms and in the use of opium. *This Place Called Absence* is an engaging, sensuous novel from a talented author with an original voice.

Lai, Larissa

Salt Fish Girl. Thomas Allen, 2002. In *Salt Fish Girl*, Lai has created a sophisticated dystopia by plundering and subverting creation stories, Chinese cultural lore, Greek mythology, fairy tales, pop culture, and current events. Crafting a picture of brooding dysfunction rather than a tale of apocalyptic prophecy, Lai effectively critiques both the disguised brutality of post-industrial capitalism and the looming threat posed by the indiscriminate application of biotechnology in the name of human progress. The female narrator, by turns a girl, a woman, and a fish, is the connecting thread weaving together two distinct narratives in the novel, one unfolding in nineteenth century China and the other set in the twenty-first century in the Pacific Northwest. In China, protagonist Nu Wa's desires for other women and a life beyond mere subsistence lead her to make violent, criminal choices. In a futuristic British Columbia, the protagonist Miranda is born into a society where corporations govern cities, factory workers are genetically engineered, corporate jobs are virtual reality video games, and people are at risk from an epidemic known as the dreaming disease, where victims cannot escape the unfiltered horror of our collective memory of past events. Miranda, an outcast born with an inexplicable scent about her of durian fruit, perpetual, sensual, and malodorous, eventually separates from her family and rebels against her society in ways that allow her to uncover devastating truths about her own origins and the world around her. In crafting this paranoid and darkly comic novel, Lai demonstrates that she is both a gifted storyteller and incisive social critic.

Lee, Sky

Bellydancer: Stories. Press Gang, 1994. The political and explicitly lesbian *Bellydancer: Stories,* Lee's second book, was barely noticed. It compares well to the work of Angela Carter; both writers produce incisive, theatrical, tongue-in-cheek explorations of violence and eroticism. Lee rewrites the world from the point of view of those rendered exotic and erotic by mainstream characterizations and caricatures, including belly dancers, sex workers, single mothers, lesbians of colour, and not-so-dutiful Chinese daughters. Lee romps across history, genre, and popular culture to create tales of different women survivors. In "Nancy Drew Mysteries," she explores the intersection of pleasure, risk, and danger through the memories of a young Asian woman who survives various brutalities prior to fleecing her white drug dealer boyfriend and picking up a woman in a bar. In "Pompei," Lee makes use of both myth and allegory to explore the choices made by village girls living in first century Rome. Veering in style from realism to magical realism, Lee's work is complex and enchanting.

Lee won the City of Vancouver Book Award in 1990.

Levine, Elise

Requests & Dedications. McClelland & Stewart, 2003. Set in both the artsy core of Toronto and a grimy boarding stable in an outlying area of the city where farms are being swallowed by subdivisions, Levine's book peels back the skin of a family of sorts whose failed intentions to one another beget dark consequences. *Requests & Dedications* is a character-driven novel with the pacing of a summer storm, a swampy humidity that implodes in a final crackle. At the center of the story is Tanis, a young butch dyke in continual conflict with her iron-ically named mother, Joy. Joy is wedged between her brother, Walker, and his lover, Mimi, an alcoholic charmer to whom Joy plays consort. Jena, Walker's spoiled daughter, is at once vacuous and the pivot on which events turn. The characters' love and tenderness are continually thwarted by their tangled loyalties and empathetically conveyed human failings. Levine's emotional logic is flawless and clear, but the structure of the novel and her style are dense and challenging. The more liter-ary minded reader will admire her ability to wring originality and cool from a vernacular that would seem to have been worn smooth as Levine glides from layered, visceral imagery to a defensive dialogue that perfectly captures the class back-ground of her characters.

Luke, Pearl

Burning Ground. HarperFlamingo Canada, 2000. *Burning Ground*, a powerfully written debut, is a quintessentially Canadian novel with sparse poetics, heavy use of landscape as a metaphor, and themes of isolation and the struggle between human beings and nature. The title of the novel is a reference to underground fires, which in this book operates as a metaphor for hidden desire. The protagonist, Percy Turner, spends her summers working in an isolated fire tower in north-ern Alberta scanning for smoke. She spends much of her time alone reflecting upon her troubled childhood, growing up in a trailer park, and her relationship with Marlea, her best friend and sometime lover. For companionship, she relies on an intense online correspondence with a man in a nearby tower. In the climax of the book, Percy discovers an underground fire and sets off to assess its destructive potential. The extensive damage appears to represent the danger of Percy's illicit desire, experienced not only in an affair with a married man, but also in her on-again, off-again lesbian relationship and in her lingering emotional response to her mother's infidelity.

Luke won the Commonwealth Writer's Prize for Best First Book (Caribbean and Canada region) in 2001.

MacDonald, Ann-Marie

Goodnight Desdemona (Good Morning Juliet). Coach House, 1990. Many Canadians have read *Fall On Your Knees*, Ann-Marie MacDonald's debut novel that managed to be both critically acclaimed and a best-seller despite the fact that an interracial lesbian relationship is the centrepiece of the story. But prior to her gripping, brooding novel, MacDonald wrote *Goodnight Desdemona (Good Morning Juliet)* a frothy and seductive play that satirizes academia and endows Shakespearean classics with a queer, feminist sensibility. Constance Leadbelly, a young, timid academic, is dumped by Professor Night, her boss whose work she has written for years. She falls into an alternate universe of the Shakespearean plays *Romeo and Juliet* and *Othello*. Constance attempts to save the heroines by changing the endings of the plays, which turns out to be quite challenging when she discovers that Desdemona is a bloodthirsty adventurer rather than a passive victim, and Juliet, far from being pure and devoted, is a lively seductress. The changer becomes the changed, as the Shakespearean female characters function as archetypes of Constance's unconscious mind while the male characters are permutations of Professor Night. MacDonald not only amuses her audience but also displays technical skill in setting the Shakespearean characters' dialogue in blank verse.

MacDonald won the Commonwealth Writer's Prize

(Caribbean and Canada region) for Best First Book in 1997 and received Oprah's Book Club Selection #45 in February 2002. She also won the Governor General's Award for drama in 1990.

MacDonald, Ingrid

Catherine, Catherine: Lesbian Short Stories. Women's Press, 1991. The eight stories in this collection are written in a deceptively simple style. Three stories, "Catherine Catherine," "True Natures," and "Seven Miracles," might very well be Canada's first works of transgender fiction. They form the Catherine Trilogy, a compelling series of interlocking stories, which was adapted into an award-winning stage production in Toronto. The trilogy is based upon the life of Catherina Margaretha Linck, an eighteenth century German woman who cross-dressed as a man. She was eventually exposed as a biological female and executed for engaging in sodomy, among other crimes. These stories are bawdy, witty, and passionate imaginings of three principal characters: the rash, hot-headed, cross-dressing Catherine; her lover, also named Catherine, who both blooms and suffers for her unquestioning faith in their relationship; and the brutal man of God who takes their fate into his own hands. The other stories in the collection are appealing contemporary tales of girls and women coming into their own as they cope with divorced parents, the loss of a best friend, and doomed romances.

Maheux-Forcier, Louise

A Forest for Zoe. Translated by David Lobdell. Oberon, 1986. Translation of: *Une forêt pour Zoé*. Le Cercle du Livre du France, 1969. Although virtually unknown outside of her home province, Maheux-Forcier is a well-regarded Quebec literary figure. Her first novel, *Amadou*, published in 1963, is Canada's first lesbian novel. Her third novel, *Une forêt pour Zoé*, is one of Canada's best lesbian novels. Both novels feature lesbians in primary relationships with men while longing for their lost female lovers. *Amadou* is lesbian pulp fiction: a humourless style is wedded to a kitschy plot filled with murder and mayhem that serves to affirm the impossibility for women to live outside of compulsory heterosexuality. *A Forest for Zoe*, in contrast, is a sophisticated literary novel that thrives upon paradox and dissonance. The narrator, Thérèse, is obsessed with Zoe, her childhood friend whom she experiences as a Doppelganger or ghostly alterego. Zoe, a reckless, courageous heathen, acts as interrogator and confessor to Thérèse as she examines the significant relationships in her life, seeking to understand the unravelling of a relationship that was once as tightly interwoven as "the strands of a web of wool." Maheux-Forcier's absurd, grimly comic descriptions of betrayals between adults and children are a sly, devastating critique of oppression, and of sexism and heterosexism. She renders the most disturbing of scenes in a splendid poetic style. The novel is infused with lesbian eroticism but the most explicit acts are often conveyed by metaphor or double entendre. Thérèse concludes that her husband is "her friend" and her illicit lover, Isis, her "denouement" but understanding does not necessarily lead to action. Thérèse appears to tell all but how reliable is she? Zoe may be real, a version of Thérèse, or a fantasy of pure, Edenic lesbian love. What is certain is the timeless appeal of this work, which may gain the recognition it deserves in translation.

Maheux-Forcier won the Governor General's Award in 1969.

Marchessault, Jovette

Lesbian Triptych. Translated by Yvonne Klein. Women's Press, 1985. Translation of: *Tryptique lesbien*. Éditions de la Pleine Lune, 1980. Contents include: *A Lesbian Chronicle from Medieval Quebec*, *Night Cows* and *The Angel Makers*. Marchessault was a rising star in the Quebec literary scene when she outed herself with the publication of *Lesbian Triptych*, a dramatic monologue in three parts. In the first part, "A Lesbian Chronicle from Medieval Quebec," which has the brutal satirical style of Valerie Solanis' *S.C.U.M. Manifesto*, Marchessault inverts the teachings of the Catholic Church to denounce the sexual oppression of lesbians. The word "Medieval" in the title refers not to the historical period of the Middle Ages but is instead a sarcastic reference to the "back-wardness" of Quebec prior to the Quiet Revolution of the 1960s when the election of the Liberal Party of Jean Lesage ushered in a period of liberalisation and a corresponding decrease in the power of the Catholic Church. Dazzling the reader with puns and metaphors linking various forms of oppression, Marchessault takes the reader on a journey through her Catholic childhood, the love she experiences for her vivacious country cousin who is made catatonic by hetero-sexuality, and the constrictions imposed by her family who reject Marchessault when she comes out. The second part of the triptych, "Night Cows," which was later adapted for the stage, is a utopian celebration of mother love and a myth of origins wherein women are cows, docile breeders by day that at night soar freely through the Milky Way entwined in erot-ic embraces. The final part of the triptych is titled "The Angel-Makers," a Québeçois expression for women who per-form illegal abortions. Marchessault riffs on the meanings of left, right, knitting, and stitching as the speaker watches her mother knit to strengthen her hands for the task of taking foetuses from the womb and returning rights to women.

Marchessault won the Governor General's Award for drama in 1990.

Marlatt, Daphne
Touch To My Tongue. Illustrations by Cheryl Sourkes. Longspoon, 1984. Betsy Warland and Daphne Marlatt have dedicated their respective books, *Open is Broken* and *Touch to My Tongue*, to each other. Engaged in the task of deconstruct-ing patriarchal language, both authors have created sensuous and cerebral collections of poetry. *Touch to my Tongue* includes

both poetry and an essay, "Musing with Mothertongue." In the essay, Marlatt examines the relationship between language and meaning in a patriarchal culture and recommends using the female body and female experiences, such as miscarriage and breastfeeding, to create new images, symbols, and meanings. Marlatt's rhythmic poems use images of nature and uninhabited, wild space to explore the dynamics of long-distance relationships and to invoke the passion of lesbian eroticism. In "eating," she writes, "a kiwi at four a.m. among the sheets green slice of cool going down easy on the tongue extended with desire for you and you in me it isn't us we suck those other lips tongue flesh wet wall that gives and gives whole fountains inner mountains moving out resistances."

Mootoo, Shani

Out on Main Street and Other Stories. Press Gang, 1993. Born in Ireland and raised in Trinidad, Mootoo moved to Canada at the age of nineteen and began a career as a visual artist and videographer. In *Out on Main Street*, her first collection of short fiction, she draws upon her hybrid identity to examine feminist, racial, and lesbian issues using a variety of voices and styles. "Lemon Scent," is a sensual and elegiac tale exploring the hidden emotions of a married woman and her lesbian lover who make love beneath a samaan tree, unobserved by the woman's husband. "Out on Main Street," written in Indo-Caribbean patois, explores different axes of privilege and discrimination as experienced by a femme/butch couple that both have East Indian backgrounds.

Mootoo won the Chapters / Robertson Davies First Novel Award in 1997.

Oliver, Kathleen

Swollen Tongues. Playwrights Canada, 1999. Oliver queers the plot of Edmond Rostand's *Cyrano de Bergeac* and the conventions of Shakespearean comedy to create a play written for the most part in heroic couplets and iambic pentameter.

While Cyrano is tongue-tied in the presence of Roxanne's beauty, the heroine of *Swollen Tongues* is rendered mute by "the love that dare not speak its name." The plot involves a brother and sister, Thomas and Catharine, being tutored by the enigmatic Dr. Wise in the art of writing poetry. Both Thomas and Catharine share the same muse and love object, Sonya, but as Catharine is fearful of revealing her lesbian desire, she reworks her brother's dreadful poems using the pseudonym Overripe. When Thomas discovers he is being plagiarized, Dr. Wise steps in to propose a duel in the form of a poetry slam. From there, the plot twists in a series of tricks, disguises, and cross-dressing as the characters discover the power of poetry and theatrical gender-bending to unearth unexpected desire. Oliver seamlessly blends contemporary queer cultural references with classic literary language. For example, when Thomas stumbles into a Sapphic hideaway, he says, "What's this decaying floor on which I stand? / What means this sign? / This 'Women only land?' / Only land where? The thought seems incomplete. / I know that cats only land on their feet, / but women...sometimes land in someone's lap, / or sometimes they might fall into a trap." *Swollen Tongues* is a hilarious marvel written by a terrific wordsmith.

Oliver won a Jessie Richardson Award in 1998.

Rule, Jane

Contract with the World. Harcourt Brace Jovanovich, 1980. Rule is best known for her novel *Desert of the Heart*, which in 1986 was made into the successful lesbian movie, *Desert Hearts*. Those familiar with the rest of Rule's work, however, will know that *Contract with the World* is her masterpiece. The "contract" in the title represents the choices and bargains individuals make with regards to the intersection of their public and private lives. Rule uses this theme to explore such diverse topics as mental illness, homophobia, intergenerational relationships, outing, class privilege, the myth and reality of being an artist and, perhaps most poignantly, the choices individuals make in terms of personal loyalties. Set in Vancouver, Rule's novel progresses using the voices of six very different men and women, gay and straight, whose "agitated" lives are interconnected in complex ways, both emotionally and sexually. Rule's talent for creating breadth and depth of character as demonstrated in *Contract with the World* is first-rate. The novel is technically polished and thematically sophisticated but written in an accessible style with colloquial dialogue and action scaled to the community level.

Rule won the Bill Whitehead Award for Lifetime Achievement Award in 2002.

Ruth, Elizabeth

Smoke. Penguin, 2005. When a young man growing up on a tobacco farm in 1950s Southern Ontario is severely burned in a fire, his sense of self is as damaged as his face. Buster McFiddie's disfigurement in an era of conformity makes him a social outcast and he is consumed with self-pity. Doc John, the town doctor, recognizing that Buster needs to be healed in spirit as well as in body, reaches out to him by recounting wild takes of infamous Detroit mobsters and bootleggers, the Purple Gang. The stories gradually guide Buster into a deeper understanding of risk, responsibility, and who or what is a true outlaw. In this warm, smart, character-driven novel, Doc John serves as Busterès foil. While Buster rebuilds his life and prepares for the future, Doc John attempts to reconcile his past with his present. Doc John and his wife Alice appear to be perfect upstanding citizens in the village of Smoke, but they are co-conspirators who hide, even from themselves to some extent, the reality that Doc John began life as a biological female. As Doc John "straddles this equator called sex," Buster and he other residents of the town address their own conflicts between their perception and that of their community. Smoke serves as an apt metaphor for both imminent danger and that which can be obscured.

Salah, Trish

Wanting in Arabic: Poems. TSAR, 2002. Salah, a transsexual lesbian with a Lebanese immigrant father, blends cultural theory with Urdu poetic traditions and queer experience. *Wanting in Arabic* is a compact examination of gender and race identity. While this sounds serious, her work slides from goofiness to anger in an instant. She wraps her poems in metaphors of mythology and pop culture and sprinkles them with parody and profanity. Her poems tackle exile, demonstrations, and transitioning as well as larger themes of sex, love, and hate; throughout, she's as attentive to rhythm and imagery as she is to content. In "Where Skin Breaks," she writes, "your stockings are white lace from Valenciennes / I hitched through there once / and your garter belt too / that was where I first thought / 'you can't hitch in to love / love is closed / like a sign, saying "Closed" '/ but you can hitch in to Valenciennes / into desire or its hook / & hitching in stockings / can teach a boy things / *& once upon a time I was*"

Scott, Gail

Main Brides: Against Ochre Pediment and Aztec Sky. Coach House Press, 1993.

Although steeped in the haunting residue of the massacre of fourteen women at Université de Montréal's École Polytechnique, *Main Brides* is also a tribute to the city of Montreal that lovingly captures its texture and essence. The novel opens with Lydia, the protagonist, coming upon the police standing beside a dead female body in the park. Following this disturbing encounter, Lydia heads to her usual haunt, a bar on Montreal's Boulevard St. Laurent, commonly known as the Main. The novel unfolds over the course of the day she spends there drinking and fabricating stories about the lives of the other women in the bar, her "Main Brides." These include a young junkie who has left home, a woman vacationing in Cuba with her sister, two incompatible lesbian lovers who are like "Canada and Quebec," a slumming

Anglophone from Toronto who resembles Marilyn Monroe, and a fierce trio of young lesbian artists. The action in *Main Brides* takes place entirely within the confined consciousness of Lydia's fantasies, which may be projections from her own life. Their purpose seems to be to help her deal with her fear and vulnerability. Details concerning Lydia's own identity are never revealed; the reader is provided at most with suggestive glimpses in the form of Lydia's dreams of incest and her attractions to her "Main Brides," despite her assertion of her own heterosexuality. Using this technique, Scott leads readers to question the assumptions, characterizations, and fantasies they bring to their interpretation of the narrator, thus leading to a contemplation of the process of creating and writing female characters.

Silvera, Makeda

The Heart Does Not Bend. Random House Canada, 2002. *The Heart Does Not Bend* explores family loyalty and the ties that bind in the Jamaican born Galloway clan. The novel begins with the reading of the family matriarch Maria Galloway's last will, in which she has bequeathed her entire estate to a seemingly undeserving great-grandson. Narrator Molly Galloway is left to contemplate this legacy and her bittersweet relationship with Maria, the grandmother who raised her. Molly remembers the intense bond she shared with her grandmother during her childhood in Jamaica, a sensuous paradise of food, beauty, and good times socializing with an extended family that included a gay uncle, her grandmother's married gardener boyfriend, and the albino girl next door. Maria was the center of Molly's childhood world but is also the source of her biggest heartbreak as Molly enters adolescence and learns more of her grandmother's vulnerabilities. Molly contrives a plan to leave Jamaica and join other family members in Canada where she is certain life will be better for both her and her grandmother. Instead, Molly must deal with the effects of teen pregnancy, alcoholism, domestic violence, familial homophobia and sexism, as well as the longing for one's homeland. Silvera creates a gracefully written, moving portrayal of a loving yet flawed Caribbean family in Canada.

Stephens, Nathalie

Somewhere Running. Advance Edition/Arsenal Pulp, 2000. In "Somewhere Running," Stephens examines the gap between what people see and what they perceive. A pair of lesbian lovers living in a city are seen by men who understand they are a threat but think they are "faggots," fundamentalists who see them as sinners but miss their joy and laughter, and an artist who intuitively captures their beauty in a photograph while refusing to recognize the nature of the relationship. A concoction of blurred photographs and cerebral prose-poetry, *Somewhere Running* examines the nature of reality and difference, and the way in which urban space offers both danger and freedom. Stephens unwinds her poems like a yo-yo. She produces the same taut groupings of words and images with slightly different inflections, an experimental aesthetic that will appeal most to students of postmodernism. In "Plate No. 29," Stephens writes, "they will laugh / laugh at the artist / the cyclops who sees with limited vision / who takes two women and renders them mute / in the image / the woman are mute / they say nothing / only later do they speak and earlier."

Tulchinsky, Karen X.

Love Ruins Everything. Press Gang, 1998. *Love Ruins Everything* is a fast read that skids from one genre to the next: romantic comedy, family drama, and political thriller. Nomi, a Canadian lesbian, is working illegally in a bar in San Francisco when her lover dumps her for a man. Given that Nomi's experience as a single lesbian consists of a string of bad dates, she contemplates buying a gun and ending at all. Fortunately, she decides instead to return to Toronto to attend her widowed mother's upcoming wedding and reunite with her extended Jewish family. In Toronto, she meets a gorgeous Asian femme activist and spends time with her gay cousin Henry, who is in the hospital following a gay bashing that may or may not be connected to work he has done to uncover a government AIDS conspiracy. Tulchinsky's comic dialogue is entertaining, and she is particularly adept at describing the complex and bittersweet relationship of her gay characters with their families, but the femme love interests are disappointingly one-dimensional. Nonetheless, *Love Ruins Everything* is an engaging read that will appeal to a wide audience.

Tulchinsky won the City of Vancouver Book Prize in 1996.

Warland, Betsy

Open is Broken. Longspoon, 1984. Warland dismantles the rules of syntax, the etymological meanings of words, and the taboo of expressing lesbian desire in order to reclaim and celebrate what she characterizes in rather essentialist terms as "women's sensual experience." Although she uses traditional symbols of femininity such as nature, water, the moon, and circular shapes, the result is as subversive as it is conventional, both in terms of scope and trope. In "Receiving the Seed," Warland writes: "I want her evident in me / her seed / ring in my ring / I have never desired it before / before was not her / we enter, inter–/ course: 'intercurrere, to run between'/ ring's turning boundary to become / vortex (inner course)."

Webb, Phyllis

The Naked Poems. Periwinkle, 1965. As an early example of Canadian literature with lesbian content, *The Naked Poems* created controversy when it was published. *The Naked Poems* is a slender volume of verse and paradox. Webb's subject is the progression and dissolution of a love affair between two women. Her writing style is cool and philosophical, and the book ends with a mock interrogation of the poet. Purporting to be confessional, *The Naked Poems* is marked by its spareness; the poems are rarely longer than a haiku. Webb reveals that the object of her love is a woman while deflecting attention from this fact by avoiding pronouns and using codes such as in this savoury erotic description—"Hieratic sounds emerge / from the Priestess of / Motion / a new alphabet / gasps for air. / We disappear in the musk of her coming." Webb uses simple language in a remarkably subtle and allusive style. She captures the lover's absence in a single sentence when she writes, "The room that held you is still here." She intimates a reason for the loss of her lover when she writes, "the way of what fell / the lies / like the petals / falling drop / delicately," but as in all of her poems, with restraint and reticence, she withholds as much as she tells.

Webb won the Governor General's Award for poetry in 1982.

Woodrow, Marnie

Spelling Mississippi. Alfred A. Knopf Canada, 2002. In *Spelling Mississippi*, Woodrow has enriched Canadian lesbian literature by providing a much-needed lesbian love story that is both sexy and well written. Woodrow pays loving homage to the city of New Orleans, which is the setting for this juicy novel. Cleo, a typically shy Canadian, witnesses a woman dressed in an evening gown hurl herself into a river. Cleo stands by, unable to act but equally unable to put the image of the woman out of her mind. Her obsession eventually unravels in a steamy tale of dysfunctional mothers, forbidden love, and the will to overcome a deeply ingrained desire for self-destruction.

Zaremba, Eve

A Reason to Kill. Paperjacks, 1978. *A Reason to Kill*, the first of lesbian mystery to be published in Canada, features private investigator Helen Keremos, a woman Margaret Atwood described as a cross between Philip Marlowe and Lily Tomlin. Zaremba writes convincingly about a range of crime and characters. *A Reason to Kill*, written and set in the 1970s, deals not unexpectedly with homophobia and coming out, and the classic reenactment of the crime becomes an exercise in collective decision-making. Written in a timeless hard-boiled style with dry, terse dialogue, Zaremba's work emphasizes plot rather than the more typical tropes of lesbian murder mysteries, i.e., alcoholic detectives dealing with romance and recovery. Keremos is much more convincing as a quintessential loner who likes to travel, drink beer, and enjoy brief sexual encounters with women.

The full bibliography can be viewed at www.canadianlesbianliterature.ca   I would like to thank Andrea Zanin for contributing an entry for Jeanne D'Arc Jutras.

Biographies

Lise Beaudry recently graduated from York University's MFA program. Her photographic work has been exhibited in several Canadian cities, the United States, Romania, and Arles, France, during Les Rencontres Internationales de la Photographie. In 2002, her first video: *Le tourbillon* (Life's Whirlpool of Days) won her the Best Upcoming Toronto Video/Filmmaker at the Inside Out Toronto Lesbian and Gay Film Festival as well as the Audience Award at the Dublin Lesbian and Gay Film Festival. *Le tourbillon* has now toured to 26 festivals in Canada, US, and Europe. In 2003, she co-founded Alley Jaunt—local art in local garages—a Toronto alternative annual art event transforming the back alley garages surrounding Trinity Bellwoods Park into venues that showcase visual art, installations, performance, and film and video.

Nairne Holtz is a Montreal-based writer whose short fiction has appeared in numerous literary journals and anthologies. She has created the *Annotated Bibliography of Canadian Literature with Lesbian Content*, an on-going project that contains reviews of more than one hundred books and reflects her love of reading and literature. She holds graduate degrees from McGill University in both literature and library science and has recently completed her first novel. She doesn't always write about lesbians, but she believes that to remove the effect being a lesbian has had upon her life, and therefore her creativity, would be akin to pulling a thread on a dress only to watch the entire garment unravel.

Susan Knutson is Professor of English and Dean of Arts and Sciences at Université Sainte-Anne, a francophone university serving the Acadian communities of Nova Scotia. The author of numerous articles and one book, *Narrative in the Feminine: Daphne Marlatt and Nicole Brossard* (Wilfrid Laurier University Press 2000), now in its third printing, she is currently researching how and why Canadian authors re-encode canon-ical literary texts. Recent publications include "Trickster Shakespeare? Canada and the Bard," forthcoming in litera-ture**compass**, an online journal from Blackwell Publishing; "Feminist Legends of natureculture: Brossard, Haraway, Science," in *Nicole Brossard: Essays on Her Works*, ed. Louise Forsythe (Guernica, 2005); "Putting Poetry at the Centre: Three Biotextual Readings of Charles Olson's 'In Cold Hell, in Thicket,'" in *Alley Alley Home Free : Open Letter* 12, 2 (2004); and "Canadian Women's Histories," in *An Historical Companion to Postcolonial Literatures*, eds. Prem Poddar and David Johnson (University of Edinburgh, 2005).

Catherine Lake is the editor of QPress, an Insomniac Press imprint focusing on lgbt Canadian literature. She is the editor for Anthony Bidulka—Lambda Book Award-winning author of the Russell Quant mystery series. Catherine Lake holds a Master of Arts in English/Creative Writing. Her previous anthologies include *Rice: Explorations Into Gay Asian Culture + Politics* and *ReCREATIONS: Religion and Spirituality in the Lives of Queer People*. A writer and editor residing in Toronto, Catherine's poetry, fiction, and essays have appeared in liter-ary journals and anthologies.

Acknowledgements

We are grateful to the following authors and publishers for permission given to reprint:

Dionne Brand's excerpt from *In Another Place, Not Here* published by Random House Canada, 1997.

Nicole Brossard's excerpt from *Baroque at Dawn*, English Translation by Patricia Claxton, published by McClelland & Stewart, 1997.

Ann-Marie MacDonald's excerpt from *Fall On Your Knees* published Random House Canada, 1997.

Ann-Marie MacDonald's Writer Notes excerpted from an interview with Sara Cassidy published in *Herizons*, Winter 2004.

Shani Mootoo's "The Upside-downness of the World as it Unfolds" from *Out on Main Street and Other Stories* from Raincoast Books, originally published by Press Gang in 1993.

A few words of heartfelt thanks to:

the writers who have honoured us by participating in this stunning project

Nairne, Susan, Lise, and the Insomniac Press crew for your hard work, commitment, and brilliant contributions which collectively created this anthology

and to my beloved Karen & Nigel whose support encouraged me through this project and whose love gives me joy each and every day.

—Catherine Lake